D1440981

Ethics, Public Policy, and Agriculture

The National Agriculture and Natural Resources Curriculum Project Ethics Group

Jeffrey Burkhardt, *The University of Florida*

Lawrence Busch, *Michigan State University*

Stanley Curtis, *The Pennsylvania State University*

Glenn Johnson, *Michigan State University*

H.O. Kunkel, *Texas A&M University*

Patrick Madden, *Madden Associates, Glendale, CA*

Robert Matthews, *Rutgers University*

Robert McDowell, *North Carolina State University*

Roy Morris, *RJR-Nabisco*

Thomas Ruehr, *California Polytechnic Institute, San Luis Obispo*

Mark Sagoff, *The University of Maryland*

Paul Thompson, *Texas A&M University*

Eileen van Ravenswaay, *Michigan State University*

Ethics, Public Policy, and Agriculture

Paul B. Thompson
Texas A&M University

Robert J. Matthews
Rutgers University

Eileen O. van Ravenswaay
Michigan State University

Macmillan Publishing Company
New York

Maxwell Macmillan Canada
Toronto

Maxwell Macmillan International
New York   Oxford   Singapore   Sydney

Editor: Sherri Walvoord
Production Supervisor: Helen Wallace
Production Manager: Su Levine
Text Designer: Jill Bonar
Cover Designer: Cathleen Norz
Figure Illustrations: Wellington Studios

This book was set in ITC New Baskerville by Digitype, Inc., and printed and bound by
Book Press. The cover was printed by Book Press.

Macmillan Publishing Company
866 Third Avenue, New York, New York 10022

Macmillan Publishing Company is part
of the Maxwell Communication Group of Companies.

Maxwell Macmillan Canada, Inc.
1200 Eglinton Avenue East
Suite 200
Don Mills, Ontario M3C 3N1

Library of Congress Cataloging-in-Publication Data
Thompson, Paul B.,
    Ethics, public policy, and agriculture / Paul B. Thompson, Robert
J. Matthews, Eileen O. van Ravenswaay.
        p.   cm.
    Includes index.
    ISBN 0-02-420695-4
    1. Agriculture—Moral and ethical aspects.   2. Agriculture and
state—United States.   I. Matthews, Robert J.,   .   II. van
Ravenswaay, Eileen.   III. Title.
    BJ52.5.T54   1994
    174'.963—dc20   92-41259
                                                               CIP

Printing: 1 2 3 4 5 6 7 8   Year: 4 5 6 7 8 9 0 1 2 3

Dedicated to our families

Foreword

This book grew out of the work of the National Agriculture and Natural Resources Curriculum Project (NANRCP), which established a course development team on Ethical Aspects of Food, Agriculture, and Natural Resources. Though the need for such a book has long existed, it was made evident as a result of the ten or more national conferences in the last decade concerned with what is now known as *agroethics*. These conferences were stimulated by the increasingly prominent problems and issues that face farmers and their families, nonfarm rural people, rural communities, agribusiness, and the consumers of the products of agribusiness, including natural resource services. These problems and issues include food chain contamination; disadvantaged farm and nonfarm rural people (Caucasian, Hispanic, Native American, and African-American); environmental degradation; rural education problems for both advantaged and disadvantaged rural Americans; difficulties with our national production, price control, and agricultural credit institutions and programs; problems of rural youth (substance abuse, alienation, and teenage pregnancy); adverse impacts of long-term national fiscal deficits—the list goes on.

Another related project, the Social Science Agricultural Agenda Project (SSAAP), has recognized that such problems cannot be defined or solved without attention to values and ethics. To that end, SSAAP's agendas include:

- Establishing appropriate teaching programs at undergraduate and graduate levels in colleges of agriculture to include, for example:
    Agricultural ethics modules for use in regular biophysical agricultural and rural social science courses.
    A senior-level agricultural ethics course open to graduate students, taught at the college rather than the departmental level.
    A college-level seminar for researchers, teachers, graduate students,

extension workers, and practitioners concerned with values and ethics in agriculture and rural societies.

- Expanding the ethics training behind:

  Agricultural extension programs to improve public understanding of ethical aspects and values important in resolving the public and private problems faced by decision makers in agriculture and rural societies.

  The advising, consulting, entrepreneurial, and administrative activities of rural social scientists.

- Improving the teaching of the rural social sciences to deal with ethical questions and values through:

  Professional upgrading via sabbatical leaves and collaborative research and education (1) among rural social scientists and (2) between rural and basic disciplinary social scientists, on the one hand, and philosophers and humanists on the other.

  Restructuring undergraduate and graduate teaching programs in the colleges of agriculture to include agroethics.

  Modifying extension/public service activities to increase public awareness of ethical issues confronting agriculture and to deal more adequately with such issues.

- Developing (through basic research in the social sciences and humanities) techniques to (1) augment present capacities to acquire, validate, and verify descriptive knowledge of values by using rigorous philosophic reasoning to interpret and analyze past experiences and (2) refine decision-making models and decision rules governing interaction among groups using value knowledge to prescribe private and/or public actions to resolve issues and problems.

SSAAP's agroethics agendas underscore the importance of this commendable book by Paul Thompson, Robert Matthews, and Eileen van Ravenswaay. They make substantial contributions to the attainment of the objectives of the course development team on Ethical Aspects of Food, Agriculture, and Natural Resources, as well as to attainment of SSAAP's agendas that complement those of the course development team.

This book provides brief, succinct descriptions of philosophic theories and concepts pertaining to rights, duties, and the social contract as it relates to the organization of societies. These expositions are generally logical rather than empirically descriptive. Another important contribution of this book is found in the empirical content of the case study chapters—particularly the ones on selenium in the Kesterton Reservoir (Chapter 6), food safety (Chapter 5), and animal welfare (Chapter 7). The empirical content of these chapters pertains largely to the value-free (relatively, at least) nature of conditions, situations, and things, though some experiential knowledge about values is provided.

Chapter 2 provides an introduction to the conduct, structure, and performance (CSP) approach to the evaluation of policies, programs, and institutions. The chapter will prove helpful to biological and physical agriculturalists, philosophers, and some activists who are less familiar with the CSP approach than are teachers, researchers, and extension workers concerned with agricultural policy. Such policy workers have concentrated on iterative and interactive policy work with affected and concerned people on programs dating back to the 1920s (in the case of research) and to the end of World War II (in the case of extension). Increasingly, these workers are now expanding the CSP approach to make it a part of the public choice/transaction cost (PC/TC) approach for which Nobel laureates in economics have been awarded (Herbert Simon, James Buchanan, and Ronald Coase). Readers of this introductory book will be better prepared to seek elsewhere for more advanced information about the PC/TC approach in relation to agricultural ethics.

In our agricultural establishment institutions, the pragmatic education philosophies of John Dewey play important roles in the extension services, the 4-H clubs, in high school vocational agriculture teaching, and, to a lesser extent, in college-level resident instruction programs. Agriculturalists with pragmatic education orientations will probably find the book's case study chapters more useful than the earlier, more conceptual chapters. In the case studies, knowledge of exchange (extrinsic) values tends to emerge out of historical processes in a manner consistent with Dewey's pragmatic concern with problem-solving processes. The conceptual chapters stress logic more than experience as a source of knowledge about values.

Economists will note that this book makes little distinction between exchange values and intrinsic values, or between monetary and nonmonetary values. Hence, the book's treatment of efficiency is elemental. Since equilibrium prices change with changes in the ownership of income-generating property rights and privileges, the commonly used "efficiency" calculations based on exchange values (market prices) are invalid across redistributions of the ownership of income-producing rights and privileges. Therefore, efficiency measures for the ethics of making choices that harm some to benefit others need to be based on intrinsic rather than exchange values.

Because this is an introductory book, the issues involved in measuring intrinsic values are not addressed with a high level of economic sophistication. Such measures must be used (along with relatively value-free knowledge of the type found in the case study chapters) to solve problems whose solutions necessarily harm some in order to benefit others. It is precisely these kinds of problems and issues for which public choices and decisions are required. Problems whose solutions leave all participants better off or unharmed can generally be solved rather well by a competitive market-mechanism, without recourse to public processes. The ethics of which choices should be left to the market place and which to the public agencies is touched on in this book. For public and private decisions, attention is needed for (1) the validation, verification, storage, and distribution and use of knowledge, with (2) special stress on knowledge of values. Finally, attention is also needed for making the decision rules used to convert knowledge of values and value-free (relatively, at least) knowledge into prescriptions as to what is the right action as opposed to the wrong action in solving a problem or resolving an issue.

This book will prove very helpful in leading biological and physical agriculturalists toward the consideration of more advanced topics in agricultural ethics. As such, it has an important role to play in our agricultural educational institutions.

Glenn L. Johnson
Michigan State University
East Lansing, Michigan

Preface

This book is an introduction to ethics as applied to public policy problems in agriculture. Agriculture is understood broadly to include food production, distribution, and consumption, as well as renewable resource management. The topics discussed here emphasize agricultural production and food safety largely because no other textbook treatment of ethical issues in agricultural production is available. Far from being a complete treatment of agricultural ethics, this book is intended to introduce concepts from philosophical ethics and to illustrate how they can be used in an analysis of public policy problems in agriculture. The real work in agricultural ethics will be done by people who combine the concepts and framework presented in this book with detailed empirical knowledge of problems in agriculture.

American agriculture has undergone change throughout its history. For 400 years, that change was largely expressed in land use patterns, technology, and production practices. A demographic dimension to agricultural change became increasingly visible in the twentieth century. Change in the size of farms and in the economic organization of rural America accelerated after World War II, turning the United States into an unarguably urban nation, with relatively few citizens having life experience in farming, ranching, and production agriculture. The demographic transition in rural America has eroded agriculture's political power at the same time that urban Americans have become less knowledgeable about the circumstances of agricultural production. The result is that American farmers, agribusiness, and agricultural scientists or public administrators must, for the first time in our history, bring agricultural policy problems before a skeptical urban public.

To complicate this task even further, the public discussion of agricultural policy takes place in a political environment clouded by our recently acquired knowledge of the true environmental costs of industrial agricultural practices. From the 1930s to the 1950s, changes in agricultural production technology were widely perceived as an unalloyed success. The public rhetoric of agricultural leaders continued in this vein long after it became clear that agricultural technology should be regarded as a qualified success—as indeed producing abundant food, but not without social and environmental costs. During the 1980s, American agriculture was torn by environmental and social problems—problems that must now be solved.

One of the key tasks in improving agriculture and winning public acceptance is to make the goals and intentions of policies more explicit. The shared life experience of a largely rural nation made it unnecessary for people in agriculture to explain their goals or to defend them with carefully reasoned arguments. In the past, policy analysis in agriculture has too often been limited to the economic planning analysis an industrial firm would undertake in preparing an investment. This kind of analysis implicitly accepts the goals of producers, leaders, and agribusiness, but why should an urban public support them? How does something that is good for agriculture also further the public interest? Although economic analysis is an important component of the answer to such questions, it must be supplemented by a careful policy argument couched in explicitly normative or ethical terms. The argument must show why a policy should be adopted, and to do this, it must connect with the general ethical norms that underlie government action and political debate.

This book has been written to provide undergraduate students with some of the essential tools that are needed to make an explicit, publicly defensible analysis of and argument for policy choices. It is a skill that agricultural leaders will need in abundance in the coming decades. These tools also provide background knowledge that should produce more informed and more discriminating citizens, whether rural or urban. The concepts and ideas presented here are a component not only of ethical thinking, but also of critical thinking as it applies to civics and public life. We hope that our readers will include this material in their courses for undergraduates, whether or not they choose to adopt our presentation of it.

The book includes six case study chapters that take up issues in food safety, environment, animal welfare, agricultural development, sustainability, and farm structure. The first four case study chapters present one or more specific policy issues and include discussion of key actors, political conflicts, and actual policy proposals. These chapters provide an excellent opportunity for students to role-play the cases, to reenact or simulate the debates. This can be done by assigning the various key actor roles to a few students who then make their case before the class, which collectively takes the role of a key decision-making body—the Food and Drug Administration, the U.S. Agency for International Development, or simply the voters. Sustainability and farm structure lend themselves less well to this kind of treatment for reasons that are explained in the relevant chapters, but even there, we encourage teaching that allows students to debate actively the issues defined and presented in those chapters.

We have received a great deal of advice in the writing of this book, all of it helpful and much of it useful. One of the most persistent themes in advice from faculty in colleges of agriculture was the absolute necessity of providing a concise introduction to the terminology and general structure of ethical theory. It also became clear that agricultural economists and extension educators would be an important subset of readers, so it seemed advisable to link this review of ethics to the structure-conduct-performance format for policy analysis. Our concise review of ethical theory as it relates to policy analysis is presented in the first four chapters. We are, as authors and teachers, of two minds about this material. On the one hand, we feel that producing this review resulted in the most important theoretical advance in the work, an explicit linking of policy analysis to themes in ethical theory, completed in Chapter 4. On the other hand, the decision to organize the book this way meant that we were committed to a selective summary of two major fields, each with practitioners numbering in the thousands, and with hundreds of volumes of important work in the existing literature. We were forced to make judgments about what to include and where to simplify. Because the three of us have made many compromises, we know that these judgments will not win everyone's approval.

The summary and synthesis of concepts from ethics and economics must be comprehensive enough to permit application by teachers who bring diverse backgrounds, interests, and skills to the study of agricultural ethics. We have tried to provide enough economics and philosophy so that specialists in these fields can link our introduction to material with which they have more familiarity and expertise. We have also attempted to present virtually all of these concepts from the ground up, presuming no prior familiarity with philosophy, economics, or indeed agriculture. We have, in short, written a truly introductory textbook, one with simplifications that are intended to get readers started, rather than presenting theories that are expected to cover every need. At the same time, it is the case study chapters, rather than the theoretical chapters, that get to the heart of ethics, public policy, and agriculture. It is these chapters that are most likely to spark student interest and excitement. As teachers experienced in presenting this material, we advise our colleagues not to get bogged down in the first four chapters. The concepts will come to life when issues of true import are addressed.

Acknowledgments

This book has been almost five years in the making. The list of individuals who have helped in its research, review, and production has grown quite long, and we must beg the forgiveness of many people who we will not mention by name. Among our institutional supporters, we acknowledge our respective universities, but also the University of Kentucky and the University of Florida, which hosted early planning meetings of the interdisciplinary group that we came to call the *E-Team*. Our principal institutional benefactor was the U.S. Department of Agriculture's Office of Higher Education, which supported workshops and research on integrating ethics with agricultural issues. Dr. K. Jane Coulter of the U.S. Department of Agriculture has been a personal inspiration, a guardian angel, and a keen source of insight for us. The Center for Biotechnology Policy and Ethics of the Institute for

Biosciences and Technology at Texas A&M University lent extensive technical support to the preparation of the final manuscript.

A few individuals deserve a special note of thanks for their advice on the planning and presentation of the text. They are William Aiken, Jonathan Bennett, Fred Buttel, Ed Harris, Joe Havilicek, Ray Lanier, Alan Randell, Tanya Roberts, and Don Vietor. Students at Texas A&M University, the University of Florida, Rutgers University, the University of Illinois, and the University of Tennessee have been subjected to various drafts of this book, and their reactions and advice may have been most important of all. Though many secretaries and graduate assistants have helped with various portions of the research and writing, the book became a reality especially with the help of Kelly Hancock, Mandar Jayawant, Ryan Soissen, and Caroline Pomeroy.

Finally, we would like to express our appreciation to our colleagues who reviewed this text and gave us helpful comments: Robert G. Hays, University of Illinois at Urbana–Champaign; Steven E. Kraft, Southern Illinois University at Carbondale; William M. Park, University of Tennessee; E. Wesley F. Peterson, University of Nebraska, Lincoln; and Daryll E. Ray, University of Tennessee.

As Glenn Johnson notes in his Foreword, the National Agriculture and Natural Resources Curriculum Project's initiative on ethics in agriculture began to conceptualize issues in agricultural ethics four years before this book was even contemplated. Each of the three authors participated in that project, and the shared vision of agricultural ethics that is expressed in this book was a group product. We express our gratitude to other members of the E-Team for their wisdom, support, and encouragement: Jeff Burkhardt, Larry Busch, Stan Curtis, Glenn Johnson, Harry Kunkel, Pat Madden, Bob McDowell, Roy Morse, Tom Ruehr, and Mark Sagoff. Without the many hours spent in group sessions and in the two-week workshop hosted by the University of Kentucky in 1987, this book would have never been possible. We extend our special thanks to the director of the Curriculum Project, Richard Merritt, who nurtured our project during the slow periods and went far beyond the call of duty in cultivating an audience for the book. Beyond our gratitude, we want to recognize the substantive contribution of the entire group. They are, in a true sense, collaborators in this book. They have corrected many of the errors that the three of us brought to this project. Those that remain we will take credit for ourselves.

Paul B. Thompson
Robert J. Matthews
Eileen O. van Ravenswaay

Contents

Ethics, Public Policy, and Agriculture

1

Introduction

American farm and ranch families have enjoyed a reputation for productivity, good will, and moral purity throughout history since European settlement began. Thomas Jefferson celebrated American farmers as God's chosen people, a thought echoed by President Theodore Roosevelt, who wrote, "If there is one lesson taught by history it is that the permanent greatness of any State must ultimately depend more upon the character of its country population than upon anything else. No growth of cities, no growth of wealth can make up for a loss in either the number or character of the farming population." (1) Roosevelt also convened the National Commission on Conservation, chaired by Gifford Pinchot, which reported in 1909: "The permanent welfare of the Nation demands that its natural resources be conserved by proper use." (2) Even, closer to our own time, President Dwight D. Eisenhower's Secretary of Agriculture, Ezra Taft Benson, wrote in the 1950's, "Rural people are a bulwark against all that is aimed at weakening and destroying our American way of life. The future of agriculture and the preservation of a sound economic system depend upon the vigorous re-emphasis of the principles, benefits, and values of private competitive enterprise. No group in America is in a better position to contribute to this need than those who live on farms." (3)

Political and rural leaders have persistently linked agriculture to key democratic values throughout American history. The statements of Jefferson, Roosevelt, and Benson each assume and draw upon philosophical visions of democratic society, and each portrays farms and farmers as having a special ethical status in the American political system. The way ethical ideas influence a person's understanding of agriculture says a great deal about what kinds of farm policies or new technologies that person will support. Yet systematic education on ethics and agriculture has only recently been initiated in agricultural colleges. This book digs beneath the apple pie political

1

rhetoric that ties farming to democratic values and develops concepts for rigorous and coherent statements of how philosophical goals and political values ought (and ought not) to influence agricultural practice and policy.

Leaders such as Jefferson, Roosevelt, and Benson made their statements about agriculture as components of arguments about how public policy in the United States should be constructed, maintained, and modified. Their remarks are part of a democratic constitutional tradition of politics that holds that power ultimately resides with the people. Government and policies are formed when the people, or their representatives, reach agreement about the rules and procedures that will guide them. While seated at the negotiating table, these representatives propose and defend policies that, in their judgment, serve the public good. They are also charged with the responsibility to hear, evaluate, and respond to the arguments of others. As such, philosophy and ethics enter into the deliberations because they provide the basis for understanding notions such as *the good, fairness,* and *justice* that are the underlying substance of democratic politics.

The constitutional conventions that transformed the thirteen original colonies into a federal republic are themselves models of how philosophy figures in a democratic political process. The founding fathers who came to these meetings were familiar with philosophical arguments for monarchy, aristocracy, and democracy. They had read the writings of Thomas Hobbes and John Locke that proposed the idea of society as an agreement among individuals. They met, drafted structures and procedures for government, and offered arguments about how government should be established. This book is an introduction to the philosophies that informed the deliberations of the founding fathers, with an eye to the way that these ideas are especially relevant to agriculture.

The Plan of This Book

In emphasizing the role of ethics in political life, this book takes an approach to ethics that may deviate from the expectations of readers. In popular use, the term *ethics* is used to refer to personal conduct. Senators and Representatives are criticized for ethics violations when they are caught in sexual imbroglios or when they bounce checks, not when they fail to live up to the principles of the founding fathers. In other fields of applied ethics such as medicine and business, ethics often refers to choices made by individuals, rather than to the public policies that structure and regulate medicine and business. Farmers and agribusiness employees do face choices like those of doctors and especially business executives. Farmers choose production practices that affect their neighbors and employees, and professional entomologists have professional responsibilities for recommending pest control strategies that replicate physicians' responsibility for securing informed consent. However, there is a sense in which the important issues in agriculture are ones in which government policies severely constrain individual choice. Chemicals, natural resources, use of animals, the development of technology, and even levels of production are so thoroughly affected by agricultural policies that it is difficult to separate public and private decision making. There is, furthermore, little reason to repeat work on public health and business ethics that is widely available.

The theoretical portion of the book is developed in Chapters 2 through 4. Chapter 2 presents a condensed framework for identifying some key elements of public policy. In this book the term *public policy* will be used to refer to the way that a society organizes its affairs and accomplishes collective, cooperative, or even competitive interaction. People who buy and sell may not think of their transactions as part of public policy, but buying and selling are possible only when a society has collectively adopted a set of rules for recognizing who owns property and when ownership can be transferred to another. Although many of the rules for social cooperation are encoded in the society's laws, others are not. It is easy to take both laws and informal norms for granted and to overlook the structure of public action that is implicit in any form of social interaction. When new laws, regulations, or practices are proposed, however, they must be evaluated against a status quo in which existing loyalties, property claims, and even rules of etiquette are already shaping incentives, decisions, and the results of individual action.

Chapter 3 is a summary of key ethical concepts. These concepts are presented as components of a social contract. A *social contract* is either an explicit or implied agreement, much like the U.S. Constitution, that is taken to serve as the basis for social cooperation, governance, and the rule of law. Thinking about a social contract introduces ethical ideas by suggesting that we frame questions based on how philosophical goals and political values ought to influence practice and policy in terms of agreements ordinary people accept as a basis for resolving differences of opinion. As noted in Chapter 3, the social contract is only one way to think about how ethics relates to agriculture. In pointing the discussion toward social agreement, the social contract approach is more useful for a philosophical understanding of government and public policy than for personal morality. While questions regarding the personal morality of America's farming people are important, this book emphasizes the role of ethics and philosophy in framing our understanding of government, of cooperative action, and of public policy.

In Chapter 4, the framework for understanding public policy developed in Chapter 2 is integrated with alternative ways to understand the social contract developed in Chapter 3. The result is a tool for analyzing public policies in light of norms and values. The integrated framework shows how ethical concepts and arguments can be used to argue for either general public policies or for decisions and applications in specific cases. The framework helps us understand why good people support different policies, not only for agriculture but for all aspects of public life. People sometimes have conflicting interests, but they may also feel highly justified in promoting their own interests over the interests of others when they have ethical arguments to support their position. In showing how ethical arguments can be used to promote specific policies, the framework can be employed as a tool for the policy analyst, who is interested in understanding how interest groups influence the policy process.

The integrated framework also provides a way for those who have ideological commitments to specific political values to understand how their beliefs should be applied in policy initiatives. The language of American politics is often extremely general. Terms such as *liberal* or *conservative* are used to describe all sorts of political views. Even when political ideas are given some substance in political theory, however, it is often difficult to see how a philosophical or ideological commitment to values such as free markets, efficiency, or opportunity specify norms that point decision makers toward one policy choice rather than another. Without a framework for integrating values and policy, one risks supporting self-defeating initiatives. Policies that appear consistent with certain values may undermine an individual's ability to apply those values in practice. Specific examples of how the framework is applied are taken up in case study chapters that examine food safety, environmental quality, water rights, animal well-being, and agricultural development aid. Although all these examples deal specifically with agriculture, the framework itself can be applied more generally. The concepts presented in this book should be useful for anyone interested in normative policy analysis.

Using the Cases

Chapters 5 through 8 take up issues in agricultural and public policy by describing specific cases that focus on particular public policy decisions. The description of each case provides information on the interests affected by the policy and on the goods at stake. Cases illustrate how different interest groups interpret the ethics of public policy. Few individuals think that a policy is right simply because it serves their interests. People usually view policies that do not serve their interests as unfair, unjust, inefficient, or corrupt. Ethical concepts are part of the way they view public policy, and when groups are in conflict, there are usually conflicting ethical arguments for alternative policy proposals. Cases illustrate how interests develop arguments within the political context of a specific policy debate.

The case chapters serve three purposes. First, they are examples of how ethics can be applied in understanding public policy and in supporting policy proposals. Second, each case has been chosen because it is one instance of conflicts between interests or ideas that have significance for American agriculture. Battles over food safety, soil and water resources, agricultural animals, and foreign aid have been fought for decades, and there is no end in sight. This book traces the issues by choosing one or two instances of conflict and illustrating the ethics and politics of an issue in microcosm. Third, the cases present a way for students and analysts to "try on" the perspective of alternative interest groups and to see how ethical concepts justify and reinforce that point of view. In the abstract, debates over distributive justice or economic efficiency seem like vague ideological disputes. When one interpretation of justice or efficiency favors and justifies one interest over another, these ideas have the effect of defining the terms of political and ethical debate. It is therefore important to understand philosophy as it influences the world views of interest groups.

Two other topics are extremely important for contemporary discussions of agriculture, but they are less well adapted to the framework of case studies. Sustainability and saving small farms are themes in many recent criticisms of U.S. agricultural practice, policy, and technology. Sustainability critics have stated that current practices sow the seeds of their own undoing. Current policies and technology undermine the long-term viability of an industry that could stress the use of renewable and regenerative resources. Like Theodore Roosevelt and Ezra Taft Benson, small farm critics have stressed the need to preserve the rural population. They see small farms as victims of technological and economic forces that have transformed these highly regarded family enterprises into failing businesses. With respect to sustainability and small farms, critics see contemporary agriculture failing to meet broad philosophical tests of adequacy. To date, the commitments to sustainability and to small farms have had more importance for the broad values with which one understands agriculture than for specific policies where conventional ethical values are applied. It is also possible that in emphasizing ecological health or small-scale community, these critics are proposing ethical ideas that run counter to the mainstream ideas of the social contract.

Analysis of issues such as small farms, food safety, world hunger, resource conservation, sustainability, and animal well-being may be of primary interest for those who contemplate careers in farming, ranching, government, or agribusiness. An ability to understand the ethics of these issues can be integrated with traditional courses in policy and communication or can supplement a scientific understanding of the technical subject matter. The issues, however, are important to everyone, regardless of training, background, or expected career. The adage "If you eat, you are involved in agriculture" holds true here. It is people from urban backgrounds who will vote for the public servants who make the farm policy of tomorrow. Jefferson assumed that an understanding of agriculture's capacities, influences, and goals was part of the knowledge necessary for every citizen in revolutionary America. It should be so today as well.

This book has been written to appeal to the broadest audience of people involved in agriculture: those who eat. Those preparing for agricultural careers should supplement the case studies with their own knowledge of agriculture. They also should realize, however, that their career choices give them a special interest in the issues, and that their special knowledge only serves to reinforce the difference between their perspective and that of an ordinary person. The ability to see these issues with others' eyes will prepare one for more sensitive and effective ways to interpret and present one's own interests. To the extent that public policy is a social contract, the ability to listen with comprehension and to speak with conviction is a crucial component of citizenship. This book is committed to equipping its readers for citizenship, rather than to specific proposals for the issues covered.

References

1. George S. McGovern, ed. 1967. *Agricultural Thought in the 20th Century.* Indianapolis: Bobbs-Merrill. p. 28.
2. Ibid., p. 42.
3. Ibid., p. 428.

Suggestions for Further Reading

Applied ethics in medicine and business tends to stress personal conduct rather than public policy, but even there public policy surfaces as an important issue. Anthologies of work in these fields provide the best introduction. See Tom L. Beauchamp and LeRoy Walters, eds., *Contemporary Issues in Bioethics* (New York: Wadsworth, 1989) for a survey of medical ethics, and A. Pablo Iannone, ed., *Contemporary Moral Controversies in Business* (New York: Oxford University Press, 1989) for the business field. Charles V. Blatz has edited a large anthology of articles on ethics and agriculture appropriately titled *Ethics and Agriculture* (Moscow: University of Idaho Press, 1991). *Agriculture and the Undergraduate,* ed. Harry Kunkel (Washington, D.C.: National Research Council, 1992), examines whether ethics education for agriculture students should focus on personal conduct or public policy. See the essays by Harry Kunkel, Ray Thornton, and Otto Doering, as well as the articles by two coauthors of this volume, Paul Thompson and Robert Matthews.

2

Analyzing Public Policies and Issues

Public policy constrains the choices and conduct of farmers, agribusiness, and food consumers. The general goal of this book is to examine alternative criteria for evaluating public policies that affect agriculture and natural resource management. But the term *public policy* is itself often used in vague or contradictory ways. Since people who are affected by policy often have different ideas about what policy is, a vague or unspecific account of public policy can itself create public disagreement about what policy should be. This chapter will introduce a framework for identifying and analyzing public policy. A vocabulary for policy analysis will be developed that will reduce the vagueness and permit a consistent discussion of specific policies.

What Is Public Policy?

Suppose that there were no government. How would your life, and the lives of your family and friends, be changed? You might expect that there would be violence and looting. People might take up arms to protect what they believe is theirs since there would be no government to prevent theft. Or perhaps they would use weapons to seize what they believe they have always deserved but were never able to have. Imagine how difficult it would be to defend your home or business. What might happen after a few years of such anarchy? Would the roads be paved, the mail delivered, the children educated? How reliable do you think the water supply, the flow of electricity, or the phone system would be? And what about the long-term future? Would we still have research to find cures for life-threatening diseases or ways to produce food to feed a growing population?

If there were no government, some things would not change. We would still have basic biological needs for food, air, and water, and the earth would still be a source for those needs. These fixed characteristics, which we will call our *situation,* would not change, but our use, our exploitation, of our situation would change dramatically. What people do or plan to do in the future depends on what they expect they can and may do with regard to one another and the resources of the planet. If, for example, you expected that whatever you could not guard with your life would be prey for others, you probably would plan either to have few possessions or to find a way to defend against theft.

Perhaps you think this vision is overly simplistic and dramatic. You might think that people are too ethical and civilized to resort to conduct such as physical violence or theft to get control of resources and other people. But where do these shared expectations of what is ethical and civilized behavior come from? What happens when these behavioral expectations conflict and there are no rules on whose view will prevail?

Shared expectations about what we and others can and may do come from shared rules or views about what is permissible or required behavior between and among human beings. These rules define the structure of civilized society. They define who is a member of society and what members must or may do under certain sets of circumstances. Choice among different types of structures involves ethical considerations. Different structures include different rules or principles about correct behavior and different punishments for rule breakers. The rules may or may not be written. The punishments for rule breakers can vary from mere social disapproval to expulsion from the group or even death. These shared principles of behavior are transmitted and learned by individuals seeking to retain membership in the group. The group's structure helps members to develop stable expectations about what they can and may do.

Most of us belong to several groups whose structures we seek to learn and abide by. We belong to families, ethnic groups, religions, communities, states, and nations. But the principles of behavior and the methods used to enforce these principles may not always be clear or agreeable to everyone in the group, so conflicts can and do arise within these groups. There can also be conflict between groups. Often such conflict arises from conflicting interests, but sometimes it arises because the rules that structure the behavior of the members of different groups are unknown, unclear, or simply unfamiliar. It is the possibility of unbounded misunderstanding and conflict, and thus of violence and theft, that leads to the desire for explicit, written rules that are agreeable to and enforced by group members. Explicit rules enhance the value of resources, goods, and services because people can develop expectations about their use. We have come to know these formal sets of rules as *laws* and the system of enforcement as the *legal system.* Together, the laws and the legal system used to enforce laws create a formal structure that people can look to for defining the principles of behavior and, thus, for developing expectations about what they and others can and may do.

Formal legal structures are not the only principles of behavior that rule people's conduct. Unwritten rules of behavior are implicit in the social norms and customs of our culture, our families, and our religions. Knowledge of the legal structure alone is insufficient for understanding and predicting the conduct of individuals. However, unlike social norms and customs, the legal structure is formally and consciously chosen through a public process. Its fairness and rightness can be judged. It also contains a mechanism for the resolution of conflict that arises when people misunderstand, disobey, or disagree with the principles of conduct. It is thus a powerful tool for directing the conduct of individuals.

Because the legal structure directs the actions of individuals, it is a tool that can be used to coordinate and plan activities of group members. Consequently, the legal structure can be used to accomplish goals or ends desired by group members. This feature of the legal structure has led to the formation of many types of self-governing groups or *associations*. Some associations are called public associations, where membership is a matter of birth, citizenship, or residence, and thus is to a certain extent involuntary (i.e., nations, states, counties, cities, townships, and special districts). A second class of association is called private, where membership is largely voluntary (for example, owners of for-profit and nonprofit corporations, members of mutuals and cooperatives, and members of families). Like individuals, associations can choose actions and goals, but the choice-making process is collective in nature. For example, an association of individuals could decide to pool their financial resources to engage in the business of processing food (the action) for the purpose of making a profit (the goal). To do this, they could decide to hire employees to carry out the tasks. It is only the association members (for example, stockholders) who ultimately decide (that is, vote on) what their collective purpose will be. Similarly, an association of individuals could decide to pool their resources to engage in the business of providing education (the action) for the purpose of improving the knowledge and skills of their children (the goal). They may decide to hire employees to carry out the tasks. They may decide to elect a few of their number (i.e., the school board) to oversee the enterprise. Again, it is the association members (here, the school district members) who ultimately decide what their collective purpose will be.

When a group uses the legal structure for the purpose of pursuing collective goals, it is making policy. A policy is a planned course of action for achieving some goal. When a policy is adopted by a private group, it is usually called a *corporate policy* or *hospital policy* or *family policy*, depending on the group that adopted the policy. When a policy is adopted by a public association, it is called *public policy*. Public policies are contained in statutes and rules adopted by the group or its appointed legislative bodies. This contrasts with judge-made or common law, which grows out of the judicial resolution of specific conflicts between private parties.

Public policy, as the name implies, is a plan or course of action for achieving some public purpose, goal, or end rather than some individual goal or end. The distinction between law and public policy is subtle. In essence, every action of every individual is subject to the law, and since the law is publicly decided, every law is essentially a public policy directed to one or more public goals. However, some individual behavior is relevant to the attainment of public or collective goals that are not stipulated by law. For example, we all want food, but we do not have to decide collectively what food each of us will eat. Each individual decides personally what to eat, and these individual decisions collectively determine what farmers and ranchers will be able to sell. If prosperity is chosen as a public goal, the individual choices of producers and consumers affect the attainment of this goal, but stipulating these choices by law is not the only way (or even the best way) to achieve the goal.

Public goals are end states that are agreed to be desired collectively by the public. Examples of broad public policy goals are peace and prosperity. Examples of more specific public policy goals are "increasing the gross national product" and "reducing inflation." Public policy goals specify not only what desired end state should be achieved, but also for whom it should be achieved. For example, the goal may be "peace and prosperity for all citizens" or "decreasing malnutrition among children." Public goals suggest criteria for evaluating the performance of public policy.

Formal legal structures and public policies are created by and apply to the behavior of people within a specified public. This association of people is defined by a jurisdictional boundary and thus constitutes a political unit. Different jurisdictions may have different legal structures. At present, the largest jurisdictional boundaries are empires, commonwealths, or nations. Smaller jurisdictions, such as states or provinces, may be created within nations. Within these may be counties, townships, cities, and villages. And within these are the jurisdictions we know as families and corporations. The smallest jurisdictional boundary is the individual. Some jurisdictional boundaries overlap, as is the case with regional planning authorities, conservation districts, or school districts.

The Means of Public Policy

Public policies consist of public goals and the means to achieve those goals. In many cases, the means to attain public goals involve rules on the allocation of some good or service such as law enforcement, clean air, waste disposal, land, health care, food, and dollars (yes, dollars are a good, just like food or clothing). There are many possible rules or structures that various jurisdictions could adopt, and throughout recorded history many have been developed. To understand these structures, it is useful to think of the laws they consist of as being of two types: procedural and substantive. Similarly, public policies are either procedural or substantive.

Procedural Law and Policy

Procedural laws define principles of behavior with regard to who within the association or jurisdictional boundary may make or change the laws, what laws they may make or change, under what circumstances, and in what manner. These procedural laws are often written in a formal constitution or similar document and thus are often called constitutional laws. Examples of different types of procedural systems are autocracy, oligarchy, democracy, theocracy, and republic. For example, in an autocracy, only one person within the jurisdiction is given the power to make laws on behalf of all other members, with or without their approval. In a pure democracy, all members of the jurisdiction must collectively agree what the laws will be. In a republic, members of the jurisdiction elect representatives to make laws on their behalf.

In this country, the power to make formal laws is given to certain publics—groups of people sharing some common interest or purpose—defined by geography (e.g., the nation, state, county, city, township, and special districts) or by social function (e.g., families and private associations of various types). But the types of formal laws each of these jurisdictions can make are delimited by the larger jurisdiction of which they are a part. For example, the U.S. Constitution limits, as well as grants, the power of states to make certain laws; likewise, the constitution of each state limits the powers of its counties, cities, and other municipalities.

Substantive Law and Policy

Substantive laws define principles of behavior with respect to who may use the resources of a given jurisdiction, what resources they may use, under what circumstances, and in what manner. For example, a law may spell out who may own (i.e., get to use and to control the use of) a particular automobile, as well as obligate automobile users to follow certain rules of the road or to have certain qualifications. Thus, substantive law addresses behavior associated with the consumption, exchange, and production of goods and services. Substantive law may address the use of all sorts of resources within a jurisdiction, including the use of our bodies and minds and the bodies and minds of others. For example, a legally established community may prohibit, regulate, or allow the consumption and production of foods, drugs, transportation, music, waste disposal sites (e.g., air, water, and land), communication services, education, human labor, and human bodies or their parts.

Principles that specify control over the use of goods are often referred to as property rights or simply **rights**, although they prescribe obligations and responsibilities as well as rights. Property rights address both rights to use and responsibilities to use the jurisdiction's resources. Since the use of resources involves their production, exchange, or consumption, property rights specify who may (not) or must (not) produce, exchange, or consume particular resources, goods, and services. For example, laws may specify that all people within a jurisdiction must organize to provide collectively educational services of a certain type, that the educational services must be distributed to people between the ages of 5 and 18 who live in a specified area, and that all people between the ages of 5 and 18 who live in a specified area must consume particular types of educational services. Alternatively, the laws may specify that anyone in a jurisdiction may produce educational services, that the educational services must be distributed to people who offer money to obtain them, and that anyone who wants to consume educational services may do so if he or she pays for them.

Examples of different types of systems of property rights are capitalism, communism, and socialism. For example, under capitalism, ownership of (i.e., rights to use and control the use of) goods and services is given to individuals as well as to public and private associations. Under pure communism, all resources and goods are owned in common, meaning that all individuals within the jurisdiction have the right to use all resources and goods within the jurisdiction. Under pure socialism, all resources and goods are owned by the state, which must allocate those resources and goods to individuals on the basis of their need. These different systems show that principles of behavior may allow for collective or individual production, exchange, and consumption of resources, goods, and service. Most systems are a mix of different property right systems. One reason for this is that some uses of resources, goods, and services differ in their production, exchange, and consumption characteristics—a subject we shall discuss in more detail later in this chapter. For example, it is difficult to exclude people from some uses of goods like oceans, air, radio broadcasts, and street illumination, thus making individual ownership of some aspects of their use impractical. Formal understandings of property rights evolve over time as our use of resources changes. Several hundred years ago, most societies were primarily agrarian. Today they are industrial. The types of resources used and the manner of their use have changed. These changes result in unclear property rights and thus unclear expectations about what people can and may do. As questions arise, conflicts occur as people disagree over what the property rights, and thus what the substantive law, is or should be.

In this book, we are concerned with understanding public policy issues related to agriculture and food. Such issues, we now see, could involve disagreements about either procedural or substantive laws. Most of the public policy issues that will be discussed concern substantive law. They deal with issues concerning the production, exchange, and consumption of resources, goods, and services related to agriculture and food.

Disagreements regarding substantive law can be of two sorts. On the one hand, there can be disagreement regarding what property rights individuals *in fact* have. Such disagreements are typically resolved through a judicial process whereby parties to the disagreement seek to find what existing laws say or imply about who has the right or duty to use the resource in question. Lawyers help clients to develop and defend a particular interpretation of the law. Judges decide whose interpretation is correct. If the conflicts are over *violations* of the principles of conduct specified in the current set of property rights, the judicial process also is used to discover whether someone has broken the law and, if so, what the appropriate punishment is.

The second sort of disagreement has to do with what property rights of individuals *should* be recognized. These disagreements typically concern proposals to change the property rights that society recognizes and/or their degree of enforcement. These disagreements are resolved by means of a legislative process in accordance with the decision-making rules prescribed by a body of procedural law. In this case, competing petitions for different sets or revisions of property right rules are brought to decision makers, who then choose whether and how to revise the set of property rights by enacting new laws. It is the latter type of conflict—conflict about what the law should be—that most clearly involves ethical choices and thus will be the subject of later chapters. We will be interested not only in what laws should be placed on the books, but also the degree to which the laws are enforced or carried out, since this determines the practical societal consequences of enacted law.

Controversy over what and whose ends public policies should serve, and what and whose conduct should be used and regulated to attain those ends, creates public policy issues. Public policy can embody many possible goals or ends. Depending on who controls the making of the group's laws, the law can serve the goals of the many or the goals of the few. The goals served can represent either the most noble ends or the most evil ends of people. The goals can be broad and vague or narrow and specific. Public policy can also embody many possible means for achieving goals. The principles of conduct can be chosen for their effectiveness and efficiency in achieving the goals of public policy, or they can be chosen for the kinds of behavior they encourage or discourage in certain individuals (e.g., honesty and equity versus lying and enslavement).

The Policy Process

Policy analysts call the decision-making process whereby problems deserving of public action are identified and public policies addressing those problems are formulated, adopted, funded, implemented, and evaluated the *policy process*. As commonly conceived, the process has five distinct stages, each of which involves a different set of controversies and a different set of key actors. Since most public policies evolve over time as conditions change, policies tend to cycle through the five stages of the policy process many times. Some cycle through on a regular basis (e.g., social security updates, defense); others cycle through on a very irregular basis (e.g., flood and drought policies). If a totally new public policy were being crafted for the first time, it would probably go through each of the five stages in order. Some policy issues may never make it through all five stages. Older public policies may have issues being raised in all five stages at once. The five basic stages of the policy process are much the same regardless of the level of government involved. For the sake of simplicity, we will focus on the policy process at the federal level. We begin our discussion of the policy process by considering the **key actors** in the policy process.

The policy process in the United States involves many people from many different segments of our society, which helps to explain both why policy change can be so agonizingly slow and full of compromise and why our process is perceived to be open and democratic. Individuals and groups who initiate change in policy, or who influence the choice of policy, are called actors. For most policies, key actors are the legislative branch, the executive branch, interest groups, and the press. These categories of key actors exist at different jurisdictional levels (national, state, local). More than one jurisdictional level may be involved in a particular policy issue; however, in order to simplify the following discussion, we will assume that only one level of government is involved.

Each group of key actors can be viewed as being horizontally specialized by policy subject area. For example, the two houses of the legislative branch are organized into committees on agriculture, health, transportation, taxation, and so forth. Each of these committees has decision-making authority for issues that fall into the subject area in which it specializes. The executive branch is specialized similarly into departments of agriculture, health, transportation, budget, and so on. Likewise, interest groups and different segments of the press tend to specialize in particular interest areas.

Each of the sets of key actors can also be viewed as having a hierarchy of decision-making authority. For example, at the top of the federal executive branch hierarchy is the President, followed by cabinet secretaries, their assistants, the aides to the assistants, and so on down to the lowest level of decision-making authority. The legislative branch exhibits a similar hierarchy of decision-making authority that runs from the overall leadership of a legislature (the Speaker in the case of the U.S. House of Representatives), to the chairs of the various committees, and finally to the various staffs. Interest groups and the press have similar internal authority structures that differ only in the extent of the resources that they command.

Policy issues vary in terms of the subject area they concern, the scope of impact they have, and the interest they hold for people. The key actors likely to be involved in the decision-making process for a given public policy issue are determined by the subject matter of the policy process and the organization of the institutions. Policy issues concerning a particular subject such as agriculture are likely to include key actors already involved in that subject area. For example, a problem dealing with farm commodity programs will involve the committees on agriculture in the legislature, the department of agriculture in the executive branch, and interest groups representing producers and consumers of the commodity and the farm press. If the policy issue has wide impact and interest, it is likely to involve the attention of the highest levels of authority in each of the key groups; if it has little impact and interest, it is likely to involve the attention of only the lowest levels of authority. Most policy issues fall somewhere in the middle of the continuum.

Knowledge of the horizontal and vertical specialization of the policy arena and the individuals who occupy the niches within this arena is important for identifying those who are likely to be the key actors in a particular policy process. In most cases, policy issues involve key actors who have come together on related issues many times in the past and thus are aware of each other's points of view and abilities. The wider the interest and impact of an issue, the greater the number and importance of the people likely to be involved in the policy process. The greater the number and importance of the people involved, the more divergent will be the views of what the problem is, whether its resolution requires a change in policy, and what level of government action is appropriate, and the more time-consuming will be the ensuing policy debate. Knowing the key actors and their views enables one to anticipate the outcome of such debate.

At the federal level, then, the key actors include the U.S. Congress, including congressional staffs; the President and the departments and agencies in the executive branch; national interest groups; and the national press, including television news bureaus, magazine reporters, and major newspapers like the *The Washington Post* or the *The New York Times*. Let us examine each of the five stages of the policy process and the differing roles that each of these key actors play in these stages.

Problem Identification

There must be a reason for government to act and thus to adopt formal policies that guide human conduct. The policy process begins when a problem or opportunity becomes recognized as something that government should act on by developing or modifying public policy. Thus, the first stage of the policy process is **problem identification**. By a problem or opportunity, we mean the perceived or anticipated lack of some desired state or condition. As discussed earlier, public policies consist of goals or ends coupled with public means to achieve those goals or ends. Thus, there must be a perceived absence of some desired goal or end for a problem to be recognized. However, the mere existence of problems or opportunities for some people does not necessarily mean that there is a perceived need for government to act on them. There must be some sense that action by government is the proper approach to the problem. There also must be a sense that the proper action for government to take is to develop or modify public policy to deal with the problem. In many cases, there may be a felt need for government to act, but there is no need to develop or modify public policy because adequate policies are already in place. Thus, for example, there are welfare policies to aid the poor, environmental policies to deal with the problems of polluted air and water, public health programs to deal with disease, and so on. Some of these programs may not be dealing with some problems in a way that is considered adequate. However, the reason for this inadequate response may be underfunding or mismanagement rather than public policy. In such cases, more money or better management is the solution, *not* developing or modifying public policy. In other words, the laws and regulations need not be changed; rather, they need to be enforced. These are problems of program implementation and enforcement, not problems for policy making.

The first stage of the policy process thus involves the recognition of a need to develop or modify existing laws or regulations of government. Changing laws is the responsibility of the legislative branch of government (Congress on the federal level). Changing regulations is usually the responsibility of regulatory agencies in the executive branch that have been delegated certain limited quasi-legislative powers by the legislative branch. There are many such regulatory agencies at the federal level, including the Environmental Protection Agency, the Food and Drug Administration, the Federal Trade Commission, the Consumer Product Safety Commission, and the Securities and Exchange Commission. At the state level, the legislative body is the state legislature and, as with the federal level, there may be regulatory agencies in the executive branch with specifically delegated quasi-legislative powers. At the county or township level, specific legislative powers may be exercised by commissions or boards. At the city or village level, legislative powers are exercised by a city or village council or board. The existence of these different levels of government implies that for the policy process to get underway, not only must there be a consensus that there is a problem that requires public policy development, but there must also be a consensus about the appropriate level of government at which to address the problem. In a multilevel political system like our own, policy initiatives often stall precisely because there is no consensus on the appropriate level of government.

Policy Formulation

Policy formulation is a political undertaking in which a consensus is developed for a particular policy option; such an undertaking requires organizing the support of many actors. Once a policy problem is identified, a whole host of policy options are likely to emerge. These can be initiated by any of the key actors involved. However, the formal proposals that finally get on the legislative and quasi-legislative decision makers' formal agenda usually involve negotiation among all the key actors interested in that policy issue. The more important the issue, the more actors involved and the longer the process of policy formulation. Usually this is a bottom-up rather than a top-down process. That is, alternative proposals are formulated at lower levels in the hierarchy of institutions, and higher levels of authority become involved only at the stages of adoption and funding. For policy issues involving the highest authority levels, elaborate procedures may be involved in the policy formulation stage. For example, the President has an annual call for legislation that follows a detailed and well-known process of developing policy alternatives originating at the bottom of the executive branch hierarchy and working their way up.

Policy formulation builds on and modifies prior policy commitments. This includes prior commitments to goals as well as means. In most cases, policy formulation does not involve a change in goals or means, but rather marginal changes in the level of commitment. Called *incremental formulation*, it involves policy changes such as expanding or contracting a policy goal commitment or consolidating or splitting the various means used to achieve the goal. In other cases, policy formulation involves a new goal, but previously used means are borrowed and adapted to the new goal. An example is applying the idea of loan guarantees for small businesses to the area of education. In still other cases, policy formulation involves innovation in the means used without a change in the underlying goals. This has happened in the environmental area, where experience has taught us that "bricks and mortar" approaches, that is, approaches that mandate the use of certain kinds of pollution abatement technologies, are not as effective in reducing pollution levels as approaches that enforce regionwide pollution standards but allow market mechanisms to determine how the "rights to pollute" created by these standards are to be distributed among the region's polluters.

Policy Adoption and Funding

The authority of a legislative body to adopt and fund policies derives from the constitution of the jurisdiction the authority serves. In the case of the federal government, this authority derives from the U.S. Constitution. In the case of state government, authority derives from a state's constitution. Municipal legislative authority is delegated by the constitution of the state in which the municipality is located. Most policies have to be approved not once, but twice—once when they are adopted as law and again when public funds are authorized to carry them out. The adoption process in the case of the legislative bodies requires the introduction of a bill by one of the elected members of the body. It is disagreements over the words in this bill that are the focus of all subsequent negotiation and decision making. The words may be amended, approved, or disapproved. The bill is assigned to a committee, and most likely the committee will assign the bill to one of its subcommittees. Most of the negotiation on the words of the bill occurs in the committees and their subcommittees. In 90 percent of the cases, the legislative body endorses the decisions of the committee; thus, the committee is a key actor in the adoption process. In cases of particular importance, the legislative body itself may debate the bill, thereby becoming itself one of the key actors in the policy process. Once past the legislature, the bill must be signed by the

President (governor at the state level) to become law. Known as a *public law,* it is codified in the *U.S. Code* unless it deals with appropriations.

If the law authorizes action by government, monies must be appropriated by the legislature before they can be spent by the executive branch. In Congress, this appropriations process occurs every year and is ruled by special procedural laws. The annual appropriations process offers additional opportunities for the policy's supporters and opposition to fight over the policy.

In the case of federal regulatory agencies, the Administrative Procedures Act prescribes that the adoption process begin with the introduction of a proposed rule. This proposed rule must be published in the *Federal Register,* and a period of time must be allowed for public comment on the rule. A hearing is then scheduled in which public comment is invited. The decision to adopt the rule is then made by the commissioners of the agency involved. Once adopted, the rule becomes part of the *Code of Federal Regulations.* (Similar processes occur at the state level.)

Program Implementation

Most public policies require some action by government to carry out or implement the provisions of the policy. The policy, coupled with funds appropriated to carry it out, mandates and authorizes the executive branch to implement programs. In general, program implementation activities involve distributive, redistributive, or regulatory actions.

Distributive policies require government programs to produce and distribute some good or service. Examples include defense, law enforcement, roads, and education. The goal of these policies is to increase the supply of these goods or services beyond what people themselves could produce. Normally they involve taxing all people, producing the good or service through government agencies or contracts with private firms, and then providing the good to all or some of the people in the jurisdiction. In some cases, distributive policies involve production only for those who pay user fees for the good (as in, for example, water and sanitation services).

Redistributive policies require government programs to redistribute wealth. The redistribution can be in cash (money) or in kind (goods). These policies require that wealth be appropriated or taxed from one group of citizens. Government workers determine who is qualified under the terms of the policy to receive this wealth and then distribute it to them. For example, programs that subsidize farm production are based on a redistributive policy that redistributes wealth by channeling tax dollars to qualifying producers. Food stamp programs redistribute wealth by channeling tax dollars to qualifying food consumers. The goals of redistributive policies vary. Sometimes, as in the case of farm subsidies and food stamps, they are intended to encourage the production or consumption of certain goods; in other cases, as with the case of public assistance (welfare), they are intended to serve philosophical objectives of equality or opportunity.

Regulatory policies prohibit or require certain production and consumption activities by private individuals. For example, regulatory policies may require that all drivers be licensed, or they may grant exclusive patents. While regulatory policies focus on directing the conduct of private individuals, the conduct involved may be very specific; thus, quasi-legislative powers may be delegated to agencies in the executive branch to establish programs that specify and enforce those regulations.

Program Evaluation

Once a program is implemented, its consequences become apparent. These consequences may have been anticipated by policy analysts in the earlier stages of the policy process or they may have been unanticipated. In either case, all the key actors will have yet another day to seek the provisions they wanted in the first place. This is done through the process of **program evaluation**.

Program evaluation occurs each year if only because, each year, budget and appropriations decisions must be made. However, because the entire budget is huge and complex, annual evaluation may be very limited. More in-depth program evaluation may be undertaken by any of the key actors. In Congress this activity is called *oversight*, and there are special oversight committees that oversee the actions of executive branch officials. Congress also created a special agency—the Government Accounting Office—to check on the implementation of programs. The executive branch has the Office of Management and Budget. There are private watchdog groups as well, such as Common Cause. Finally, the judicial branch may be called upon to determine whether the executive and legislative branches of government are obeying both procedural and substantive law.

Different types of issues arise in each of the five stages of the policy process. Knowing whether a particular issue has to do with problem definition, developing policy alternatives, adopting policy alternatives, implementing programs, or evaluating programs is crucial for understanding the issue. In this book we will be mainly concerned with evaluating policies rather than programs.

A Framework for Analyzing Public Policy

Many types of questions may arise in analyzing public policies. For example, questions may be raised about their efficiency, effectiveness, equity, political feasibility, and implementability. The ability to ask and answer such questions can be greatly facilitated by the use of a suitable analytical framework.

The framework to be presented is intended for use in the analysis of substantive policies. It can be used in the analysis of procedural policies, too, but the form of analysis that these two different types of policies require would be different. Thus, for the moment, we concentrate only on the problem of analyzing substantive public policies.

A fundamental assumption of the framework is that substantive public policies are concerned with the *allocation of goods and services.* In other words, substantive policies seek to develop principles of conduct with respect to the use of goods and services. These uses include consumption as well as production. Thus, substantive public policies specify *who* gets to consume or produce goods and services as well as *how.* For example, distributive policies deal with the production and distribution of goods and services by government. Regulatory policies address production, distribution, and consumption of goods and services by private individuals. Redistributive policies are concerned with the redistribution of goods and services among private individuals.

The analytical framework we will use consists of four sets of variables important to analyzing substantive public policy: situation, structure, conduct, and performance. Within each of these four categories are still other variables that help us in the job of analysis. Let us look at each of the four categories separately; we will then go back and consider how they are related.

Situation

The term *situation* will be used to identify those aspects of the world that must be taken as a given, as well as constraints that cannot be changed readily by policy. Because many substantive policies concern the allocation of goods and services, one of the key steps in analyzing the situation in which a public policy decision will be made is to identify the particular good(s) or service(s) whose production or allocation is at issue. Examples of some of the goods that will be addressed in subsequent chapters of this book include food nutrients, drinking water, irrigation water, groundwater, food safety, and farm land.

The *characteristics* of goods and services are key components of the situation. These characteristics affect people's expectations about their use of goods and services, and people's actions, in turn, depend on their expectations. Although expectations are shaped by public policy and the development of systems of property rights, they are also affected by the nature of the goods and services themselves. Three characteristics of goods and services are particularly important: rivalness, excludability, and information cost. Each will be discussed in turn.

Rivalness of Consumption.   One important characteristic is the **rivalness** of consumption of a good. Goods whose consumption by some people reduces the total quantity available to other people are *rival goods.* Goods whose consumption does not reduce the total quantity available are *nonrival goods.* For example, consumption of food is rival since food eaten by one person cannot be eaten by another. However, consumption of information about the nutritional requirements of human beings, the growing requirements of crops, or the potential toxicity of a pesticide is nonrival since consumption of this information by one person does not diminish its potential consumption by others. Hookups to electric power lines, city water lines, and irrigation canals are also nonrival. That is, if lines or canals are going to be established to deliver electricity or water, one person's hookup does not diminish the ability of others along the same route to hook up as well.

The use of the air can be both rival and nonrival since some uses of the air are incompatible while others are compatible. For example, if one person uses the air for emissions of waste products such as exhaust from a car, airplane, or factory, another person cannot use that same air for healthy breathing or drying clean clothes. Those uses are incompatible and thus rival. However, if all people use the air for healthy breathing only, many people can use the air in a nonrival way.

The rivalness of consumption of a good influences people's behavior with respect to that good. People must compete to get a unit of a rival good because only one person can have that unit. Thus, some rules of competition (i.e., physical strength, beauty, wealth) will be established among people who want that good. In contrast, people may share the use of a unit of a nonrival good, and it may be less costly for them to share a single unit than to produce one unit for each individual who wishes to consume one. However, with just one source of supply, problems of *monopoly control* develop, as well as disagreements about exactly what good or service will be provided to all consumers sharing the costs.

Excludability of Consumption. The **excludability** of a good is determined by the effort required to prevent someone from consuming it. When it is relatively easy or cheap to exclude people from consuming a good, it is called an *excludable good*. When it is difficult or costly to exclude people from consuming a good, it is called a *nonexcludable good*. For example, it is relatively easy to exclude someone from consuming a particular unit of food. All you have to do is package and hide it. It is somewhat more difficult to exclude someone from consuming food growing in your fields. You would have to post a guard or put up an electric fence. It is even more difficult to exclude someone from consuming the air around your home.

The cost of excluding consumption of a good influences people's behavior with respect to that good. If you must expend a great deal of effort to exclude others from the use of goods that you have produced, you are less likely to produce them. Similarly, if others cannot exclude you from using goods they have produced, it would be less costly to you to consume their goods than produce some of your own. You have an incentive to be a *free rider*. Most goods require at least some effort to exclude people from using them. In fact, the cost of maintaining our system of property rights, and the police and justice system that enforce those rights, are examples of exclusion

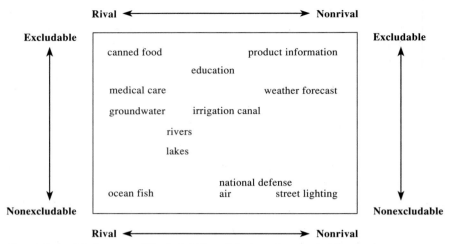

Figure 2–1   Rivalness and Excludability of Various Goods and Services

costs. However, it may be so costly to exclude people from the use of some goods that it may not be worthwhile to do so. When you cannot exclude, you cannot have a system of exchange. Figure 2-1 illustrates the relative rivalness and excludability of various goods and services.

Information Costs of Consumption.   **Information cost** is the effort or expense required to obtain information about the qualities of a good (or service) prior to its use. If it is difficult or costly to obtain information about one or more of a good's qualities, its consumption involves *high information cost.* If it is relatively easy to obtain such information, its consumption involves *low information cost.* Some qualities of goods can be directly seen, smelled, touched, heard, or otherwise sensed prior to consumption of the goods. For example, it is easy for most people to see the cosmetic quality of fruits and vegetables or to smell rotten food. Similarly, it is relatively easy to observe the color or texture of clothes. Other qualities of goods can be observed directly using the ordinary human senses, but not prior to their consumption. For example, you cannot be certain that unfamiliar food will taste good before you eat it. This requires experience, which is costly to acquire. Some qualities of goods cannot be observed directly using the ordinary human senses. For example, unless you know the exact recipe and ingredients used in preparing an entree, you cannot be certain what its caloric or nutritional content is. Similarly, a sophisticated laboratory and several days of testing are required to determine the level of pesticide residues in a particular batch of food.

The cost of obtaining information about the qualities of a good influences people's behavior with respect to that good. Low information costs make it easy for people to enforce an agreement with someone else to provide the good that they want. High information costs make it difficult for people to ensure that they will get the exact qualities they seek. People may end up consuming more or less of a good than they would if they knew what its true qualities were.

Rivalness, excludability, and information costs are normally characteristics of goods that cannot be changed. We may be able to do something about the distribution of goods by having a larger police force or requiring sellers to provide information about their goods, but such policies shift consequences from one group to another. We cannot make the characteristics themselves go away. They are realities or constraints that influence people's choices, and people must learn to live with them.

Substantive policy issues involve goods and services whose allocation has become a problem. Identifying and understanding the basic characteristics of the goods and services involved can help to clarify the nature of the problem in many cases. Identifying the basic characteristics of goods and services is also useful when trying to predict what would happen if public policy were changed. Public policies establish what behavior or conduct will be permitted. Since the characteristics of goods affect people's behavior, the characteristics of goods will affect the outcomes of public policies.

Structure

The term **structure** refers to the rights and obligations that public policies create in order to control or influence people's conduct with respect to the use of goods and services. These rights and obligations are collectively established by a community of individuals within a jurisdiction. These rights and obligations structure certain people's conduct by affecting their expectations about what they can or may or must do. Understanding the structure of rights and obligations created by a particular community's policy involves identifying *whose* conduct is being addressed by the policy and *how* that conduct is structured by the policy. The structure of rights and obligations created and imposed by a particular policy will invariably have features unique to that policy; however, such structures can usually be categorized in several broad generic classes. In other words, there are generic types of rights and obligations with respect to the use of goods and services. In a **status system**, a jurisdiction or community grants rights to use certain goods and services to individuals based on their social status. These rights are exclusive but not transferable. For example, marriage entitles spouses to exclusive rights to use certain goods and services owned in common by the household. Childhood entitles children to certain types of nurturing and care. In both cases, the social status of the person determines his or her right to use a good, but that right is not transferable (i.e., it cannot be sold) to someone else, nor does it entail any obligations to the community.

In an **administrative system**, the community grants rights to use certain goods and services to individuals based on specific administrative criteria such as residency or geographic location. For example, residency in a particular community may entitle an individual to certain educational or fire protection services. However, rights to community resources also entail certain duties as well, such as the transferral of a certain percentage of the individual's earnings to the community. Like the status system, the rights established by administrative criteria are exclusive to those who fit the criteria but are not transferable. Unlike the status system, these rights also entail certain obligations to the community. However, obligations to the community are not necessarily tied directly to use of the community's resources.

In a **bargained exchange** structure, the right to use goods and services is given to individuals, but this right is transferable at the discretion of the holder of the right. This structure allows a person to exchange the goods and services he or she currently owns for the right to use other goods and services. The terms of the exchange are the result of a bargain struck between the parties to the exchange. In a **regulated exchange** structure, rights to use goods and services may be limited to certain individuals (e.g., people with permits), the manner in which goods and services may be used may be limited (e.g., you are permitted to use your land for farming but not for a factory), or the terms of transferability may be limited (e.g., price controls). Thus, in a regulated structure, rights to use goods and services may be contingent on the fulfillment of certain duties or obligations. Finally, a **common property** structure indicates that all people have the right to use goods and services. The right to use is not exclusive, and it is not transferable.

By establishing and enforcing rights of ownership (i.e., rights to expect that you can use a good or service), governments enhance the value of resources. For example, establishment of exclusive and transferable rights can create or facilitate markets where none existed before (e.g., financial markets). Likewise, enforcement of rights makes a good or service more valuable to you because you can be more certain that someone else will not steal it from you. Most policy issues deal either with disagreements over what the structure of rights should be or with the level of enforcement. In the former case, most policy alternatives debated are some mixture of the generic rights structures: status, administrative, bargained exchange, regulated exchange, and common property. In the latter case, since enforcement activities are a service, debate usually centers on the problems of detecting and punishing parties who have violated the rights structure. Since detection is a service, policy debate usually focuses on the question of who should provide the service (e.g., private individuals versus public agencies).

Conduct

In specifying certain rights and obligations, the structure created by public policies provides rules for people to follow. It is often the case that the rules put few constraints on people's choices; and even when the rules are very specific, they cannot constrain action completely if people choose to break them. People still have free will. Policy analysis must not assume that people will act in accordance with these rules. The outcome of a policy choice depends upon how people are likely to act given a set of rules. The way people actually act under a given set of rules will be referred to as **conduct**. Understanding policy consequences requires the ability to predict conduct. One might think that predicting people's behavior under a new policy is almost impossible, yet people are very adept at predicting how others will act. For example, when you drive, you expect that other drivers will stay on the right side of the road and will obey traffic signals. When you go to a movie, you expect that other people will remain quiet while viewing it. You expect most adults to go to work by 8 A.M. on weekdays. These are but a few of the expectations and predictions you constantly and unconsciously make about how other people will act.

Part of the reason for your ability to predict how people will act is a knowledge of structure. People obey rules, such as driving on the right side of the road and showing up for work at 8 A.M. Some rules have been around for a long time, and even informal rules can be enforced by the disapproval of others. Long-standing customs, which all children and newcomers must learn, produce customary behavior. Customary behavior is predictable behavior. People will follow rules that are customary, so a full account of structure should include discussion of customs. But what if the rules are changed?

Suppose that the rules were changed so that all drivers must stay to the left rather than the right. The first thing you might predict is that some drivers would not know the rules and thus would continue driving on the right. This problem may be an example of a failure to specify a crucial aspect of structure; that is, we failed to specify if people would be fully informed of the new rule. Suppose that all drivers are notified of the rule by mail and through public announcements on radio and TV, and that the police are at every major intersection for the first month after the rule change. If this were the case, you might predict that everyone would soon have knowledge and understanding of the new rule except those incapable of understanding, such as children or the mentally disabled. But once competent individuals had knowledge and understanding of the new rule, would you predict that people would drive on the left or the right?

There are two theories of behavior that may lead you to predict that people would start driving on the left. One theory is that people always obey the rules if they feel that the rules were adopted by a **legitimate authority**. People or groups have legitimate authority only if they are rightly in a position to make and interpret rules. In our society, officers of government have legitimate authority over a limited domain of rule making. Street gangs, by contrast, may indeed make and enforce rules, but their authority is not legitimate. Under this theory, you would have to determine whether this rule change was in fact adopted by a legitimate authority with the consent of community members (note that this is a question of structure!) in order to predict that people will obey the rule. However, this theory of behavior sometimes proves to be false. For example, people who know the rules about speed limits, illegal parking, shoplifting, and insider trading sometimes break them even if they consent to the procedural policies that govern the process used to adopt these rules. Furthermore, this theory of behavior does not tell us how people will act when the rules allow wide choice by individuals. For example, a rule may create incentives to encourage soil conservation rather than require conservation. In this case, only those people seeking the incentives are required to obey the conservation rules. The theory gives us no useful propositions for predicting the incentives people might desire.

A second theory of behavior is that rational, fully informed, and competent people act in their own **self-interest**. This does not mean that they are never motivated by concern for others, but merely that if people perceive a pattern of conduct to be consistent with their interests broadly defined, they are able and motivated to consider the consequences of their actions. Under this theory, you would have to determine whether people thought that obeying the rule would be in their interest. If a person thought that others would drive on the left, it would be to that person's advantage to drive on the left to avoid a costly accident. This theory would predict conduct in conformity with the new rule as well. In the case of driving on the left, self-interest coincides with following the rules.

Some people object to this theory of human behavior because they think that self-interest implies that people think only about themselves. However, people often derive satisfaction or other benefits from serving other people's interests. Moreover, the theory does not rule out the possibility of obtaining satisfaction from sacrifice or asceticism. Self-interest theory is important in policy analysis precisely in cases where following the rules requires sacrifice. If, for example, the policy change is to lower the speed limit, those who have an interest in minimizing travel time will have an incentive to break the new rule. Legitimate authority theory tells us that people will follow the rules, but self-interest theory tells us that some at least will break them. If the rules are adequately enforced, the incentives for speeders disappear, and self-interest theory predicts compliance. An enforcement provision in the structure creates an incentive for individuals to follow rules.

A good place to start in developing predictions about conduct is to identify the people whose behavior is relevant to the policy in question. For example, since many policies involve the allocation of goods and services, we will be interested in the conduct of people who supply the good and of those who demand it. Since several goods involve many stages of production, there may be many levels involved in supplying and demanding the good or service. For example, in a complex economy, food production involves different sets of actors in every stage from breeding plants and animals to preparing and serving a meal.

The next step is to ask what opportunities and constraints different people are likely to face under the new policy. At the outset of this chapter, we noted that people's behavior depends on their expectations of what they and others can and may do, and this in turn depends on both property rights and the characteristics of goods. For example, suppose that our policy on air quality was that everyone has the right to use the air. This kind of structure is called *common property* or *ownership in common*. Under this type of structure, what kind of expectations are people likely to have about how they will get to use the air? A simplistic analysis would be that everyone could do what they wanted because everyone owns the air. But as our earlier discussion of characteristics revealed, it is very costly to exclude people from using your air. If others cannot be excluded, how is it possible for you to use the air as you want if uses of the air are *incompatible?* If person A uses the air to get rid of the smoke from her fireplace, person B will find it difficult to use that same air to breathe or dry clean clothes. If we restrict uses of the air to *compatible* uses, then some people will not be able to use the air as they want and thus will not own the air. The point of this example is that *legal* ownership alone is not a perfect predictor of who can expect to use a good or service. We have to take the characteristics of goods and services into account as well as our understanding of what motivates human conduct. Putting these factors together allows us to develop predictions about who may *expect* to get to use a good or service and thus whose interests are served by a particular structure. For shorthand, we call this set of expectations people's **opportunity set**.

In summary, then, the analysis of conduct involves four steps. First, we need to identify the people whose conduct is important in predicting the outcome of a change in policy. Next, we need to identify the opportunity set these people likely face. This is a matter of thinking through the combination of characteristics and structure. Third, using the theory that people pursue their own self-interest, coupled with plausible propositions about what types of things people are or are not likely to view as in their interest, we can make many predictions about conduct. Fourth, we may wish to test these predictions in the real world by running experiments or studying how people have acted under similar circumstances.

Performance

Once we have predicted what people's conduct is likely to be under a new policy, the last step is to ask what consequences those actions will likely produce. Often we discuss a potential change in one of the public policies within the existing structure to achieve a desired end state or goal for people. Analyzing the extent to which this goal is realized and the sacrifices required to reach this goal are what we mean by **performance**.

For example, suppose that our policy goal was to reduce water pollution. There are many possible indicators that we could use to decide whether water is polluted or not and whether we have reduced the level of pollution. How we define these indicators will depend on what we believe are the main goals or reasons for reducing the pollution. These reasons might be reduced human and animal exposure to hazards that cause illness and mortality, in which case we might measure pollution in terms of bacteria counts or chemical residues; or increased recreational activities, in which case we might be interested in measuring pollution in terms of smell or visual pleasure; or increased commercial fishing opportunities, in which case we might be interested in dissolved oxygen and algae.

Since many people are affected by a public policy, it is important to think broadly about its consequences; we must not, for example, be too narrow in deciding what we are prepared to count as a policy consequence. How we think about consequences (e.g., what we count as a benefit or a cost) will often have important implications for our decisions on how to allocate community resources. Thinking about costs is especially tricky. For example, some of the sacrifices required to reduce water pollution are obvious but others are not. We can easily account for the labor and other equipment needed by government officials to monitor pollution. It is much more difficult to account for the resources used by private individuals who have had to change their conduct. Just as important as the consequences is the question of who experiences them. In the example of water pollution policy, the benefits of the policy may go to those who did not contribute to covering the costs. Also, benefits may be widely distributed while costs are highly concentrated, or vice versa. The distribution of consequences is important not only for considering the fairness of different public policies, but also for understanding the types of politics that may come into play. Who wins and who loses certainly has an effect on who the key actors are likely to be and their desire to influence the policy outcome of the collective choice process.

Using the Framework to Analyze Public Policy

The analytical framework presented can be used to analyze the different sorts of policy questions that arise in each of the five stages of the policy process. As mentioned earlier, however, we shall concentrate on questions that arise in the first three stages.

The framework can be used to help *define* the public problem that people seek to do something about. In many cases, a public problem means that some desired performance is not being achieved. Thus, defining the problem involves defining and measuring those aspects of performance that we are concerned about. For example, we may wish to identify and measure global warming or groundwater contamination. A second part of defining the problem involves understanding why it is occurring. This involves going back to the variables of situation, structure, and conduct to identify why we are experiencing the current level of performance. For example, we can examine what human activities are causing global warming or groundwater contamination and how situational characteristics and structure create incentives for people to undertake these activities.

The framework can also be used to help *identify* and *evaluate* policy alternatives. One approach is to use the problem explanation developed from analyzing situation, structure, and conduct to identify elements of the structure that would need to be changed to obtain a different sort of human conduct and try to determine how this change in conduct might affect performance. Another approach is simply to take our knowledge of generic policy structures and see how each might affect the conduct and performance in question, trying each one out for size. For example, we could imagine how changing the right to use automobiles might affect transportation activities that influence global warming or how changing the right to use pesticides might affect farming activities that influence groundwater contamination. Thus, the framework can be used to *analyze* the potential performance of a proposed policy alternative (i.e., a change in structure) by working through the variables of situation and conduct and then comparing the predicted performance to the current performance.

Each of these uses of the framework requires a great deal of careful analysis and often the collection of facts and data about each of the four sets of variables. This exercise helps us consider the question of what public policies we think we should adopt. But even with all this information, we still need to decide what values should guide us in judging the information we have gathered. As the next two chapters will show, there are many different views about how to judge what is good government and what is good public policy.

Summary

People need shared expectations about how they and others will act toward each other and with respect to the use of the resources of the planet. One way to develop these shared expectations is for groups of people to come together to debate and adopt formal, written rules about what conduct should be used. The set of rules chosen provides a formal structure for deciding what is ethical or morally correct behavior among this group of people. This structure enhances the group members' ability to pursue certain mutually agreeable goals such as life, liberty, and the pursuit of happiness in particular ways.

People form a variety of groups or associations to decide collectively what the particular policies in this structure should be. Some of these associations, such as national governments, are formed to develop policies that form a structure for people or subgroups of people within a specific jurisdictional area. These governments adopt procedural policies, which govern people's conduct with respect to one another in proposing and choosing policies, and substantive policies, which govern people's conduct with respect to one another in the production, allocation, and use of goods and services. The collective set of public policies chosen form a structure of rights and obligations of the people within the jurisdiction.

In establishing particular public policies, a variety of disagreements and conflicts arise among the key actors within the jurisdiction during the process the association uses to arrive at policy choice. These conflicts concern what problems government ought to address, how these problems ought to be defined, and what policies ought to be selected to deal with these problems. Understanding the stages of problem identification, policy formation, policy adoption and funding, program implementation, and program evaluation aids understanding of who the key actors are and what the conflict is about.

During the various stages of the policy process, key actors present their analysis of what the problem is, what the policy alternatives are, and which ones should be adopted. This type of policy analysis is aided by having a framework for identifying important policy variables. The analytical framework provided in this chapter stresses the role of four sets of variables. First are the situational characteristics of goods and services. Changing public policies cannot change these characteristics, but they may alter the impact of these characteristics on people's behavior. A second set of variables helps us to describe the existing structure of rights and obligations and to analyze how a new policy might alter this structure. The third set of variables helps us analyze how people's conduct might be expected to change if the structure is altered. Performance variables help us describe how the consequences of people's actions might be expected to change.

While the framework helps us identify variables likely to be important in the public policy debate and provides a common set of terms to facilitate our discussion, it does not tell us how we should judge which policy is best. For example, should we judge the goodness of a policy in terms of how it changes structural variables, conduct variables, performance variables, or a combination of all three, or should only some subsets of variables within some of these categories be considered? How should changes in any particular set of these variables be judged? Chapter 3 examines different philosophical viewpoints on how to judge ethically acceptable public policies. It considers how these viewpoints apply in different stages of the policy process and how they address the role of structure, conduct, and performance variables in reaching judgments about the acceptability of policy change.

Key Terms

administrative system	opportunity set
bargained exchange	performance
common property	policy adoption and
conduct	funding
distributive policies	policy formulation
excludability	problem identification
information cost	program evaluation
key actors	program implementation
legitimate authority	redistributive policies

regulated exchange

regulatory policies

rights

rivalness

self-interest

status system

structure

Suggestions for Further Reading

The framework developed in this chapter relies heavily on the work of Allan Schmid and Grover Starling. Readers wishing to pursue their approaches to policy analysis should consult Schmid's *Property, Power and Public Choice* (2nd ed.; New York: Praeger, 1987) and Starling's *Strategies for Policy Making* (Chicago: Dorsey Press, 1988). Policy analysis and rule making is a well-developed interdisciplinary field with many textbook treatments. Three that we recommend are Kenneth C. Davis's *Administrative Law and Government* (2nd ed.; St. Paul: West Publishers, 1979), Jack Davies's *Legislative Law and Process in a Nutshell* (2nd ed.; St. Paul: West Publishers, 1986), and David L. Weimer and Aidan R. Vining's *Policy Analysis* (Englewood Cliffs, N.J.: Prentice-Hall, 1989).

Other approaches to decision making for agriculture, including public policy decision making, could be adapted, with a little work, to make use of our framework. Most of the existing books concentrate on the integration of technical components rather than on the framework itself. One approach that strikes a better balance between technique and the general framework is described in *Agricultural Sector Planning*, ed. George E. Rossmiller (East Lansing: Michigan State University Press, 1978), which also includes a chapter on values by Rossmiller and Glenn Johnson. Another book that emphasizes the process of problem formulation and presentation, rather than technical detail, is Kathleen Wilson and George E. B. Morren, Jr.'s, *Systems Approaches for Improvement in Agriculture and Resource Management* (New York: Macmillan, 1990).

3

Ethics and the Social Contract

Should you tell a lie in order to prevent some harm from coming to a friend? Is it all right to break a promise when a better opportunity comes along? When you have a few extra dollars, is it always right to spend them on yourself, or should you sometimes give money to charity? Is it okay to make a few personal calls on your employer's long distance WATS line? If you find a wallet on the street, can you keep the money, or should you return it to its owner? Questions like these often come to mind when the word *ethics* is used. Some of them raise deep philosophical questions about what we ought to do in a given situation and about the general principles that guide our moral life.

Other ethical questions are directed at people in particular walks of life. Is it ethical for a salesperson to misrepresent a product or service so long as no law is broken? Should an engineer who detects a safety problem "blow the whistle" on the employer by reporting the problem to the press? People in any of these situations might find it hard to know what to do. They might consult counselors or do some reading on ethics in order to help them determine the right action. They would find a long and distinguished tradition, dating back to the ancient Greeks, of men and women who have pondered the question "How should we act?" or "What are we morally permitted to do?" Ethical and political theories attempt to explain how we should go about answering questions like these. Because ethics deals with questions as general as "How should we act?", there are ethical aspects to almost everything we do.

As long as the choices are strictly personal, that is, questions of what an individual should do rather than what a society should allow, these questions do not involve public policy in any obvious way. Many ethical questions, however, have both a personal and a public dimension. In the case of abortion, for example, it is the individual woman who must make the choice to have an abortion, even in societies where abortion is legally prohibited. On the other hand, it is for society at large to decide whether the practice of abortion should be legally permitted, and this decision will depend partly on the collective judgment of all people in society. Similarly, it is up to the individual to decide whether to "just say no," but it is a public policy matter whether there will be laws regulating sexual conduct and drug use.

What is true in general is true with respect to agriculture as well. An individual farm family may struggle with the question of whether to continue farming or to sell out. They may see this choice as a choice between loyally carrying on a family tradition while living an economically impoverished life on the farm versus reaping a cash windfall that could be invested in ways that would reward them and their children with expanded opportunities for years to come. In other words, it may be a deeply moral choice for them. It is, in any case, a personal choice in our society. Other choices in agriculture, however, have a dual nature. An individual farmer may question the morality of using potentially dangerous chemicals in crop production or may worry about the ethics of raising a particular crop (such as tobacco) or food animal (such as veal). As far as the farmer is concerned, this is a personal choice; but the fact that the farmer has decided that DDT is morally acceptable hardly means that he or she can use it. Society has intervened in these choices and limits or regulates the choices the producer is permitted to make. The question of when society *should* intervene is one of the main questions we will address throughout this book.

It is the public policy side of these ethical issues that will be the main focus of attention here. It is not always possible to classify the problems and choices we discuss as either personal or public. People who feel that it is always wrong to raise tobacco, for example, will advance their reasons for this judgment in attempting to influence public policy. There is the added complication of public corporations that have corporate policies distinct from the personal ethics of their employees and shareholders. These corporations have a tremendous influence on the shape of agriculture and public life. Their decisions are, in that sense, public decisions. They are also private in that they are not made by government and in that the officers of these corporations are directly accountable to shareholders rather than to the public at large. Corporate policy thus represents a middle zone between the purely personal deliberations of individuals and the public deliberations of the political sphere. Like government policy, corporate policy represents or reflects a form of collective agreement on ethics. Although this book will stress how ethics influences public policy, many of the same things can be said about decision making within a corporation.

The Social Contract

The idea of a **social contract** is one way to indicate the basis of social ethics or the ethics of public policy. The social contract indicates an implied agreement among all members of society to accept a limited set of rules or principles that make social cooperation possible. The agreement is implied rather than actual. Although there are famous historical incidents (such as the signing of the Magna Carta and the writing of the U.S. Constitution) in which people did make explicit agreements about the future shape of their society, these agreements did not encompass all the rules and principles that make a society work. The U.S. Constitution, for example, does not say that we must keep our promises (aside from exceptional circumstances perhaps), but the common principle of promise keeping is clearly implicit in the way that we relate to one another as social beings. Talk of a social contract does not necessarily mean that members of a society have actually agreed to a social morality, but merely that their recognition of social practices like promise keeping and obeying the law is a form of unspoken consent to a broad set of rules that make social cooperation possible.

There are, of course, situations in which social cooperation is made possible not because people have willingly accepted an implicit way of doing things but because they have been unable to resist the power of an external force. Invaders, tyrants, and dictators have created social order throughout history by using torture, police power, and the threat of death to make people do what they would not otherwise do. The idea of a social contract is meant to exclude these forms of social order, efficient and stable though they may be. The social contract throughout history has been thought to point the way toward principles that underlie the constitution of a just society, one worthy of moral approval and obedience. One of the main philosophical problems in social contract theory is determining just what those principles might be.

The idea of a social contract is intended to recognize two essential limitations in the ethics of public life. First, it is not reasonable to think that people will agree on every matter of personal ethics. Some feel that exercise and good physical conditioning constitute a moral duty; others do not. There will be many points on which members of a society disagree. It is important to reach agreement on those rules most crucial for a stable and rewarding society and to leave other matters to personal conscience. Second, it is not reasonable to think that every person will voluntarily (and in all instances) submit to the rules once they have been agreed upon. It is essential to enforce these rules as a means of protecting citizens from the wrongful acts of others. Enforcement involves the creation of public authorities charged with executing this responsibility, not in light of their personal morals but in pursuit of the public good.

As a matter of fact, societies may adopt rules or create authorities that, upon reflection, seem morally wrong. The U.S. Constitution makes an explicit provision for chattel slavery. Even at the time of its writing, many of the founding fathers felt this provision to be morally wrong. They nevertheless agreed to its inclusion in the Constitution because they felt that a morally imperfect agreement was preferable to no agreement at all. In the intervening years, the moral wrongness of human slavery has come to be recognized by virtually everyone, and the provision for human slavery was eliminated by the Fourteenth Amendment. One of the main reasons for thinking slavery wrong is that the slaves were denied any opportunity to consent to the original agreement. They were not given the minimum protection from others (particularly their owners) that the social contract is supposed to guarantee. The social contract is not, therefore, a one-time agreement. The statutes and practices of a society are susceptible to criticism and reform, and one of the main types of criticism that can be leveled is that current laws are not true to the spirit of the social contract.

The social contract is important to food and agriculture in a variety of ways. Obviously, a society cannot function without a safe and adequate supply of food. Protection of the food supply may thus be a primary goal of public authorities. Thomas Jefferson thought agriculture was important to the social contract for a very different reason. He felt that any just society must provide any citizen who was willing to work with an opportunity for economic independence and an economically viable life. This meant that a person need not be dependent upon the whim of an employer (though it was perfectly all right for one to accept wage labor voluntarily) and that there should be alternatives to wage labor whereby persons could support themselves and their families. In the postcolonial United States, this opportunity was guaranteed in the form of small subsistence farming. If farming was to serve as a fundamental "safety valve" for the social contract, however, it was a duty of government to ensure that opportunities to farm continued to exist. This thinking has continued in different forms throughout U.S. history and will be discussed in more detail in Chapter 10.

If we are to provide content to the idea that ethics has its basis in an implied social contract, then two philosophical issues must be addressed:

1. *What are the terms of the contract?* The social contract is a statement of the fundamental principles that are to guide public policy. Alternative accounts of the social contract will entail different sets of terms.

2. *Why would someone agree to the contract?* Social contract theories present an argument for accepting the terms of the contract by describing why someone would or should accept it.

The presentation of social contract theory in this book presents paired analyses of these issues. Libertarian terms of the contract are paired with a state of nature argument for accepting them. Egalitarian terms are paired with an original position argument. Utilitarian terms are paired with a prisoner's dilemma argument.

Specifying the Terms of the Social Contract

Given that we need rules and principles to organize and operate our society, and that the rules we choose can come relatively close to (or fall sadly short of) the just ideal, what rules are we to choose? The main task of this chapter is to look at several different ways of answering this question, each of which has philosophical considerations that weigh in its favor and against rival views. In fact, our society seems to reflect each of these different sets of views at different times and under different circumstances, and this raises the further question of how we know which to choose at a given time. For the sake of clarity, each of these views will be discussed in a pure form; that is, each will be discussed as if it were expected to account for the entire range of public policy decisions made in our society. This is an abstraction that will help us understand the content and logic of each view, but readers should bear in mind that our real political life is far more complex.

There are two broadly different ways of understanding the sorts of rules that the social contract is intended to specify. First, there might be rules or principles that specify the goals of our society and determine, in fairly direct application, the sorts of policies that we should adopt. Since these types of rules are aimed at the substance of our public policies, they will be called **substantive ethical theories** for public policy. Jefferson's idea that economic opportunity is a prerequisite of the just society is an example of a substantive ethical principle. It entails that some policies are required and others are prohibited. Alternatively, the rules of the social contract might say nothing about what particular policies should be, but might instead address themselves to the way that laws, policies, or regulatory principles are enacted. Since these types of rules are aimed at the procedures we use to reach agreement and adjudicate disputes, they will be called **procedural ethical theories** for public policy. A practice of deciding policy by majority rule is a simple example of a procedural principle. It does not tell us what policy will be adopted by the majority, but it does tell us that whatever the majority decides is right. In this book, we will discuss several types of substantive theories, but procedural theories will be discussed as a single type. This distinction between substantive and procedural theories parallels the distinction between substantive and procedural policies discussed in Chapter 2.

Substantive theories break down into two general types. **Consequentialist theories** evaluate policy entirely in terms of its outcome. Although there are several forms of consequentialist theory, the most common is a version of **utilitarianism**. The basic idea of utilitarian consequentialism is that policy should produce the greatest benefits or the least harm for the public at large. For example, a utilitarian would apply ethics to the regulation of an agricultural chemical by comparing the costs and benefits of its use with the costs and benefits of its nonuse. Whichever option had the best distribution of benefits and costs would be the one to choose. **Rights-based theories**, by contrast, evaluate policy according to the type of structure employed or by certain uncompromisable standards of performance. Rights can be defined in various ways, of course, but would typically include protection of the life, liberty, and property of citizens. Two different forms of rights theory will be discussed here. The first is a theory that takes a very limited view of the duties

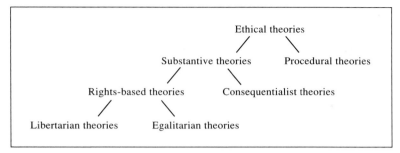

Figure 3–1 The Types of Ethical Theory

of government. Government has a duty to protect the life, liberty, and property rights of citizens from interference by others, but it has no duty to protect people from their own mistakes or to compensate them for personal inadequacies. This theory has come to be called **libertarian theory** in recent years. The second theory also holds that government has a responsibility to protect life, liberty, and property, but it asserts that these responsibilities mean ensuring a minimum quality of life. This stronger rights view also holds that government has a duty to ensure equal opportunity. Theories of this sort have been variously called *welfare theories, communitarian theories,* or *natural law theories,* as well as *Kantian* or *Rawlsian theories* after the philosophers who have advocated versions of them. Here they will be called **egalitarian theories** to indicate one of the main features that differentiate them from libertarian theories.

These theories will be given a much fuller treatment in the sections that follow. Each offers a somewhat different approach to the problem of what moral values are implicit in the social contract. The most basic differences have already been discussed, but each view entails profoundly different ideas about how a society should be run, even if all views would probably answer a large number of policy questions in the same way. The purpose of describing these theories is to develop some common vocabulary for understanding different ways of approaching ethics. These are not definitive statements of the views, but rather preliminary definitions that are intended to help the discussion reach a higher plane. The theories can be categorized with respect to one another as shown in Figure 3–1. In analyzing them, it may be helpful to remember how they contrast with one another in terms of the way that the logic of each theory is constructed.

Rights-based Theories of the Social Contract

Thomas Hobbes's *Leviathan,* written in 1651, and John Locke's *Second Treatise on Government,* written in 1697, are two of the most important books in the social contract tradition of social and political philosophy. Both Hobbes and

Locke borrowed terminology from theological ethics, and both thought that the new theories they developed were expositions of rationality or common sense. One of the main ideas borrowed from the theology was the notion of *natural rights*. Natural rights were, as the name implies, rights that people were thought to have naturally, according to God's plan of creation, or perhaps just in virtue of being rational human beings. Hobbes and Locke assumed that the principal goal of government was to establish legal protection for natural rights or, put another way, to convert natural rights to legal rights. Both philosophers deviated from the theological tradition, however, in identifying two new tasks for social and political philosophy.

The first task, they thought, was to give an account of natural rights that did not depend upon religious faith. Their goal was to give a plausible explanation of why some claims of right deserve to be recognized by government, while others do not. Locke, for instance, wanted to show why citizens' claims to rights of life, liberty, and property should be protected by law and why monarchs' claims of divine right to rule should not. One result of Locke's work was that the concept of rights has much greater importance in the emerging social contract tradition than it had in natural law theory. In natural law theory, rights were implied by one's place in the natural order or the social hierarchy. The account of rights would depend upon the more important philosophical work of describing who rules whom. In the philosophy of Hobbes and Locke, rights are concepts that should be applied before rulers are identified and questions of power have seen settled. One important result is that legitimate authority is shifted from religion to the social contract.

The second task was to show that any rational person would recognize the ethical force of rights specified. Hobbes and Locke wanted to show that everyone was ethically obligated to obey the laws that protected natural rights. This meant that people should voluntarily accept the moral force of the rights that are established; they should not accept these rights simply because they fear the power of the army or the police. Hobbes and Locke tried to complete this task by telling a story that illustrates the motivation for acknowledging these rights. The story describes how governments might arise as a result of unforced agreements made by free and informed people. If the motivation these people have for forming a government is sufficiently general, it will apply to any rational person. If every rational person is motivated to recognize the rights agreed upon in this story, then we should be willing to recognize the same rights in our own society, even though the origins of our society are quite different. Hobbes and Locke argued that if we identify universal components of human motivation, we can determine the rights that should be protected by law a priori, or in advance of any particular knowledge about the circumstances of our own situation. The important result here is that the reasons for accepting social contract ethics are consistent with self-interest.

Hobbes and Locke were not entirely uniform in the way that they met these two tasks of social contract theory, and subsequent development of the social contract approach has introduced further variations. Some philosophers have abandoned their commitment to the language of rights almost entirely. Among those who have not, the range and content of rights vary considerably. In this chapter, we will present two extreme forms of the disagreement about what rights belong in the social contract. It is possible to construct arguments for rights-based theories that fall somewhat between the two.

Libertarian Theory

Theories defined as **libertarian** limit the scope of public policy sharply, holding that such policies are justified only to the extent that they protect the life, liberty, and property of citizens against interference by others (both foreign and domestic). Governments should enforce laws against assault, theft, and other harmful acts. They should also provide for the common defense. But aside from these rather sharp and uncompromising duties, governments ought to stay out of their citizens' affairs.

In order to see how this libertarian view is developed in its full magnitude, it will be helpful to return to the story of the social contract. Social contract ethics often asks readers to imagine a situation in which individuals carry out their daily affairs in total isolation from one another. In this imaginary situation, a person would be free of all social constraints and all social enforcement. The person could act purely in accord with the dictates of his or her own conscience. If we can imagine what such a situation would be like, perhaps we will be in a position to put some meat on the bare bones of the contract idea. If people could live such radically independent lives, why would organized societies ever be formed? Would people have reasons for giving up some of the freedom to act as their personal conscience dictates? Perhaps we can get some idea of the moral notions underlying our own society by thinking about the reasons why people would leave a state of radical independence and be willing to live in an organized society.

Social contract theories that ask us to imagine a situation in which governments do not exist are called **state of nature** theories. The name derives from the contrast between life in a civil society and life bounded only by the constraints of nature. Organized or civil society is characterized as an artifact, as something of human invention. It is in this sense that civil society is unnatural. Life in the state of nature is a life unbounded by social laws or public authorities entrusted to enforce public policy. The point of describing a state of nature is to draw a contrast with full-fledged civil societies so that we can begin to think about those aspects of our society that count as advantages over the state of nature and those that count as defects.

Some philosophers in the social contract tradition such as David Hume and Edmund Burke reject the state of nature idea entirely, finding it implausible to think that people ever lived in a situation truly devoid of social relations and unlikely that any actual society was founded in any important sense upon agreements made by individuals in a state of nature. Instead they suggest that the social contract (or the true constitution of society) is an evolutionary product of small agreements and common practices that gradually build up over time. Admittedly, the imaginative construct of a state of nature is not realistic. But reality here is arguably beside the point. The idea of a state of nature is a hypothetical construct—a *thought experiment*—that state of nature theories employ in order to answer certain questions about the proper role or aims of government.

If, then, individuals *were* in a state of nature and thus free to act according to their own wisdom, what reason would they have for leaving that state and entering a civil society? In order to answer this question, we must think about what the state of nature might be like. It would be a state of radical freedom where we could truly do what we want, subject only to our own conscience. We quickly recognize, however, that everyone else could do what they wanted as well. Their conscience might tell them to take whatever they desired and to have no thought of the harm that it does to others. Since there would be no public authorities, there would be no police to call when we were threatened. Even if we felt confident about our ability to protect ourselves and our property, we would be at risk when we slept. Some would enjoy advantages of strength, some of wit, but all would nevertheless be in a situation of grave risk. It would be a life, as Hobbes described it, that is likely to be "mean, nasty, brutish, and short."

We would therefore be moved by self-interest to join in an association of mutual protection. It would be in our interest to agree not to attack the person or property of others, for the freedom we lose in making this agreement would be small compared to the assurance of our own security. It would be in our interest to have designated authorities who would enforce these promises, and whose judgment would be supported and obeyed by all members of the community. We would want some safeguards, of course, since we would not want people in authority to misuse their power. There would be many details to be worked out, but the important point here is that we, each and every one of us, would be moved to leave the state of nature and to join this association on the basis of self-interest. It would be the protection of self-interest and the avoidance of grave risks to self-interest that would be the common bond uniting all parties to the social contract.

Now, one might say, "What if someone doesn't want to join this association?" The libertarian could fairly reply that such a choice could not be in that person's self-interest. The only thing that an associate would give up is the opportunity to attack, murder, rape, or rob a neighbor. Someone who refused to join the association would be in exactly the same position as someone who does join but breaks the rules. The full force and power of the association could be brought to bear upon the outlaw; and in forcing compliance with its rules, the association could justly inflict any number of punishments, up to and including execution. Anyone who refused to join the association would be at increased risk from a large and powerful group, would have no more practical freedom than an associate, and would be sacrificing guaranteed protection of life, liberty, and property. What kind of reasoning could possibly sanction such a foolish bargain?

Since it would seem irrational not to join the association once it becomes clear that it will be formed, the libertarian may say that the contract is based upon self-interest. Any rational person would have self-interested motives to enter the contract, and the contract attains its moral force from the voluntary consent of all parties to it. Now the question of whether or not there ever was a state of nature can be put aside. The point of the story has been to show us that so long as our public policies are confined to providing these limited protections, they are justified by the fact that they are in the rational self-interest of every member of society. To violate the laws is not only to make oneself liable to punishment, but to act irrationally as well. Furthermore, by describing the motives of all rational people, the libertarian has avoided making any reference to the specific goals that would be sought by each of us in a real situation. The libertarian establishes the account of rights that should be enforced in the most general cases and among fully free and informed individuals. Even though we (i.e., real people) are neither fully free nor fully informed, even though we cannot enter the state of nature to agree upon a constitution, we can accept the structure of rights implied by libertarian theory because we can see that it is the structure to which any rational person would agree. This choice of structure can be made prior to or in ignorance of any information about our situation, including our particular preferences and life goals.

Noninterference Libertarian Rights

But what structure of rights do we choose? Thinking through the transition from a state of nature to a civil society gives us some taste of what libertarian moral theory will be like, but it does not tell us much about how it will work in a public policy decision. The working concept of the theory is that of **noninterference rights** (or negative rights, as will be explained shortly). We get a picture of how libertarian theory works, first, by knowing in general what rights are and how they guide policy decisions and, second, by knowing what particular rights appear in the libertarian catalog (or barring an actual list, a way of testing proposed rights on a case-by-case basis).

The U.S. Constitution contains the famous Bill of Rights, as well as additional amendments that establish more rights. Other rights have been recognized in legal decisions throughout history, and most Americans have an informal, nonlegal notion of rights that they would apply in a wide variety of situations. Before attempting to give any detailed account of rights, it will be useful to think about commonsense interpretations of a few examples. First, the Bill of Rights is frequently thought to guarantee the right of free speech. The right of free speech ensures each citizen that there will be no interference with the attempt to express opinions, make persuasive appeals, or otherwise offer statements. There are some implicit limitations, of course; the First Amendment does not guarantee a right to yell "Fire!" in a crowded theater. Nevertheless, this right is one we commonly understand as giving us wide latitude in what we may utter, write, or otherwise express. Second, a series of court decisions has established the right to privacy. This is in many respects a complicated right, one that is still challenged in some circles. What it means to most of us, however, is an assurance that we will not be pestered or bothered, so long as our pursuits do not infringe upon the privacy of someone else. We are to be left alone, allowed to occupy ourselves in pursuits of our own choosing.

Let us set aside, for a moment, the question of whether these rights are justified by libertarian social contract story and examine the concept of a right in more detail. The right to free speech is very much like a permission. If we have the right to speak freely, we have permission to say whatever we want. The right of free speech protects a very large set of speech acts that citizens are permitted (by law and custom) to perform. The right of free speech says nothing about whether it is advisable to speak out on an issue or about whether one should choose words in a way that is most likely to achieve one's intended objective. It is not the usefulness of speech that is at issue here, but rather its permissibility. The right of free speech guarantees us permission to say some very stupid and counterproductive things. Much the same can be said for the right of privacy. One is permitted a measure of peace and quiet to pursue one's own affairs. It may be foolish to avail oneself of that opportunity at a given time, but wise use of one's opportunities is not part of rights theory. In addition to permissibility, rights entail an obligation on the part of others not to interfere with the exercise of permitted acts and an obligation on the part of government to ensure this noninterference.

These remarks on the rights to free speech and privacy can be generalized to all rights. If we let the variable placeholder X stand for a class of actions that might be performed (e.g., voting, attending political rallies, going to the movies, owning property), then someone has a right to X just in case (i) that person is permitted to X and (ii) everyone else has an obligation not to interfere with that person's X-ing.

The foregoing definition of rights implies that there is a logical correlation between rights and obligations: If one person has a right, then everyone else has an obligation not to interfere with the exercise of that right. This logical correlation, it should be noted, does not say anything about how rights and obligations are to be distributed; it is consistent with the definition of rights that one person has all the rights and everyone else has all the obligations. The state of nature argument for libertarianism, however, implies that rights and obligations are universal, that is, they are distributed equally to all: Because the terms of the contract are general, everyone has the same set of rights and obligations.

The idea of correlative universal rights and obligations is very helpful in determining how far rights are expected to extend in the libertarian view of the social contract. Your right to free speech, for example, ends when it encroaches on the rights of others. As we noted, the right to free speech does not give permission to yell "Fire!" in a crowded theater. The reason it does not is that this act of speech is very likely to cause panic. You will have caused a situation in which people are likely to get hurt. Since some of the most important rights are the rights to life, health, and safety, your action threatens the rights of others to continue living in a safe and healthy fashion. The right of free speech ends where it threatens to violate the rights of someone else. The idea illustrated by this example of one person's rights delimiting (i.e., fixing the boundaries) of another person's rights is fundamental to libertarian social theory: Libertarian rights carve out regions of personal authority in much the same way that national boundaries carve out regions of national authority. Individual rights are constantly bumping up against one another and constraining actions that would involve crossing a boundary drawn by another's rights. Only within the region of personal authority carved out by one's rights is one free to act as one pleases.

Libertarians like to describe this last feature of their theory by saying that libertarianism allows only for *negative duties*. A negative duty is a duty to observe a constraint or *not* to do something that would violate someone else's rights. If the full force of our social rights theory is merely to constrain actions that might violate another's rights, then it seems that we can never be required to act in any particular way. We are required to refrain from acts that harm others, but we are never required to do things by this theory. It is important to note that we can define rights that fail to satisfy this criterion. We sometimes, for example, speak of a right to education. Such a right would entail that certain others in society are obligated to provide the right holder with an education. Fulfilling this obligation will require many positive acts such as paying taxes, building schools, hiring teachers, and so on. A noninterference right to an education would simply mean that others could not prevent you from becoming educated. Libertarian rights are **negative rights**, meaning that they are rights that entail only negative duties.

Farmers and ranchers often understand the ownership of their land in terms of noninterference rights. Ownership of real estate is often thought to give the owner full control over the use of the property. Others are thought to be prohibited from interfering with the owner's use. A farmer may plant cotton or sugar beets or may leave the land fallow. No one, including the government, has the right to interfere with this decision. Farmers may also think that the decision to use chemicals on their land is protected by their right of ownership. If owning land is truly a noninterference right, owners should be able to use chemicals on it if they want to do so. Restricting a property owner's use of chemicals would not be justified unless the noninterference rights of others were violated. Such a violation would occur if chemicals leave the farm in the form of runoff from the fields, groundwater pollution, or even residues on the food produced there. The ethics of a farmer's chemical use would then depend upon whether the chemicals leaving the farm interfere with other people, either by harming them or by limiting the use of water or food that they own.

Egalitarian Theory

The group of theories that we will call *egalitarian theories* are probably less well unified than libertarian theories. While few people who hold libertarian views would object to being called *libertarians*, those who hold the views discussed in this section might prefer to be called *communitarians* or even *Kantians*. Some might prefer modifications of this view that would make it more consistent with certain religious views. In the interests of simplicity, many important contrasts that might be drawn between different versions of this general view will be ignored as the view is described here. The point is not to gain a final grasp of the ethical/political theory, but to develop an initial understanding of the vocabulary and of its principal themes.

Like libertarians, egalitarians generally find much to praise in social contract theory; they, too, use state of nature theory as a launching pad. Like libertarians, egalitarians specify the terms of the social contract by giving an account of the rights and obligations of each citizen. Egalitarians also accept the validity of libertarian rights, but unlike libertarians, they do not limit their catalog of rights to negative rights. Egalitarians find some *positive rights* (such as the right to be educated, which requires action) also to be justified. The philosophical underpinnings of egalitarianism can thus be understood in terms of how it proposes to justify the recognition of certain positive rights.

Positive Rights and Egalitarianism

Egalitarian theory, we noted, is usually thought to include all the negative rights of the libertarian contract, plus certain positive rights. As one might expect, the recognition of positive rights entails a more expansive interpretation of rights and a much larger social apparatus than the libertarian theory. Consider, for example, the difference between a libertarian interpretation and an egalitarian interpretation of the right to life. For the libertarian, the right to life is simply a right not to be killed by someone else; it does not require any action on the part of another to preserve my life if I am threatened by natural causes. For the egalitarian, however, the right to life includes some assurance that society will act to help prevent my death, even when I am threatened by disease, fire, or famine. If this right is to be meaningful, it demands action from the citizens in civil society rather than merely restraint. Another way to put this is to say that egalitarians interpret rights as opportunities rather than as mere permissions. One may be permitted to do things that one has no opportunity to do. If permissions are to be meaningfully exercised, government must create conditions in which opportunities exist. For this reason, positive rights are often referred to as **opportunity rights**.

The libertarian case for restricting the contract to negative rights seems persuasive, so egalitarians owe us an argument for supposing that the social contract would include positive (opportunity) rights. Egalitarian philosophers such an Immanuel Kant and John Rawls have developed arguments that illustrate how rationally motivated people might be led to accept a social contract that included opportunity rights as well as noninterference rights.

An egalitarian theory of the social contract begins where libertarian theory leaves off. Libertarian theory, we saw, describes a social agreement focused on self-protection; the rights recognized by this agreement stress protection from harm by others. Natural law theory offers one explanation of how the social agreement might reach beyond concerns of self-protection: religious faith demands it. But in appealing to religious faith, natural law theory narrows the basis of agreement too severely. Egalitarian theory does not want a social agreement that appeals only to believers; it wants one that appeals to all rational people, regardless of creed. The assumption that the social contract should be acceptable to all rational people has important implications for what sorts of rights and obligations (duties) can appear in it. There can be, for example, no law requiring attendance at Christian services on Sunday, since such a law would hardly be attractive to Seventh Day Adventists, Jews, and other believers who are either non-Christian or who observe the Sabbath on other days, to say nothing of nonbelievers and atheists. Egalitarian theory would endorse instead a provision protecting religious freedom since rational persons, both religious and nonreligious, could agree on a right that ensures public tolerance on matters of religion.

The egalitarian theory can take the first step in constructing a social contract by generalizing on the reasoning that prohibits a law requiring attendance at church. The task is to define the terms of a contract that are attractive to all rational people and to exclude terms that are attractive only to people who share some trait (such as observing the Sunday Sabbath) that is not essential to rationality. We are looking for an agreement among all rational people, but one that also includes all the social principles to which rational people can agree. We can find this by asking what it is that people want in a society, not in virtue of being Christian or Caucasian or accountants, but merely in virtue of their being rational. This way of approaching the contract guarantees that the contract will not discriminate against anyone on the basis of race or occupation since being rational does not entail belonging to any particular race or having any particular occupation.

In addition to the libertarian protections, every rational person wants a share in the things that make a decent life possible. We shall use John Rawls's term for these prerequisites to a decent life and call them **primary goods**. Primary goods include food, shelter, security, some discretionary income, and, arguably, certain "goods" such as self-respect. They also include opportunities to learn, to work, to communicate, and to increase one's allotment of other primary goods. Every rational person wants primary goods, so it is entirely reasonable for social contract theory to take up the question of how they are to be provided. Now it is important to see that this argument in no way shows that primary goods must be provided through public policy. Government clearly does have a role, however, when providing such primary goods depends upon public action. This explains how, contrary to the libertarian view, it can be public policy to provide services like fire protection and education. Fire protection is a form of security that every rational person would want. Education is a crucial primary good since it has value both in itself and as a means for making people more capable of pursuing increased income, more rewarding jobs, and more interesting life experiences. The rational egalitarian recognizes that primary goods are not manufactured from thin air, however, so the mere fact that everyone *wants* these things is only the first move. The theory must also say how far it is reasonable to go in taxing property to provide them. Here, as one can imagine, things become a bit complicated, so the following is only a sketch of what the answer might consist of.

Property Rights and Primary Goods

The task before us is to imagine the sort of social contract that rational people would make with one another solely by virtue of being rational, and without regard to whether they, as individuals, happen to belong to a particular race, creed, or other social group. Rawls suggests that this might be done by imagining a hypothetical situation that he calls the **original position**. Since we are interested in the social contract that people would choose by virtue of their rationality, Rawls imagines the original position to be a situation in which those who are to choose a social contract have all of their rational capacities; that is, they are fully capable of making logical, intelligent choices about social institutions, yet they have no information about themselves that would allow them to favor their own interests unfairly. People in the original position would settle upon the terms of the social contract that would govern their lives, while being deprived of all information about their personal goals and interests. They choose, in other words, from behind a **veil of ignorance** that conceals information about their personal tastes and about the components of their personal identity (such as their race or sex) that might affect their choice of social contract. Thus, for example, they might have to decide whether a particular minority (e.g., convicted felons) should be permitted to vote, but they would have to make this decision in ignorance of whether they were a member of this minority.

Of course, as a matter of fact, we are *not* ignorant of such information, but this fact is beside the point. We can imagine what it would be like to make general policy choices that affect people according to their beliefs, their sex, their income group, and so on without knowing how those choices might affect us personally. We can also presumably imagine ourselves ignorant of just those facts about ourselves that might bias our policy choices in our own favor. If we can do this, then presumably we can imagine the policy choices that we would make, assuming that we were ignorant of these facts about ourselves. This is the key idea behind the original position.

So what would be the terms of the social contract that people in the original position would choose? It is virtually certain that they would recognize the libertarian rights to life and liberty, since these are important to everyone. But what about strict rights to property? If we are to propose positive versions of these rights, which would entitle citizens to aid when their lives or liberties were threatened, we might have to collect taxes to ensure them. Such taxes clearly challenge the absoluteness of property rights. From the original position, we could imagine a society in which some people have plenty of wealth and others have relatively little. Would we agree that the wealthy should be taxed so that the poor could be provided with basic health care or with access to legal aid needed to protect liberty? If we knew that we were among the wealthy, for example, we might not agree to a policy of taxation to provide health and legal services to the poor. We might feel that our wealth is our property to do with as we want. In the original position, however, we would not know whether we were to be wealthy or poor. Lacking this knowledge, would we choose a policy of providing these benefits to all, or would we choose a policy of protecting property? Rawls thinks that people in the original position would not want to run the risk of being destitute, or even poor, of being denied health and legal services. People in the original position, he thinks, would choose a social contract that guaranteed to everyone certain minimal rights, for example, the right to a healthy, secure, and free life, irrespective of one's place on the social ladder. While rational people may be willing to gamble in certain situations, Rawls thinks that people in the original position would not be willing to gamble on the basic essentials of a minimally decent life; they would choose a social contract whose terms guaranteed these essentials to everyone.

Although we do not live in a society in which everyone can have everything he or she wants, we do live in a society in which there is more than enough to satisfy everyone's essential needs. So the question must be addressed: "Should some be allowed to have more than others, or is it better for everyone to have about the same?" Surely there will be less jealousy if everyone has the same, but there may be less opportunity too. It may be that the invention of new technologies and the development of new ideas and services depend upon (i) the existence of some disposable wealth and/or (ii) the incentive for people to advance to a greater level of well-being. If everyone is equally poor, there may be no social opportunities for progress. Since a rational person would not want to preclude the possibility of economic growth and social development, it seems wise to leave room for some discretionary holding of primary goods, especially money and real property, that might provide an initial market among the better-off for something that will be enjoyed widely once the economy has expanded. It might be argued, for example, that it was the rich who provided the market for automobiles, refrigerators, and stereos until such time that these products could be produced efficiently enough to make them available to average consumers. Similarly, it seems wise to provide incentive for people who invent automobiles, refrigerators, and stereos since if there is no return in it for them, they might not think it worth their trouble. It seems useful, therefore, to countenance departures from a strict egalitarian insistence upon equal distribution of wealth since equal distribution might result in a low level of economic development.

The principle here is to insist on a limit to the practice of taxing wealth (for the purpose of providing social entitlements) at precisely the point where disparities in wealth would no more guarantee opportunity for the poor than would a government program. From the perspective of the original position, it is rational to limit our risk and, in this case, it is the risk of eliminating social mobility and innovation that we want to minimize. As a matter of policy practice, one must admit that it will be very difficult to determine precisely where this point might be. More conservatively inclined theorists may feel that reliance on markets and individual incentives makes a better use of society's wealth in the vast majority of cases. Marxists are more likely to think that discretionary wealth and incentives are important only because there are inequalities in society. If we decided to eliminate them, the same kinds of social change would occur in a communal spirit. These practical difficulties are based on factual assumptions about human nature. The difficulty of balancing market forces and social entitlements, however, and the possibility for disagreement on the facts of human nature, led Rawls to think that rational people would incorporate into the social contract certain procedures for resolving such disputes. Although discussion of procedural considerations will be postponed until the final section of this chapter, it is important to note that it is with regard to exactly this sort of dispute that they come to be applied.

Many of the central provisions of an egalitarian theory have already been discussed in describing how people in the original position come to agree on a social contract. Positive versions of the libertarian rights to life and liberty, for example, will mean that people will be entitled to fire protection, to some health services, and to legal assistance. Job training and low-interest loans for small businesses also would be among the things that an egalitarian society might want to provide. If the primary goods mentioned here can be provided only through public policy, egalitarian theory provides a reason for establishing legal rights or *entitlements* to them. Since rights in an egalitarian society are thought to provide opportunity as well as protection, they are, as noted, sometimes called *opportunity rights*; egalitarian theories themselves are sometimes called *equal opportunity theories*.

What are the key opportunity rights that must be secured? One way to specify important opportunities is to consider human capacities that are most completely developed in the process of living a full and rewarding life. One important opportunity involves knowledge and learning. Improvement of the mind is both intrinsically valuable and instrumental in accomplishing life tasks. Recall, however, the brief discussion of the right to education. One cannot readily improve one's mind without aid and support from others, who must, at a minimum, teach. So the goal of knowledge and learning entails positive obligations for others. It is likely that an entire system of education, thought, and research would need to be supported by an egalitarian society.

A second contribution to individual fulfillment comes with society's ability to participate with others in community. *Community* is the sense of common purpose and of mutual caring and support that reinforces the individual's sense of well-being. A society may provide an economic forum for exchange, as well as establish law and order, without serving the moral ideal of community. An individual living in a society that lacks community may feel alienated and may lack a sense of purpose and role in life. One might say that community is the spiritual side of society. Community may be supported by religious practices but also by public celebrations, works of art, sporting events, elections, and public services (such as fire protection). An egalitarian society will want to provide some sense of community.

While education and community are both opportunities that an egalitarian society will wish to promote, there are important differences between them. Education is probably best understood as an entitlement, whereas community is considered to be a goal. Entitlements are rights that entail obligations on the part of society (usually the government) to provide some good for the right holder. Health benefits and legal aid are entitlements. The government may not be required to provide an entitlement to people who could provide it for themselves or for people who do not want it, but the idea of entitlement means that anyone who claims the right in question will be recognized as having made a valid and binding claim on the resources of society as a whole. If education is an entitlement, then anyone who claims the right to an education has a valid claim upon that amount of the public treasury needed to secure an education. It would, however, be quite strange to talk of community as an entitlement. It seems good that both individuals and public policy should do whatever possible to promote community, but the idea of being able to guarantee the provision of community seems beyond our grasp. Although most of us have some sense of what community is, it is still vague. Perhaps we think that our society actually succeeds in achieving the kind of social unity implied by community in short bursts (e.g., on July 4th or during the Christmas season). But if we are so sporadic in our ability to fulfill the requirements of community, we can hardly (as a society) guarantee it as an entitlement. Thus it is probably better to think of community as a goal that we seek for our society, that is, as an ideal that is at present beyond our ability to guarantee as an entitlement.

This distinction between opportunity rights that can be established as entitlements and those that can only be put forward as goals provides a strategy for striking a compromise between egalitarian and libertarian theory. Perhaps it is impossible to guarantee everyone in society a good job, although it is rational to think that a truly just society would never consign anyone to meaningless work or unemployment. One may wish to recognize many of the most basic opportunity rights—rights to life and health, for example—and be willing to say that these rights are the basis of an entitlement to food and shelter. But one may also think that securing everyone an opportunity to hold a good job is something that is beyond our capacity. As such, it cannot be a demand of justice. Such a compromise theory has been called a *basic rights theory* by Henry Shue (1) because it places opportunity rights in a hierarchy. Only rights at some basic level need be guaranteed by government in order to satisfy minimal demands of justice.

Now it is important to note that goals and entitlements will differ from one society to another. Only during the twentieth century has our society been able to think of education as an entitlement rather than as just a goal. Societies that are quite poor may have great difficulty making health assistance or legal aid an entitlement. Most of the spectrum of opportunity rights may be mere goals for societies recently under the yoke of dictators or colonial powers. A society struggling to its feet may lack the resources to secure high-level entitlements and may find it more important to concentrate on the provision of security rights or the alleviation of hunger. As the society becomes stable and developed, it will be possible to address new goals and to convert more goals into entitlements.

If we imaginatively reconstruct the passage of a society from poverty to development, gaining the capacity to secure an ever larger class of its citizens' claims, we can establish a rough but useful guideline for ordering the importance of various opportunity rights in an egalitarian society. An egalitarian society should guarantee as many entitlements as possible and should set higher levels of opportunities as social goals. Basic security rights, safety of the person, and access to food are among the most basic opportunity rights, rights that every society will strive to satisfy as an entitlement. Next will come opportunities to participate in the governing of the society, which can be guaranteed by ensuring freedom of speech and assembly, access to legal representation, and the opportunity to stand for public office. Soon afterward will come the opportunity to participate in the economy, and this will mean access to jobs. We may move through opportunities for healthful lives and opportunities for personal growth to more difficult opportunities like community, full employment, leisure, and unrestricted personal wealth. We can get a sense of how to rank opportunity rights by thinking about the order in which they would be converted from goals to entitlements. This ranking deserves more careful consideration than it can be given here, but it is important to note that basic rights theory has a strategy for indicating the relative importance of different opportunities.

Consequentialism and Utilitarian Theory

Libertarian and egalitarian theories both had forceful advocates when Jeremy Bentham wrote his *Introduction to the Principles of Morals and Legislation* in 1789. Bentham's book brought utilitarianism to the language of public policy and did it by a simple and direct attack on the concept of rights. Natural rights, Bentham argued, are "nonsense on stilts." By this he meant that anyone could claim a right to anything he or she wanted. In most political jurisdictions, it would simply be a matter of power and privilege whether one's claim to a right was recognized and validated as a legal right. The basic philosophical question facing rights-based theories was what legal rights should be recognized, but such theories, Bentham argued, were unable to provide any principled answer to this question. Rights-based theories, he thought, provided no meaningful insight into social justice or the ideals to which public policy *ought* to aspire. Claims regarding rights and obligations seemed merely to reflect the distribution of political power within society, and the social contract argument, to the extent that it relied on rights, seemingly did little more than rubber-stamp the prerogatives of the rich and powerful.

Bentham proposed that we conceive the social contract not as some elaborate story about morality in the state of nature, but as an ordinary contract in which all parties agree to a package of benefits from social policy and establish the price. The contract determines the price that each must pay if the benefits are to come about. Bentham thought that the obvious standard by which to evaluate such a contract was to inquire whether it produced the greatest benefit for the greatest number of people. A policy that does so is right; a policy that does not should be sacked in favor of one that does. Bentham thought that any commonsensical person faced with the idea of a social contract could see the simple logic of such a view, and that talk of natural rights could hardly improve on common sense in this regard.

In the two hundred years since Bentham's book, utilitarianism has flourished. By most accounts, it is the social theory that has dominated U.S. public policy in the last fifty years. As utilitarianism marked its peak in actual policy applications during the last couple of decades, it began to be questioned and attacked vehemently by social philosophers, to the point where many philosophers today regard it as totally discredited. The 200-year biography of this idea, complete with its variations and the complaints of its critics, is largely omitted from the discussion of utilitarianism that appears here. Utilitarian theory is sketched in only the broadest of strokes, and only some of the major variations on and criticisms of the theory are described.

The Logic of Utilitarian and Consequentialist Theory

Utilitarianism was described previously as one type of consequentialist theory. In general, consequentialist theories decide the correctness and value of a public policy based upon the consequences of the policy. A rights-based theory, such as libertarianism or egalitarianism, by contrast, would decide based upon the acceptability of the structure of legal rights and obligations imposed by the policy, without regard to the consequences that such a structure might produce when conduct is taken into account.

If we are to evaluate a policy in terms of its consequences, then we must have some idea of (i) what is to count as a consequence and (ii) what the consequences are consequences of. A specification of (i) and (ii) defines the **scope** of a consequentialist theory. There is considerable controversy among consequentialists regarding (ii). We could choose human *acts* as the focus of the theory, letting them be the object of evaluation, but we could as well choose *rules* or even motives as the focus of the theory. The choice may have important ramifications. For example, if it is acts that are to be evaluated, it seems that one must decide whether or not to keep a promise one has made only after assessing the consequences of doing so. To many people, this seems to drain the promise of any moral force. An alternative way to look at promises is to evaluate the general rule "Keep your promises," and here it seems that the rule has good consequences overall if it is followed. In thus shifting the focus from acts to rules, we shift from so-called *act consequentialism* (restricting the scope to acts) to *rule consequentialism* (restricting the scope to rules). In the present context, where we are concerned with public policy, the scope of our consequentialist theories will be restricted to policies, that is, to structures of legal rights and obligations.

There is general agreement that all consequences of the act, rule, or policy being evaluated should be counted. In practice, however, it is easy to neglect consequences for parties who are not explicitly identified or salient in the problem identification stage of the policy process. When we make choices for ourselves, for example, it is easy to neglect consequences for others. When public officials make choices for our society, it is easy to overlook consequences for those in other countries. It is also easy to overlook consequences for nonhuman animals and future generations. The question of whether or not consequences for all these parties should be included is settled once the scope of a theory has been adequately defined. Except in special cases, the scope of consequentialist theories will remain unspecified in the following discussion, and readers may presume that we are interested in all the consequences of choosing a particular policy structure.

A second component of a consequentialist theory is an **axiology**, a theory of value used to determine the relative value of consequences. This axiology provides the basis for a form of moral arithmetic in which various consequences can be treated as "credits" or "debits." At its most basic level, an axiology determines whether any given consequence is to be counted as desirable (e.g., because it is pleasurable) or undesirable (e.g., because it is painful or harmful). Utilitarian axiologies often use the terms *benefit* to designate a desirable consequence and *cost* to designate an undesirable consequence. The choice of the word *cost* is apt inasmuch as some undesirable consequences are in no interesting sense bad, painful, or harmful.

The term *utility* is used to refer to any kind of valued consequence, desirable or undesirable. Increasing someone's utility means either providing benefits or reducing costs. Reducing utility means either imposing costs or depriving the person of benefits. Consequentialist theory usually assumes that the utility (e.g., costs and benefits) of different policies can be quantitatively compared, and it is convenient to use symbols to express these comparisons. If the symbol a stands for the act or policy under evaluation, then the utility of a would be the net value of a's consequences once both benefits and costs had been taken into account. The utility of a is expressed as $U(a)$.

Most consequentialists believe that utility judgments are transitive. Consider a case where a decision maker has three possible choices: a, b, and c. If the utility of a is larger than the utility of b and the utility of b is larger than the utility of c, then if utility judgments are transitive, the utility of a is larger than the utility of c. Expressed symbolically, if $U(a) > U(b)$ and $U(b) > U(c)$, then $U(a) > U(c)$. If utility judgments are indeed transitive, then there will be one act or policy that has a utility that is at least as great as that of all the others.

Consequentialist axiologies can be classified on the basis of how desirable and undesirable consequences are identified. Bentham thought of good and bad in terms of pleasure and pain; desirable consequences were pleasure-producing, undesirable consequences pain-producing. An axiology that evaluates consequences in terms of pleasure and pain is called *hedonic*. The pleasures and pains in question can be sensory or mental; they are not restricted to the base pleasures and pains that we would commonly associate with the hedonist. The possession of a hedonic axiology is the defining characteristic of *hedonic utilitarianism*. Hedonic utilitarian theory says that it is the pleasures and pains of all affected parties that must be accounted for in assigning a utility value to a policy or a policy option. The right action is the one that produces the most pleasure and the least pain for all people. Thus, for example, a policy of providing low-interest loans for small farms would produce a certain amount of pleasure for the recipients of the loans and a certain amount of pain for the taxpayers who provided the funds for these loans. The hedonic utility of this policy would be assessed by weighing the pleasure of the farmers against the pain of the taxpayers (who might also be getting some pleasure from lower food prices, and who in some cases would be farmers who were also getting pleasure from the loans), and when all pleasure and pain had been accounted for, one could assign an overall utility to the policy.

Two further points should be noted about hedonic utilitarianism. First, everyone's pleasure or pain counts equally. One thing that distinguishes utilitarianism from other forms of consequentialism is the presumption that each person's pleasure or pain must be weighed impartially. Second, the axiological assumption that it is pleasure and pain that matter means that value arises from the way that individuals experience a state of affairs. The value judgment here seems, in an odd way, to be both subjective and objective. It is an objective fact that a person has pleasure or pain as a result of some experience, yet the pleasure or pain itself is a subjective experience. It seems impossible to make any kind of precise comparison of the pleasure and pain that individuals feel.

The obvious difficulty of measuring and quantifying the subjective pleasures and pains of others creates a practical problem for hedonic utilitarianism. An alternative axiology, which has proved particularly useful in evaluating public policy, largely avoids this difficulty. According to this axiology, a positive consequence is one in which one has been able to do what one would have chosen, and a negative consequence is one in which freedom to do what one would have chosen has been frustrated. Here we assume that people decide for themselves what is good or bad *for them*, and the ethical problem is simply one of placing them in a position to satisfy themselves. This is an axiology of preference satisfaction, and it defines a *preference utilitarianism.* Given the preference axiology, a theorist could say that a good outcome is one in which people can choose for themselves or one in which people get what they want. Either formulation comes to the same thing.

In one version of preference utilitarianism, we do not try to compare the degree of benefit and cost, but simply look at the number of people who have been satisfied. This makes comparison much easier, but it also means that important differences in the degree of satisfaction may be lost. Jill would prefer not to have a hangnail, and Jack would prefer not to be tortured and maimed, for example. There is something wrong with a theory that rates Jack's preference equally with Jill's. It seems more reasonable to talk about the intensity of an individual's preference, too, but this can make preference utilitarianism quite complicated since now we must provide a quantitative measure of the relative values of satisfying one or another preference.

Both hedonic utilitarianism and preference utilitarianism share the axiological assumption that each person's utility is to be counted equally in assessing the net utility for an option or policy choice. For contrast, it will be momentarily useful to think about a version of consequentialist theory that does not make this assumption. *Egoism* is a consequentialist theory that places extra weight on the benefits and costs that fall directly to the decision maker. An egoist will do whatever provides the best personal outcome, and the rest of society be damned. The pleasures and pains, satisfactions and dissatisfactions of friends, neighbors, and fellow citizens simply do not count. Put another way, all consequences to others have zero value; they are neither credits nor debits in the moral arithmetic. It is important to see that egoism meets the formal requirements of consequentialist axiology. It tells us how to evaluate and rank consequences. Admittedly, egoism does not seem to be a very promising theory for public policy. It can only tell what is good for some particular person, never what is good for society as a whole. Egoism is mostly relevant to policy as a claim about personal psychology. (The self-interest theory of behavior discussed in Chapter 2 can be interpreted as saying that regardless of what we ought to do, most of us behave like egoists most of the time. Self-interest theory is not a normative theory of ethics but an empirical theory of behavior.)

The axiology indicates what are to count as benefits and costs, good and bad, but it does not provide a decision maker with any basis for action. We saw how an axiology could provide a ranked list of all the options facing a decision maker, but the ranked list does not tell the decision maker how to choose. In addition to a scope and an axiology, all consequentialist theories must contain a **decision rule**. The decision rule is needed for guiding action or policy choice that will have desirable or undesirable, good or bad consequences. The decision rule makes the transition from the good to the right. Our understanding of benefits and costs tells us whether (and to what degree) an outcome is good, but it does not tell us that an option having a good outcome is the right one to choose. It may even be wrong to choose an option with a good outcome, for example, if there is another option with an outcome that is remarkably better. The decision rule tells the decision maker which option is the right one based upon the rankings of good and bad that have already been compiled according to the axiology.

The most obvious decision rule is simply to choose the option at the top of the list, to do the thing or adopt the policy that will have the greatest number of benefits, that is, the greatest utility for the greatest number of people. This decision rule was in fact the one proposed by Bentham and Mill, and it has come to be known as the **utilitarian maxim**. If you combine the utilitarian maxim with a hedonic axiology, you get a hedonic utilitarianism that defines right action in terms of maximal pleasure. If you combine the utilitarian maxim with a preference satisfaction axiology, you get a preference utilitarianism that defines the right action as one that maximizes the satisfaction of individual preferences. The decision rule plus the scope and axiology is thus action guiding, or prescriptive, meaning that together these three features tell the decision maker what policy to choose. They produce more than just a statement of what is good; they produce a prescription for what ought to be done.

The utilitarian maxim is clearly the most obvious decision rule, but others have been suggested. Perhaps we should not expect policy to aim at the best option. After all, our policies aim at such a broad variety of social goods that it would be difficult to compare them all. Should we cancel public expenditures for agricultural research and put the money into defense? Strictly speaking, the transitivity of utility tells us that one of these policies is quite likely to produce more utility than the other, so if we are truly maximizers (i.e., if we apply the utilitarian maxim), it seems we should be interested in comparing agricultural research and defense expenditures. As a practical matter, however, this seems unreasonable. As a substitute decision rule, we might simply require that a policy produce more benefits than costs. We might not insist that a policy achieve the best possible outcome, but merely that it do more good than harm. Such a rule differs from the utilitarian maxim in telling us that policies that produce net benefits are good enough to be called right even if they don't produce the maximal good. This rule makes sense when we are being asked to compare options that have very different aims and outcomes. It helps us in choice situations where we do not know how to assign value rankings that would make the transitivity principle apply. On the other hand, citing such a simple decision rule would be a poor defense for the bureaucrat who knowingly chooses an inefficient policy over an obviously better one. It would not be adequate for the bureaucrat to say that "it provided more benefit than harm" when a clearly better choice could have been made.

A second alternative to the utilitarian maxim is one that says that it is always wrong to do harm and that policy choices in which anyone is made worse off are to be avoided entirely. It is important to notice that the utilitarian maxim can justify policies in which people are harmed in one of two ways. First, in cases where all options make people worse off, the utilitarian maxim still chooses the least disliked option from the top of the ranking. For example, a military commander may choose between a tactic that will cost ten lives and a tactic that will cost one hundred lives. The utilitarian maxim tells him to select from the top of the ranking, to do the best possible, even if, as in this case, it means doing the least bad that he can. Second, and more typically, public policies achieve social goals only at someone's expense. For example, suppose that a new reservoir will provide electric power and recreation for many, but a few will lose farms that their families have lived on for generations. The utilitarian maxim would say that it is right to build the reservoir so long as the benefits to the many outweigh the harms to the few.

It is possible to describe a decision rule that does not allow this type of result. Suppose that a decision maker decides to accept only outcomes that make at least one person better and make no one worse off. We may maximize utility among those choices that make no one worse off, but the decision rule tells us to refuse all choices that make even one person worse off. We will call this rule the **Pareto principle**, after the sociologist Wilfredo Pareto, who first proposed it. The Pareto principle has some initial plausibility and attractiveness, since the restriction on harming people seems consistent with important political ideals. It is in some respects a concession to libertarianism since it accepts that theory's emphasis upon doing no harm. It is important, however, to note a significant limitation of the Pareto principle. If there is no policy that does not make someone worse off, the Pareto principle does not tell us what to do. But in fact, each of the policy options that typically confronts policy makers makes at least one person worse off, so the principle gives policy makers no guidance. Social theorists who have been attracted to Pareto's ideas have, as a result, modified the principle in ways that make it more practical but also weaken its attractiveness as a decision rule. For example, we might have a modified version of the principle that says that the right option is one in which the winners from a policy choice *compensate* the losers. Here the reservoir could be built, but users' fees, for example, might be used to pay the displaced families for the loss of their farms. This modification of Pareto's idea is called a *pure Pareto improvement*. It seems in the spirit of the Pareto principle, since once the losers have been compensated, they are no longer losers. The policy has identified an option consistent with the Pareto principle where no one is harmed. A second modification has been proposed for situations in which practical considerations make it impossible for winners actually to compensate losers, but in which they have received enough benefits that losers could have been compensated if it were possible to do so. This principle is called the *Kaldor-Hicks criterion*. Even though the Kaldor-Hicks criterion allows for uncompensated harms, it insists that the benefits be great enough to compensate losers for the harms they suffer, at least in principle. It produces an outcome that is called a *potential Pareto improvement* (as discussed in Chapter 4).

There are other axiologies and other decision rules besides those just discussed. But even with the two different axiologies described here (hedonic and preference satisfaction) and the three different decision rules (the utilitarian maxim, the Pareto principle, and the Kaldor-Hicks criterion), it is possible to construct six different combinations, each of which might be used as a guide for public policy. The traits that mark these combinations as utilitarian, rather than simply consequentialist, are (i) an impersonal axiology and (ii) decision rules that optimize outcomes. The axiologies are impersonal in that effects are counted equally for all persons; benefits and harms are not weighted in favor of any particular group or individual. The decision rules optimize in the sense that they encourage decision makers to choose options that have relatively better outcomes. The utilitarian maxim is a very strong optimizing principle, while the Kaldor-Hicks criterion is relatively weak. Even weak optimizing is in marked contrast to the rights-based decision criteria of libertarian or egalitarian theory. Under these theories, policies are permitted (even required) without any regard to whether they produce benefits that outweigh the costs of implementing them. In this sense, utilitarian theories place a greater burden on the decision maker than rights-based theories do. There are, at the least, far fewer policies that can meet the standard of right.

It should be clear, on the other hand, that virtually any version of utilitarianism will permit (and even encourage) some policies that might be rejected by a rights-based view. Conservation policies, for example, are far easier to justify on utilitarian grounds. Soil loss frequently can be prevented when individual producers adopt conservation practices. Let us assume that soil conservation will be good for a very large number of people over the long run. Adopting conservation practices may impose costs on a small number of producers over the short run. If we adopt a hedonic axiology, we would describe these benefits and harms as the pleasures obtained from having a secure and stable food supply versus the pleasures foregone by spending on conservation rather than something else. If we adopt a preference axiology, we would compare the preferences of many consumers (who want a secure food supply and are willing to pay for it) with the preferences of a few producers (who would rather spend time and money on something else). Any of the three decision rules would lead toward a policy favoring conservation. The utilitarian maxim and the Kaldor-Hicks criterion would achieve this result immediately. If the choice is between conservation and nonconservation, then by our assumption, the benefits of conservation outweigh the costs; hence a conservation policy represents the greatest good for the greatest number. The Pareto principle would lead one to balk at harming the producers, but it clearly points one toward an alternative conservation policy in which producers are compensated by consumers (who are willing to pay), and we are thus able to move toward a situation of maximal utility.

Under a strong version of libertarian theory, by contrast, government probably has no business promoting the conservation of privately owned resources unless it can be shown that nonconservation harms others. The producers hold the property rights to the land, and public policy has no warrant for interfering in their use of their land unless it can be shown that the non-interference rights of others are being violated, perhaps by deposits of eroded soil. An egalitarian view is more complicated, since society has an obligation to help ensure the subsistence of all citizens. Although it is reasonable to think that present citizens enjoy an entitlement to nourishing food as a component of their (positive) right to life, it is difficult to say how far this entitlement extends into the future. We cannot control the future or guarantee that future generations will have food, no matter what we do. It therefore seems that the long-term sustainability of our food system may be a social goal, but it is not an entitlement that can be claimed on behalf of future generations. This makes the rationale for conservation relatively weak, particularly when it runs up against the clear property rights claims of the producers, who even in an egalitarian society would have some right to control the use of their land. For now, it is important to see that utilitarian theory has a fairly direct and clear route to a justification of conservation, provided that our factual assumptions about the consequences of conservation are correct. Rights-based theories, it seems, could arrive at a justification of conservation only by a rather tortured and convoluted path. The point here, of course, is *not* to decide whether conservation is good or bad but simply to note that utilitarian theories readily justify some policies that are not easily justified by rights-based theories. In itself, this fact does not weigh in favor of utilitarianism since it may be that these are just the sorts of policies that rational people in the state of nature, or the original position, would want to avoid. This is the topic we will now consider.

Utilitarian Theory and the Social Contract

How would any of these six utilitarian theories fare in a social contract? Is there any reason to think that rational people would agree to be governed by utilitarian principles? There are several simple reasons for thinking that they might, and these reasons should not be overlooked merely because they are simple. First, there is an element of common sense in the idea that public policy ought to seek the greatest good. It seems likely that a group of people in the state of nature might hit upon this straightforward idea long before anyone would think through the arguments supporting libertarianism or egalitarianism. Second, as Bentham noted, social policies expressed in terms of rights have an open-ended character that should make us uneasy. It seems likely that those wealthy and powerful enough to hire expensive lawyers will be better able to manipulate the language of rights to their advantage. The more direct language of consequences may keep us better informed of what our policy is intended to do. Third, the social contract is a common endeavor, and it seems natural to express its principles in language that speaks directly to the common good. Talk of the greatest good for the greatest number might bind a group of people together, while talk of individual rights and entitlements seems to set them against one another.

Although these simple reasons might create an inclination toward utilitarianism, they might not win the day against the more sophisticated contract arguments we have already discussed. The strength of contract theory is that it explains why anyone might be motivated to accept the terms of a particular social contract. A similar argument for utilitarianism might begin by noting that the reasons given earlier seem commonsensical precisely because they appeal to the special motives of people (like ourselves) who, having learned to live in a democratic society like our own, accept the idea of acting for the common good. Many of the most valuable benefits of living in a civil society, it might be argued, are the fruits of social cooperation. Whether it is national defense, police and fire protection, or health care, not to mention cooperative arrangements that put food on our tables, cars in our driveways, and pictures on our TVs, these are benefits that could not be achieved without social cooperation. Few of us, for example, could afford to keep a personal ambulance in our backyard for emergencies, and even if we could, in the absence of social cooperation there would be nowhere to go if an emergency were to arise. If there is one thing that public policy must do, it must facilitate such social cooperation. As the conservation example discussed previously illustrates, rights-based views offer little positive guidance regarding the structure of policies that would create the institutional arrangements necessary to secure the benefits of social cooperation.

A hypothetical situation called the **prisoner's dilemma** illustrates vividly the need for social institutions if we are to secure social cooperation and its benefits. Two prisoners are being held in separate cells for a crime that they have jointly committed. They have no way of communicating with one another and no reason to trust one another's actions. Each prisoner is offered the same deal by the prosecuting attorney. The prisoner may confess to the crime and testify against his confederate. If the prosecuting attorney uses the testimony, the prisoner will receive a light sentence of one year in jail. If the prisoner confesses but the prosecutor does not use the testimony, the prisoner will receive a sentence of three years in jail. If each prisoner refuses the deal and thus does not testify against his confederate, neither can be convicted. If, on the other hand, one prisoner refuses the deal and is convicted on the basis of the testimony of the other, that prisoner will receive a

Prisoner A

		Confess	Not confess
	Confess	3, 3	1, 20
Prisoner B	Not confess	20, 1	0, 0

Figure 3–2   The Prisoner's Dilemma

sentence of twenty years in jail. The prisoner's dilemma can be graphically illustrated by the matrix in Figure 3–2, where (0,0) represents the collectively best result (for the prisoners) in which both go free, (3,3) represents the outcome where both prisoners confess and hence the prosecutor does not need either prisoner's testimony, and (20,1) and (1,20) represent outcomes where one confesses and the other does not.

The best possible outcome (from the prisoners' perspective) would be the one that resulted from each prisoner's choosing not to confess. This is the outcome that any rational person in a prisoner's dilemma, acting purely out of self-interest, would prefer. But paradoxical as it may seem, this is not an outcome that is accessible to the prisoners if they are rational. Since the two prisoners cannot communicate with each other, they will have to base their choices on their expectation of what the other will do. If Prisoner A thinks that Prisoner B will confess and testify, then clearly he will have a very strong incentive also to confess, since only by so doing can he avoid what would be the worst outcome for him personally: twenty years in jail. If, on the other hand, Prisoner A thinks that Prisoner B will not confess and testify, he has some incentive not to confess: the opportunity of avoiding two additional years in jail. But given that he cannot rely on the actions of his fellow prisoner, he has a much greater incentive to confess and testify: the long sentence he will receive should he be mistaken about what Prisoner B will do. Thus, whatever B does, A has a significant incentive to confess and testify. Since B has exactly the same incentives as A, he too will have a significant incentive to confess and testify. So, if A and B are rational, they will both confess, with the result that they will end up with an outcome that is less than optimal.

In order to secure the desired optimal outcome, the prisoners would need what is unavailable in the imagined situation: a way of coordinating their individual choices and entering into a binding agreement not to confess. They would need an institutional arrangement—in effect, a "government"—that would effectively regulate their choices in the imagined situation. Consider how organized crime organizations such as the Mafia avoid the prisoner's dilemma. Knowing that situations such as this can arise in their line of work and knowing also that persons such as themselves are not trustworthy, members of such organizations enter into an institutional arrangement that effectively guarantees that as prisoners they will not be tempted to confess,

Prisoner A

Confess Not confess

	Confess	Not confess
Confess	death, death	death, 20
Not confess	20, death	0, 0

Prisoner B (left label)

Figure 3–3 The Prisoner's Dilemma with Mafia Enforcement

thereby ensuring that if they should find themselves in the described situation, they would be able to secure the desired optimal outcome. Their institutional arrangement is quite simple: They retain an "enforcer" whose job it is to murder anyone who confesses and then testifies against a confederate. The existence of the enforcer changes the *contingencies* (i.e., the payoffs associated with the various choices of the prisoners) in the imagined situation to guarantee that a rational person, acting purely out of self-interest, would choose *not* to confess (see Figure 3–3).

The foregoing description of the prisoner's dilemma and the Mafia's rather effective (but brutal) scheme for avoiding the dilemma points to a potential role for government in fostering and maintaining the institutional arrangements necessary to secure benefits that depend on social cooperation. Social cooperation and coordination require communication, but distance in time and space, as well as social distance, can prevent people from communicating in real life. If people are spread across a broad expanse, they may not have easy ways to communicate with one another about the choices they must make. A more serious problem may be brought about by *social distance*, a situation in which people can in principle communicate with one another but do not because they belong to different social groups. Clearly there will be many cases in which social cooperation will be possible only if some person, group, or organization steps in and provides the needed channels of communication that make it possible to coordinate individual choices; often government will be the appropriate social institution to undertake these tasks.

Even when people in a prisoner's dilemma can communicate and are inclined to agree that they should choose a course of action that produces the greatest good, a further problem can prevent them from reaching the best outcome. They must be confident that others will make the choice that corresponds to the prisoners' refusal to confess and testify. If one persons thinks that the other may defect from an agreement not to confess and testify, that person will have a strong incentive to confess and testify. This aspect of the prisoner's dilemma is called the **assurance problem**. It suggests that in addition to the role of facilitating communication and coordinating individual choices, government has a role in enforcing the agreements that are made.

The policy options for dealing with prisoner's dilemma situations are quite varied; specific examples are discussed in later chapters. The point here is to see how persons who can imagine themselves in the prisoner's dilemma would have an incentive to form a government that would coordinate individual choices and actions and enforce compliance with collectively chosen courses of action intended to produce social benefits. Consider a version of the social contract story in which the state of nature and the original position are replaced by a very large, very general version of the prisoner's dilemma. According to this version of the story, parties to the social contract understand, even before having entered society, that they stand to gain considerably from social cooperation. They know that in the absence of social institutions that effectively coordinate their individual choices and actions and enforce compliance with collectively chosen courses of action, they (like the prisoners in the described situation) are virtually certain to make many suboptimal choices. They recognize that government offers an effective means (perhaps the only means) to ensure the cooperation needed to secure the desired benefits because it has the coercive powers needed to ensure that individuals make choices that produce mutually beneficial outcomes. Thus, understanding both prisoner's dilemma situations and government's potential role in helping them avoid such situations, rational individuals, acting purely out of self-interest, would be motivated to form a government that would provide the needed coordination and enforcement.

Procedural Theory

Each of the three theories that have been discussed provides different principles for making policies and a different picture of what society would look like in the ideal case. They differ from one another in that the two rights theories offer principles that serve as constraints upon the resources and power of public officials, while the utilitarian theory offers guidelines that aim at producing benefits. The final approach to policy ethics differs from all of these in that it makes no attempt to describe what the ideal society would look like, nor does it provide rules that prescribe certain types of policy decisions. Instead, the theory confines itself to processes of conflict resolution. It aims to specify when a procedure for resolving conflict, for coming to agreement, is fair and impartial. Because this theory focuses on procedure rather than on the substance of policy, it is called *procedural theory.*

Each of the social contract arguments that have been discussed involves the resolution of conflict among individuals. Whether it is the state of nature, the original position, or the prisoner's dilemma, social contract theory begins with a situation in which individuals have interests that are potentially in conflict with one another. It first describes the kind of society people would agree to live in and then formulates policy rules or principles that would bring about that society. In each case, social contract theory hypothesizes a process whereby parties to the contract set aside certain differences and agree to certain terms of a social contract. Procedural theory directs attention toward this process while setting aside questions about the terms of the agreement reached. The main moral claim of procedural theory is that what people agree to is less important than the way they have reached the agreement. Put another way, if the process for reaching agreement has been fair and impartial, then whatever is actually agreed upon is just and right. A simplified example will illustrate the main idea behind procedural theory.

Imagine a negotiation between two people, Jack and Jill. Jill is willing to trade several hours of yard work to Jack in exchange for Jack's used bicycle. This is a familiar sort of trade, and we can easily imagine that Jack and Jill have individual interests at stake. Jack would prefer that Jill do more work rather than less, for example, and Jill might prefer that the flat tire on the bicycle be fixed before the trade is made rather than afterward. What would be a fair trade? A substantive approach to this question, such as the libertarian, egalitarian, or utilitarian theories would provide, looks at the terms of the bargain itself. We might want to know what sorts of property rights are at stake, how the market value of Jill's labor compares to the market value of the bicycle. A procedural theory sets all this aside and looks only at the circumstances under which Jack and Jill reach agreement.

There are several procedural circumstances that would lead us to call any deal between Jack and Jill unfair. Suppose, for example, that the negotiations just described have never taken place, but that Jack leaves the unrepaired bike at Jill's house along with a note explaining that she owes him four hours of work. We would say that this deal was not fair because Jill had not actually participated in the negotiations; she had no chance to accept or reject Jack's terms. **Participation** is a crucial requirement for the validity of the process of arriving at agreement. Participation, however, is only part of a more comprehensive requirement because the real objection here is that since Jill has not participated, she could not have consented to the exchange. Suppose that Jill goes to Jack's house and offers three hours of work for the bicycle. Jack refuses, saying it is not enough. Jill works for three hours, Jack all the while shouting from the window that they do not have a deal. After finishing, Jill puts the bicycle in the back of her truck and prepares to leave. Jack comes out and tells her to put down the bicycle, saying that he did not agree to the trade. Jack has clearly participated in this transaction, but he has rejected Jill's offer equally clearly at every turn. Participation is important because it is a necessary condition for **consent**, and it is the consent of all parties to the agreement that validates the terms of the agreement.

If we generalize this simple kind of negotiation to the social contract situation, where many individuals must agree on terms that will govern the shape of society, we discover that procedural theory's emphasis upon consent remains in force. None of the three substantive theories denies the importance of consent. Indeed, in each of these theories, the point of the social contract argument is to describe the terms to which individuals in a state of nature, or in an original position, or facing a prisoner's dilemma would consent. A procedural theory turns attention away from the contract per se and examines the circumstances under which people do consent to the terms of the agreement. According to procedural theory, an agreement is valid when its circumstances satisfy the criteria of consent. Any of the three substantive forms of the social contract would be valid so long as parties consent to the terms specified by libertarian, egalitarian, or utilitarian principles, respectively.

Circumstances of Consent

What are the circumstances in which rational persons would agree to be bound by a collective decision? One of these circumstances is participation, just discussed. Someone who has had no opportunity to participate in an agreement cannot be said to have consented to its terms. A second circumstance is *unanimity*. All the parties to the agreement must have consented to it. This might appear to be a very difficult criterion to satisfy; however, unanimity here is not required for specific policies, only for rules about how disagreements over policies are to be resolved.

Consider an election of officers for a garden club. The election is an agreement of members to be led by a specific group of people, but elections of club officers are rarely unanimous. How, then, can elections be described as valid instances of consent? The answer is that the club has rules for electing officers, and when members formed or joined the club, they agreed to abide by these rules. One of the most common principles for resolving disputes is *majority rule*: Officers are elected and activities decided by what a simple majority of the members prefer. Other principles, of course, can be formulated: Some actions of the club, such as changing by-laws, might require a *two-thirds* majority; business meetings may require a *quorum* in order that votes be binding. The requirement of unanimity demands that everyone who is a member agree to abide by the club's rules, so at this level there is unanimous consent. In most clubs, there are also procedures for changing the rules, and members have unanimously agreed to abide by these rules too. Once the procedures for running the club have been agreed upon, the entire range of club activities can be justified on the grounds of consent, even though there may not be unanimous support for any specific club project or activity.

Procedural political theory states that what goes for the garden club goes for the social contract. Society is a large and diverse group of people who cannot be expected to agree on everything. A civil society is nevertheless a group in which people who live and work within society's boundaries have agreed to be bound by a fairly extensive set of principles for resolving disputes and deciding upon policies. These principles include procedures for electing representatives, who in turn have procedures for making law, for raising public revenue, and for spending revenue in pursuit of public policies. In this respect, there is little philosophical difference between the elected officials of government and the elected officers of a garden club. The garden club officers raise money by assessing club dues, the Congress by assessing taxes. Each group also proposes and debates certain activities that the group should use its revenue to support. As long as the leaders follow the rules in deciding what to do, according to procedural theories, their policies are fair and just. A society, of course, is more comprehensive than a garden club. Its procedures must include an executive branch and a judicial system charged with carrying out and enforcing the laws. All of these activities, however, are founded upon the unanimous consent of all citizens both to be participating members of the society and to be bound by higher-level procedures, as well as the specific policies these procedures produce.

There is one additional criterion for establishing the circumstances of consent. Consider again the garden club. The club may have begun as an organization of people who enjoyed growing flowers and vegetables in their yards. There are rules for electing officers and for deciding upon activities, and anyone who joins the club accepts these rules. It may be that the members of the club elect officers who decide to change the club's direction, perhaps turning it more toward campaigning for zoning laws or to sponsoring contests to see who can grow the best violets. If this change in club policy is supported by the membership in general, following agreed-upon rules for electing leaders and deciding upon activities, it can be said to be procedurally valid. Some members, however, may not want to participate in the new activities. As long as they remain members of the club, the requirement of participation guarantees that they are free to express their displeasure with the change; however, they are bound to accept whatever is decided. If these dissident members really object to the club's new course, they may have no other course of action but to quit the club. The opportunity to leave the group, releasing oneself from both its benefits and its obligations, is an additional requirement for consent. This requirement will be referred to as **exit**. One cannot be said to have consented to a group's policies if one does not have the power to revoke one's lower-level consent to the group's procedures by leaving the group entirely.

Again, what goes for the garden club goes for society as a whole. At the society level, exit means that citizens must be guaranteed an opportunity to leave society, though to do so may also mean that they forego the opportunity to reside within its boundaries. At the level of civil society, exit amounts to a right of emigration. If one cannot leave, then one can hardly be said to have consented to what happens if one stays. The guarantee of an opportunity to emigrate means that people who no longer feel that they can accept the policies of their society may withdraw their consent, leave the society, and join another civil society. This is an extreme measure for an individual, one that will not be taken lightly. There are, however, many historical examples of individuals who chose to leave their society rather than be bound by its actions. Draft resisters who opposed U.S. involvement in Vietnam left the country rather than accept conscription. Many Jews and intellectuals fled Nazi

Germany when they found the policies of Hitler's government intolerable. Exit continues to be the ultimate rejection of a social contract. Exit is an indispensable element of consent theory and the procedural interpretation of the social contract.

Varieties of Consent

Participation, unanimity, and opportunity for exit are crucial requirements for consent, but the procedural theory that has been developed so far leaves the basic idea of consent largely undeveloped. Much more needs to be said about when an individual can truly be said to have consented to an agreement or state of affairs. If we recall the agreement between Jack and Jill, for example, we would want to know exactly what actions by each of them are said to *convey* consent. Is it enough simply for them to nod their heads, or must they say the words "I agree" in order to have consented to the terms of the contract? Perhaps they must have actually signed a contract. We often feel that written consent is more binding, but this is only because the written document serves as palpable proof of consent. Verbal agreements that can be proved, as when a witness is present, also can be binding.

Discussions of consent in the context of political theory focus on the notion of *meaningful consent.* To be meaningful, consent must satisfy two basic conditions. First, it must take the form of a mutually recognized sign of consent, though as we shall see, meaningful consent does not have to be explicit. Second, it must be given freely. A person who consents to an agreement under the threat of physical violence or other forms of coercion can hardly be said to have truly consented to the bargain, even if he or she does mouth the words "I agree."

Consent must often satisfy other conditions as well, though these additional conditions may vary from case to case. The requirement that valid consent be informed, for example, requires that all parties, at the time the agreement is made, be in possession of relevant information about the terms of the agreement. You cannot meaningfully consent to an agreement that you do not understand. The requirement of *informed consent* underlies disclosure laws that require patients undergoing certain medical procedures to be informed beforehand of the risks associated with those procedures.

When a person votes for a proposition, amendment, or bond issue, that vote conveys a willingness to be bound by its terms; voting is thus one way that people can express their consent. Many people, however, never vote, do not register to vote, and furthermore never intentionally perform any public acts that would convey their willingness to be bound by the laws and procedures of their society. These people's actions may not express consent but they may nonetheless imply consent, inasmuch as one may infer justifiably from these actions that these people have consented to the laws and procedures of their society. This is the idea of *implied consent.* Procedural theory assumes that everyone who takes advantage of society's benefits has implicitly consented to the terms of that society's social contract. Clearly, to be justified, this assumption must presume that individuals whose consent is only implicit have an opportunity for exit.

There is one additional variation on the idea of consent that should be discussed here. It is sometimes possible to describe hypothetical, counterfactual (i.e., contrary to fact) situations under which a person would consent to an agreement or policy. The agreement or policy in question is one that the individual would have consented to *if* this hypothetical situation had been real. Consent to such agreements or policies is called *hypothetical.* Hypothetical consent becomes particularly important in situations where the knowledge conditions required for informed consent cannot be satisfied. Thus, for example, a patient might be said to have hypothetically consented to an emergency procedure, even though she was not informed of the procedure (perhaps because she was unconscious), on the grounds that had she been informed of the procedure, she would have consented to it.

The introduction of hypothetical consent arguments into procedural theory, which standardly concerns itself with procedures that depend upon *actual consent*, would represent a major modification of procedural theory. Such a modification would significantly narrow the difference between procedural theories, on the one hand, and substantive theories (e.g., libertarianism, egalitarianism, and utilitarianism), on the other, since the justification of the latter relies heavily on arguments to the effect that parties would agree to certain social contracts in certain hypothetical situations. Actual consent theories insist that the terms of a proposal or policy are validated solely by the process of reaching an agreement. Hypothetical consent theories, by contrast, validate a proposal or policy by offering a plausible story about why people would consent to the terms of an agreement under some idealized, hypothetical set of conditions. Since the conditions are hypothetical, the consent is not actual; however, if the story includes all the considerations we think important to giving consent and eliminates all the considerations we think weaken the force of agreements we make in the real world, then we may be persuaded to accept the idealized, hypothetical picture of consent as morally binding. We have, of course, already heard three stories of this sort: the state of nature, the original position, and the prisoner's dilemma. This brings us full circle.

Free-choice (Free-market) Theory

A hypothetical consent argument is sometimes used to justify an economic system of unregulated exchange. This argument will be referred to as **free-choice theory**. (Free-market theory is just our society's particular form of free-choice theory.) In completing our discussion of procedural theory, it will be useful to examine the argument for free choice in more detail. Throughout this discussion, we should bear in mind that the rejection of actual consent in favor of hypothetical consent marks a significant departure from the purely procedural considerations that have been discussed in the first two sections. Our discussion will reveal deep philosophical links between procedural theory and each of the substantive theories, principally libertarianism and utilitarianism.

The free-choice argument begins by considering exchanges just like the one between Jack and Jill discussed earlier. Jill's deal with Jack is offered as a paradigmatic example of consent. We assume both that Jack and Jill have all relevant information and that it is easy for them to get together to make the trade (it wouldn't do to have Jack in Ottawa and Jill in Rangoon). When some common and plausible assumptions are made, we come to see Jill's trade with Jack as an indisputable case of individual consent. If individual consent is the key moral criterion, as procedural theory suggests, then it seems logical to have a social contract that makes the most of bargaining situations like this one. It would be crazy to have a social contract that interferes in a perfectly good instance of exchange where both parties have settled upon terms. Each is perfectly willing to abide by the terms of the exchange; each has consented wholly to the bargain. What could better satisfy the criterion of consent?

This individual transaction is so satisfactory, as far as consent goes, that a society might do well to rely entirely upon voluntary individual exchange. Let the procedures of individual bargaining simply *be* the procedures for social governance, at least as far as this is possible. To the maximum extent possible, let individual bargaining be the procedure for resolving disputes, and keep voting, representative government, and public policy out of it entirely. The result will be a society of open, unbridled exchanges in which people exchange their wealth and their labor in whatever transactions they are willing to enter. They will be constrained only by the willingness of others to bargain. It is as if the consent of one is constrained only by the consent of others. No one is coerced into any particular exchange so long as there are other traders in the market. Now if one can offer something to trade that is highly prized by many, one can find traders who are willing to give up more to get it, while if what one can offer is very common, one may have to accept less of other goods to trade it. This, of course, is an elementary point of economics. What is important for the free-choice argument is to see even these less favorable trades as instances of individual consent. Jill would prefer to get the bike for fewer rather than more hours of work in Jack's yard, but if there are several willing workers, she will have to weigh that fact in her negotiations with Jack. Whatever terms she finally accepts will be terms to which she has consented. When this picture is generalized to society at large, the implication is that government has no business regulating or interfering in voluntary exchange. The minimum wage, for example, is what the market will bear, not what some group of legislators decides is fair. If people want clear water, they must be willing to buy it. The list of free-market political claims can go on indefinitely and should be familiar enough to require no further elaboration here.

It is also important to see how the free-choice argument involves hypothetical rather than actual consent. Procedural theories hold that whatever people agree upon is just, so long as the procedures are based on consent. Jack and Jill agree upon a value-for-value exchange, it is true, but they might have agreed upon any number of other procedures for consummating their deal. They might have set the terms by the flip of a coin; they might have allowed a third party to set the price. On a social level, a group of people might agree on a procedure of free-market exchange, but they might also agree to a socialist system or to having astrologers set prices by looking at the stars. Actual consent theory says that whatever procedures they agree to are socially valid as long as the requirements of participation and exit remain open. Odd as it sounds, we can unanimously consent to procedures that minimize individual consent on day-to-day matters. Anyone who enlists in the military consents to just such an agreement. There is, therefore, no necessary relation between actual consent and procedures that maximize consent.

The free-choice argument, as outlined, sounds a bit like libertarianism. Although the former makes no mention of a state of nature or of noninterference rights, it seems to justify a very minimal state. It does not, for example, ascribe any role to government in regulating the way that individuals make exchanges with one another. Indeed, the free-choice argument does not ascribe any role for government; it simply assumes that people who wish to make trades will keep their promises and that individual property rights will be secure. The free-choice argument portrays markets as procedures for guaranteeing consent, but in failing to portray any means of regulating exchange and protecting property, it fails to be a theory of even the minimal state. When coupled with libertarianism, the free-choice argument provides such a theory.

The free-choice argument can be given a twist that moves it away from libertarianism and toward preference utilitarianism. Utilitarianism, we will recall, takes the goal of public policy to be the maximization of utility, where according to a preference axiology, utility is defined in terms of the satisfaction of individual preferences. The free-choice argument proposes to structure society on a model of free-market exchange according to which individuals freely consent to exchanges in order to obtain goods that they desire. This free-choice argument is quite compatible with preference utilitarianism inasmuch as the free-market exchanges contemplated by this argument can be expected to move a society in the direction of maximal utility. The exchange between Jack and Jill is instructive. If they have reached their agreement under conditions stipulated in the free-choice argument, there is no other agreement that would be preferred by both of them. If both have consented to the deal, then we may safely presume that they have reached an equilibrium point that maximally satisfies their preferences. For this two-person case, then, when a preference axiology is assumed, the free-choice argument yields a result in which Jack and Jill have maximized their utility. Free-choice theory presumes that it is reasonable to generalize (at least partially) to society as a whole and to conclude that free exchanges maximize utility for society as a whole. The idea that free exchanges maximize social utility for everyone who participates in such an economy is called **allocative efficiency**.

By supporting the goal of allocative efficiency, the free-choice argument provides a bridge between procedural theory and utilitarianism. Unregulated markets, *provided* that they are not beset with various market failures, can be understood both as a social procedure for securing consent and as a way of maximizing social utility. It should be clear, however, that despite this coincidence, procedural theory provides no basis for deciding policy on the grounds of any substantive criterion (including allocative efficiency) since people may give actual (and universal) consent to social ideals and governmental policies of a quite different sort. Furthermore, it is not clear that people always choose what is in their own interests or what will benefit them the most. The preference utilitarian's assumption that free choice leads to the maximal satisfaction of individual preferences is therefore open to challenge, although the affinity between the two doctrines should be apparent.

Free or unregulated markets are an example of public policy; such markets exist only if there has been a public choice to allow individuals open opportunities to exchange goods and services. Our brief survey of free-choice theory illustrates how libertarianism or utilitarianism might lead one to endorse a policy of unregulated markets. And although we have not bothered to outline it, egalitarians also might be led to endorse such a policy. The important point to note here is that each of the three substantive ethical theories discussed in this chapter could be combined with a free-choice argument in favor of unregulated markets. Our purpose, it should be emphasized, has not been to present an argument in support of free or unregulated markets since there are both philosophical arguments and factual considerations that militate against unregulated markets in particular circumstances. In the application chapters that make up the second half of the book, a number of alternative policy options are discussed, and the ethical and political theories that have been presented in this chapter bear on these options in different ways. The next chapter shows how the framework for policy analysis that was presented in Chapter 2 can be integrated with both substantive and procedural theories to provide a method for analyzing the normative dimensions of public policy and for evaluating policy options on a case-by-case basis.

Summary

Social or political ethics differs from personal ethics. One way to understand this difference is to imagine how social ethics might take the form of a social contract, understood as an agreement into which all members of society enter. On this view, ethical theory specifies the terms of the agreement. There are, however, several different ways to specify these terms, so any version of the social contract should be supported by an argument. The argument has the task of specifying why one set of terms is to be preferred over another. Four approaches to ethical theory are outlined. Each specifies the terms of the social contract in a different way. Each is also supplied with an argument that attempts to show why people in a presocial bargaining position would accept terms of a given sort.

Libertarian theory limits the social contract to negative or *noninterference* rights. These rights protect individuals from harm or interference by others. Standard noninterference rights include rights to life, liberty, and property. The argument for libertarian theory is that all are vulnerable to threats from others in a *state of nature*, a situation in which there is no government. Rational individuals will agree to not to harm others if they can be assured that others will not harm them. Government is an agreement in which all members of society agree to respect the noninterference rights of others, and that grants government the power to enforce compliance with the agreement through the power of the police and the courts. Government's powers are limited to the protection of noninterference rights, however, since it is unlikely that every member of society will agree to more expansive government activity. *Egalitarian* theory expands the rights protected by government to include positive or *opportunity* rights. Opportunity rights entitle citizens to certain *primary goods*, such as food, shelter, education, and income, which are necessary to live a decent life. Opportunity rights may also specify *social goals* (such as the elimination of poverty) to which governments should strive, even if it is impossible to guarantee achievement of goals as an entitlement. Unlike noninterference rights, opportunity rights require government to do certain things on behalf of citizens, so egalitarian theory must therefore extend greater power and latitude to government than does libertarian theory. The argument for egalitarian theory is that if people were to evaluate the terms of the social contract from a truly impartial perspective, they would wish to limit the inequality of access to primary goods that is allowed by libertarian theory. John Rawls's *veil of ignorance* is a thought experiment designed to simulate conditions of true impartiality. Behind the veil of ignorance, people must choose the terms of the social contract without knowing their social role, whether rich or poor, male or female, black or white. Rational choice from behind the veil of ignorance would select terms for the social contract that limit the risk of being in the worst-off social group; hence opportunity rights would equalize the life chances of all. *Utilitarian* theory evaluates the terms of the contract according to the welfare or well-being of citizens. Well-being can be evaluated in terms of happiness or in terms of satisfaction. Since this criterion evaluates an action in terms of its consequences, utilitarian theories are *consequentialist* theories. Alternative versions of utilitarian theory would use different decision rules to compare alternative forms of the social contract. The *utilitarian maxim* says that government should provide the greatest good for the greatest number of people. The *Pareto principle* says that government should make choices that make at least one person better off but that make no one worse off. The argument for utilitarian theory is that there are situations in which individuals seeking their own interest will make choices that fail to provide benefits. These situations are called *prisoner's dilemmas*, and their terms are specified in the chapter. In a prisoner's dilemma, the role of government is to help individuals coordinate their choices so that a socially optimal result occurs.

When we cannot agree on the terms of the social contract, attention shifts to a set of rules for resolving disputes. *Procedural* theory focuses only on rules that are used to make decisions and does not evaluate the content of a decision in ethical terms. Policy choices are assumed to be legitimate and defensible so long as they follow the rules or procedures for decision making. The most basic procedures specify rules for ensuring that parties have had an opportunity to express or otherwise signify their consent to the rules that will be used to make policy decisions.

Key Terms

allocative efficiency	Pareto principle
assurance problem	participation
axiology	primary goods
consent	prisoner's dilemma
consequentialist theories	procedural ethical theories
decision rule	rights-based theories
egalitarian theories	scope
exit	social contract
free-choice theory	state of nature
libertarian theory	substantive ethical theories
non-interference rights	utilitarianism
opportunity rights	utilitarian maxim
original position	veil of ignorance

References

1. Shue, Henry. 1980. *Basic Rights.* Princeton, N.J.: Princeton University Press.

Suggestions for Further Reading

There are many introductory texts on ethics, ethical theory, and political theory. Although most will agree with this book on the principal terms of ethical theory, each takes a somewhat different approach to the presentation and categorization of alternative views. Burton F. Porter's *Reasons for Living: A Basic Ethics* (New York: Macmillan, 1988) provides a textbook treatment of ethical theory, along with selections from the great philosophers including Bentham and Mill. C. E. Harris, *Applying Moral Theory* (2nd ed., Belmont, Calif.: Wadsworth, 1992), is available for those who wish an alternative introduction to applied ethical theory. The classic works of philosophers discussed in this chapter are Hobbes, *Leviathan*; Locke, *Second Treatise of Government*; Rousseau, *The Social Contract*; Bentham, *Principles of Morals and Legislation*; and Mill, *Utilitarianism* and *On Liberty*. All are widely available in a number of editions. Recent works suggested for those wishing a higher level treatment of these issues are as follows:

Libertarianism
Machan, Tibor. 1982. *The Libertarian Reader.* Totowa, N.J.: Rowman and
  Littlefield.
Nozick, Robert. 1974. *Anarchy, State and Utopia.* New York: Basic Books.

Egalitarianism
Nielsen, Kai. 1985. *Equality and Liberty.* Totowa, N.J.: Rowman and Allanheld.
Rawls, John. 1971. *A Theory of Justice.* Cambridge, Mass.: Belknap Press.

Utilitarianism
Griffin, James. 1982. "Modern Utilitarianism." *Revue Internationale de
  Philosophie* 36:331–375.
Sen, Amartya Kumar and Bernard Williams, eds. 1982. *Utilitarianism and
  Beyond.* Cambridge: Cambridge University Press.

Procedural Theory
MacLean, Douglas. 1986. "Risk and Consent: Philosophical Issues for
  Centralized Decisions," in *Values at Risk*, Douglas MacLean, ed. (Totowa,
  N.J.: Rowman and Allanheld), 17–30.
Rawls, John. 1985. "Justice as Fairness: Political Not Metaphysical," *Philosophy
  and Public Affairs* 14:223–251.

4

Ethics and Policy: How They Fit Together

The aim of this chapter is to develop an understanding of the role of ethical considerations in the policy process, where this process is understood to encompass problem identification, policy formulation, policy adoption and funding, program implementation, and program evaluation. Our task is to understand how the ethical theories discussed in the previous chapter influence and receive expression in the policy process described in Chapter 2.

How Ethical Theory Bears on Public Policy

Public opinion polls conducted across the United States over the last several years consistently find that an overwhelming majority of Americans believes that abortion is morally unacceptable (except perhaps in cases of rape or incest). A clear majority also believes that the decision on whether to have an abortion should be left to the woman, that is, that there should be no legal restrictions on abortion beyond those expressed in the famous Supreme Court decision *Roe v. Wade.* Similar findings could be presented for any number of other issues of public concern. Most Americans apparently believe that the goal of public policy should not have as its chief or even a major goal the codification of their personal moral vision.[1]

Many social philosophers would concur with this judgment, especially as applied to a pluralistic society founded on the notion of government by consent. They would point out that public policies that can find justification only in the fact that they enforce a certain moral orthodoxy are precisely those for which there would be no public consensus. Such policies could achieve their moral goals only at great cost to the society they are intended to serve. And

[1]Supreme Court Justice Sandra Day O'Connor put the point well in a recent decision when, speaking for the Court, she said, "Our obligation is to define the liberty of all, not to mandate our own moral code" [*Planned Parenthood of Southeast Pennsylvania v. Casey* (112SC 2791)].

even if the public consensus necessary to implement moral orthodoxy did exist, as sometimes it does for specific issues, there would be little reason to suppose that society should undertake to police the morality of its members.

Social contract theorists would state this position as follows. Moral orthodoxy is not one of the rationales that would lead one to abandon the state of nature, no matter how strongly held one's moral beliefs might be. Not only is it difficult to imagine a plausible argument for supposing that parties to the social contract would endorse a contract that took such moral orthodoxy to be one of its goals; but also, given the acknowledged lack of consensus in such matters, it seems likely that these parties would adopt only contractual goals that did not presume such orthodoxy. The challenge facing those in the contractual situation is precisely that of fixing upon a social contract that secures the benefits of social cooperation and organization despite the existence of deeply held differences in moral vision among the contractors.

Yet if the institution and enforcement of moral orthodoxy is not one of the goals of public policy, how does ethical theory bear on policy? The answer to this question is to be found by examining the analytical framework developed in Chapter 2. This framework, we will recall, identified four sets of variables important to analyzing substantive public policy: *situation, structure, conduct,* and *performance.* These variables are related in the following way: Public policy imposes a certain *structure* of legal rights (and obligations) upon a pre-existing *situation,* defined in terms of (i) the characteristics of the goods and services whose allocation is to be modified by the policy, (ii) the characteristics of the persons and institutions affected by the policy, and (iii) the existing structure of rights and obligations of those persons and institutions, established by law, custom, and covenant, to the goods and services in question. The imposition of this structure upon a pre-existing situation determines a new set of opportunities that leads actors in the situation to act in novel but predictable ways. This *conduct* has certain consequences, which in the analytical framework we called the *performance.* Ethical theory bears on public policy not in the guise of a goal of such policy, but rather as a constraint upon acceptable policy or as a criterion for being the right policy: Good public policy must among other things be ethically acceptable, if not the best policy ethically. Our task in this chapter will be to understand just what ethical acceptability or rightness means here, if not conformity with a single moral vision.

Ethical theory constrains acceptable public policy in three different ways: in structure, in conduct, and in performance. In effect, there are three basic questions that can be raised regarding the ethical acceptability (or rightness) of a particular public policy. First, is the structure of the policy ethically acceptable? Second, is the conduct that the policy elicits, or can be expected to elicit, from actors in the situation ethically acceptable? Third, is the performance that eventuates from the conduct of actors in the situation upon which the policy structure is imposed ethically acceptable? Let us look at each of these questions in turn.

Acceptable Structure

Public policies are instruments for effecting societal change because they create, destroy, or redistribute some of the legal rights of certain individuals (and hence the legal obligations of others) affected by the policy. (Recall that by *legal rights* we mean the rights of individuals, established by law, with respect to their access and control over the resources of their community.) Questions of the first sort, having to do with the ethical acceptability of the policy's structure, ask whether both the legal rights created by the policy and the changes in rights brought about by their creation are ethically acceptable, in themselves and without regard to their consequences for conduct and performance. The idea here is that we can assess the ethical acceptability of a policy independently of its consequences. Only certain structures of legal rights, or changes to such structures, are thought to be ethically acceptable. Consider, for example, a land use policy that limits development by zoning areas currently under cultivation for agricultural use only. Such a policy changes the property rights and hence the opportunities for affected landowners. Farmers who might have anticipated lucrative sales to developers find themselves limited in their options: They are able to sell only to buyers who contemplate continued agricultural use of the land. In effect, these farmers have lost the developmental rights to their land that they once enjoyed. The ethical acceptability of this zoning policy can be assessed both with respect to the impact of this zoning policy (i.e., conduct and performance) and with respect to the changes in property rights that this policy creates (i.e., the policy structure itself).

Policy structure is assessed by reference to some antecedent philosophical specification of ethically acceptable configurations of legal rights (or modifications thereof). The described land use policy might be held to be ethically unacceptable not simply because it fails to compensate farmers for the lost speculative value of their land, a value that farmers could reasonably have assumed to be appurtenant to land ownership, or because it may deprive some farmers of what in effect is their retirement savings, but also because land ownership, it is claimed, should entail the right to develop the land in any way whatever, so long as the development does not constitute a public nuisance or hazard.

The plausibility of any proposed assessment of the ethical acceptability of a policy's structure of legal rights will, of course, depend crucially on a number of things, including details about both the policy's structure and the situation on which it is imposed. The important point here is simply that the structure of a proposed public policy can be assessed independently of the impact (i.e., the conduct and performance) of the policy. Such structural assessments clearly presuppose the existence of certain acceptability criteria against which the structure of a policy can be evaluated. Rights-based theories of the sort described in the previous chapter (e.g., libertarianism, egalitarianism) typically provide the basis for such criteria. Libertarian theories, for example, would count as acceptable only those policy structures that are consistent with the limited role of government that such theories presume. Policy structures that provide for necessary police protection would be acceptable (perhaps even mandatory), while those that either restrict or curtail such protection or go beyond the provision of protection would not. Egalitarian theories, on the other hand, would count as acceptable only those structures that are consistent with the more expansive role of government that these theories presume. Policy structures that provide citizens with the opportunities and services that they deserve as a matter of right would be acceptable (perhaps even mandatory), while structures that either restrict or curtail such things or go beyond their provision would not. In effect, then, the structure of legal rights imposed by a policy must be consistent with the moral rights antecedently imputed to the individuals affected by the policy.

Acceptable Conduct

Public policies bring about societal change by virtue of the conduct that the policy elicits from actors in the situation upon which the policy is imposed. Questions of the second sort propose to assess the ethical acceptability of policies by asking about this conduct. A policy will be ethically acceptable only if the elicited conduct is ethically acceptable. The basic idea here is that policies that elicit unethical conduct are themselves ethically unacceptable, although clearly this idea needs to be qualified. A policy is not ethically unacceptable simply because it may lead some to act unethically in ways that they would not (and indeed could not) have acted in the absence of the policy. Tax policies, for example, do not become ethically unacceptable because these policies afford the dishonest an opportunity for unethical conduct that they would not otherwise have had (e.g., evading just taxes instituted by the policy). Yet a tax policy that forced many otherwise honest people to break the law would be ethically unacceptable. Ethically acceptable policies should not expose individuals to known weaknesses of human moral psychology.

Assessments of policy acceptability that focus on elicited conduct are comparatively rare in our society, presumably because the virtue-based ethics and moral psychology necessary to underpin such assessments are simply not a significant part of society's conceptual resources. While comparatively rare in our society, such assessments have played a dominant role in other societies, most notably in ancient Greece. Some philosophers recently have called for their revival in our own society, noting that it is only through such assessments that one is able to examine the impact of policy on individuals treated as **moral agents**. Policy assessments in our society, they argue, tend to overlook the role of public policy in creating the circumstances in which specific ethically significant acts on the part of individuals become possible or impossible, likely or unlikely. Thus, for example, statutes that hold individuals liable for harm that they do while attempting to render emergency assistance to others may tend to discourage persons who would otherwise be Good Samaritans from such actions.

Acceptable Performance

Public policies have societal consequences by virtue of the consequences of the conduct elicited by the policy. Questions of the third sort aim at assessing the ethical acceptability of a policy by asking about the ethical acceptability of those consequences, that is, the performance that eventuates from the conduct of actors in the situation upon which the policy structure is imposed. Criteria that address this end state evaluate policy performance. A policy is ethically acceptable only to the extent that its performance is ethically acceptable. The most obvious performance assessments are consequentialist in character, and as such rely on consequentialist—typically utilitarian —ethical theories of the sort described in the previous chapter to provide the basis for assessment. The expected policy performance is assessed with reference to an antecedently chosen *scope, axiology,* and *decision rule,* which respectively determine which aspects of policy performance are ethically significant, what their ethical significance is, and how their significance is to be aggregated in order to permit an overall, usually comparative, assessment of the policy performance. Thus, for example, a performance-focused assessment of the land use zoning policy discussed earlier would begin by identifying the ethically significant consequences of the policy (say, the financial impacts on farmers, on local and regional development, and hence on businesses and trades dependent upon such development, on the local tax base, and hence on the availability of public services; the environmental impacts on local residents and on wildlife habitats; and the political impacts on other policies whose performance may be affected by the adoption of this policy). The assessment would attempt to evaluate these consequences quantitatively so as to enable comparison with alternative proposals. The chosen decision rule would then indicate which policy proposal to select.

The option of assessing the ethical acceptability of a public policy from any of the three different perspectives described previously (that is, with respect to structure, conduct, or performance) raises the possibility that the choice of assessment perspective may reflect fundamental ethical differences since the ethical theories associated with each one of these perspectives are largely incompatible with the theories associated with the other two. The possibility of conflict is magnified by the fact that each of these perspectives has associated with it a number of ethical theories (or versions of a theory), each of which is itself largely incompatible with the others. Thus, libertarians can come into conflict with egalitarians regarding the specific sorts of rights of individuals that public policies should respect, protect, or advance.

Libertarians and egalitarians can come into conflict with consequentialists (i.e., utilitarians) regarding the appropriateness of rights-based or consequentialist assessments of public policy. Utilitarians can come into conflict among themselves regarding the appropriate choice of axiology and decision rule. All of the foregoing can come into conflict with proceduralists regarding the priority of procedural as opposed to substantive constraints on public policy.

Ethical conflict over public policy is more than a mere possibility; it is the focus of much of the policy debate in our society. That we nevertheless succeed in shaping and pursuing a public policy on most issues of public concern suggests that these conflicts are typically managed, if not resolved, in the course of the policy process. The obvious question is: "How is this done?" To answer this question, we need to understand the manner in which ethical considerations both influence and receive expression in the policy process.

How Ethics Figures in the Policy Process

The policy process consists of five stages: *problem identification, policy formulation, policy adoption and funding, program implementation,* and *program evaluation.* Ethical considerations influence and receive expression in each of these stages, though in ways that differ from stage to stage.

Public policy is an institutional response to a perceived problem or opportunity that is thought by those with policy-making authority to require or deserve public action. The various ethical theories discussed in the previous chapter provide a *criterion* for determining whether a particular problem (or opportunity) is of the sort that *should* receive public action. As proposed specifications of the content of the social contract, these theories each claim to specify the proper scope of public action and hence of public policy. Thus, for example, libertarian theory would include items on the policy agenda that are intended to improve public safety but would probably exclude items that are intended only to diminish disparities in individual wealth. Egalitarians, on the other hand, would probably include both sorts of items on the policy agenda.

To say that ethical considerations are decisive in determining which problems should be included on a policy agenda is not to say that such considerations are decisive in determining which problems (or opportunities) are in fact included. Whether ethical considerations actually influence the policy agenda depends on the degree to which agenda setting is responsive to such considerations. In practice, the distribution of influence and access in any political system, including our own, has inherent biases, which are reflected in the system's policy agenda: certain problems and opportunities will receive institutional attention; others are simply organized out of the system. Rarely, if ever, do these biases conform closely to the ethical norms of any recognizable ethical theory. Rather, they reflect a complex interaction between ethical norms, raw political power, institutional expediency (for example, older issues get preferential treatment because the institutional bureaucracy knows how to deal with them), political opportunism, and no doubt some measure of historical serendipity. Ethical norms, therefore, are rarely decisive in determining which problems and opportunities are placed on a policy agenda. Yet these norms nonetheless do play a significant role in determining what gets placed on the policy agenda, especially in political systems like our own, where political power is widely dispersed among groups with competing interests and where accepted political ideology holds that exercise of political power should conform to ethical norms.

It is some measure of the influence of ethical considerations in setting the policy agenda that public debate regarding the inclusion of particular problems on an agenda is typically formulated in ethical terms. The fundamentally ethical character of such debate is most obvious in cases that concern the possible inclusion of new sorts of problems on a policy agenda. In such cases, the public and politicians alike are typically quite explicit in their reliance on ethical theory when attempting to justify their proposal to include a problem on a policy agenda. Thus, for example, during the farm credit crisis of the last decade that saw hundreds of farmers forced into bankruptcy and their farms into foreclosure, many proponents of federal assistance to debt-ridden farmers argued that these farmers' plight demanded federal action for basically consequentialist reasons: the country needed to preserve this seemingly endangered way of life because, for one reason or another, to do so was in the public good. Wendell Berry and others in the new agrarian movement (see Chapter 10), for example, are fond of quoting Thomas Jefferson's famous letter to John Jay, of August 23, 1785, in which he offers a clearly consequentialist rationale for preserving farming as a way of life:

> Cultivators of the earth are most valuable citizens. They are the most vigorous, the most independent, the most virtuous, & they are tied to their country & wedded to its liberty & interests by the most lasting bounds.

When, to take another example, American soybean producers lobbied Congress for restrictions on U.S. international agricultural assistance to third-world countries (see Chapter 8), they argued that such assistance was unacceptable on the grounds that it promoted the development of third-world competitors in U.S. export markets. International agriculture assistance, they assumed, should not cause harm to members of the state providing such assistance. It is unclear whether this assumption will withstand careful scrutiny; however, the point to be noted here is that these soybean producers made their case to Congress on basically ethical grounds: the agriculture assistance was ethically wrong because it was harming American citizens, and it should therefore be prohibited.

Once a problem has been identified as requiring public action, the task facing policy makers is to formulate a policy consistent with their definition of (i) the problem, (ii) the situation (as defined previously), (iii) available public resources (for funding, administration, enforcement, etc.), and (iv) goals and values. Ethical considerations influence each of these four types of constraints on policy formulation. Such considerations obviously influence policy goals and values directly: ethically acceptable policies can aim to achieve only certain goals, to promote only certain values. Acceptable goals and values are those consistent with one or another of the ethical theories described in Chapter 3. Ethical considerations also constrain the means that can be employed to achieve these goals or promote these values. Thus, for example, many economists argue that U.S. farm price support policies, whether in the form of surplus purchases, acreage restrictions, or direct subsidies, impose an unacceptable burden on society. Federal outlays for support programs, they point out, topped $30 billion in 1986 and accounted for roughly five-sixths of net farm income in that year. These economists argue that the best thing to do for U.S. agriculture would be to eliminate all forms of price support, even if such a policy would force a lot of medium-sized farms out of business. Many policy makers endorse the stated goals of such a policy; however, they have reservations about the equity and fairness of the proposed means by which the farm sector would be reduced to a reasonable size. Owners and operators of medium-sized farms, they point out, would bear the brunt of the imposed costs: they would be the ones who would lose most of the equity in their farms; they would be the ones forced into non-farm employment. Such inequities, these policy makers argue, make the proposed policy ethically unacceptable.

Ethical considerations influence the other three constraints on policy formulation (i.e., problem definition, situation, and available resources) more indirectly. Consider, for example, the issue of federal Medicaid funding for abortion. The deep ethical disagreement within our society regarding this issue defines not only the political context within which a funding policy must be crafted, but also the very problem, not to mention the availability of resources, which such a policy is to address. The issue of whether poor women in our society deserve such public assistance is a nonissue if, as many argue, abortion should be prohibited by the state. The question of resource availability is similarly mute. Given the intensity of feelings on this issue, it is not surprising that the debate over public funding quickly becomes a debate over the underlying issue of the ethical acceptability of abortion itself.

The influence of ethical considerations on these four constraints on policy formulation explains the general attentiveness of policy makers to the ethical acceptability of the policies that they formulate. To the extent that policy makers are not attentive to considerations of the ethical acceptability of both the goals of public policy and the means by which these goals are to be achieved, they can expect such considerations to be forced on them in one way or another. Policies that are perceived by a significant portion of the public to be ethically unacceptable must survive a hostile environment in which adoption, funding, and implementation are achieved only at great political cost to those who support the policy. Sometimes, of course, such costs are justified; sometimes policies deserve support in the face of strong public opposition. At other times, however, policies do not deserve support, either because the policies are ethically unacceptable or because, while acceptable or even good, they are too costly. Sometimes even a good policy is simply not worth going to the wall for. Deciding which policies deserve support and which do not is, then, at once a political and an ethical question, if for no other reason than that political and ethical questions are not easily distinguished and demarcated, especially in a pluralistic society like our own, where the ethical foundations of our political institutions are as much procedural as substantive.

Policy Evaluation: Two Views of What Constitutes the Right Policy Ethically

Policy evaluation encompasses all five stages of the policy process; in fact, it is a component in the ongoing political process by which public policy is continually restructured, reformulated, modified, and corrected in an attempt to fit current policy to an ever-changing situation. Policy evaluation is as much the precursor as the successor of new policy. Whatever their status (e.g., proposed, current, past), public policies are typically evaluated either with respect to their structure or with respect to their performance (evaluations with respect to conduct, we noted, are comparatively rare). *Structure-focused* evaluations will typically be rights-based, while *performance-focused* evaluations will typically be consequentialist.

This difference in focus entails an important difference between these two sorts of policy evaluation. Structure-focused evaluations of policy seek to determine whether the policy's structure is consistent with some antecedent specification of ethically acceptable configurations of rights and obligations. Rights-based ethical theory (e.g., libertarianism) specifies a class of acceptable configurations, and the task of a policy evaluation is to determine whether the structure of the policy in question is included in this class. If it is, then the policy is ethically acceptable; otherwise, it is not. The question to be answered by a rights-based evaluation is simply this: Does the policy structure in question satisfy the conditions for ethical acceptability established by the adopted rights-based ethical theory?

Whereas structure-focused evaluations answer the relatively narrow question of whether a given policy is ethically acceptable, performance-focused evaluations typically answer the broader question: Which of the available alternatives is ethically the best policy? The consequentialist theories upon which performance-focused evaluations are based typically incorporate an optimizing decision rule that effects an ordinal ranking of policies in terms of their relative ethical acceptability. Thus, for example, classical utilitarian theory, which incorporates the utilitarian maxim, defines the morally right policy as the one that maximizes net aggregate utility and provides a scheme for ordering policies in terms of their net aggregate utility. (Decision rules, such as the Pareto principle discussed in Chapter 3 and later in this chapter, are exceptions inasmuch as they count as ethically acceptable any policy that satisfies the chosen criterion.) Rights-based ethical theories, it should be noted, provide no basis for ranking policies as more or less ethically acceptable, given that these theories make no provision for an ethically acceptable violation of one's rights.

Determining which of a set of alternative policies is ethically the best is not necessarily more difficult than determining whether a given policy satisfies certain conditions for ethical acceptability. In some cases, it may be unclear whether the acceptability conditions established by a given rights-based theory are satisfied by a particular policy; in other cases, it may be unclear how these conditions are even to be understood and applied. (Consider, for example, the difficulty that our courts have had in determining the scope and application of constitutional rights of free speech, freedom of religion, and due process.) Nevertheless, consequentialist evaluations typically do demand a *comparative* evaluation of alternative policies that rights-based evaluations do not. In effect, the consequentialist evaluation of one policy requires the evaluation of all the alternatives. Such comparative evaluations are often extremely difficult and time-consuming, in part because they require that the individual policies be evaluated in terms that will permit their comparison. Let us look more closely at some of the issues and problems associated with both rights-based and consequentialist evaluation.

Rights-based (Structure-focused) Evaluation

Rights-based evaluation seeks to determine whether a policy's structure is consistent with the specification of acceptable configurations of rights (and obligations) provided by an antecedently adopted rights-based ethical theory. Any policy structure that is consistent with the specification is ethically acceptable. Rights-based evaluation can be thought of in terms of template fitting: Rights-based theories provide templates against which policy structures are evaluated. If the structure fits within the template, the structure (and hence the policy) is acceptable; otherwise, it is not. The ethical acceptability of one policy, it should be noted, does not preclude the ethical acceptability of one or more alternative policies. Thus, for example, there are a number of policies that a city or municipality might adopt regarding political rallies, parades, and demonstrations, each of which would be entirely consistent with constitutionally recognized rights of free speech and assembly.

Consistency with an antecedently adopted rights-based ethical theory is an acceptability criterion whose stringency depends on the nature of the rights and obligations specified by the theory. The more specific and extensive the specified rights and obligations, the fewer the acceptable policies.

The principal difficulty encountered in rights-based policy evaluation arises from the typically abstract nature of the rights-based theory's specification of acceptable configurations of rights and obligations. It is difficult sometimes to ascertain what specific rights and obligations are entailed by the theory. Thus, for example, egalitarian theories require that as a matter of rights, individuals have equal opportunity of access to the various roles and positions within society by means of which the benefits of society (wealth, status, self-respect, etc.) are distributed. But what precisely does this entail in regard to ethically acceptable tuition policy in public universities? Should there be free tuition? If not, how precisely are tuition levels to be set? Or, to take another example, consider the now repealed Highway Beautification Act of 1965, which restricted, without compensation to the landowner, construction of billboards within 660 feet of an interstate highway. Was this statute consistent with a libertarian theory that permits coercion only in order to prevent harm to others or their property?

Difficulties in ascertaining what a particular rights-based ethical theory entails by way of specific rights and obligations are similar to the difficulties faced by our courts in ascertaining the specific rights and obligations entailed by legal statutes or provisions of the U.S. Constitution and of state constitutions. These theories, like statutes and constitutions, are not self-interpreting. We come to understand their content only through a sometimes lengthy process of interpretive definition. Through a series of decisions about how the theory is to be applied in concrete cases, we come to understand how the rather abstract provisions of the theory are to be construed; through interpretation, the provisions of the theory receive an increasingly concrete definition. Of course, there is one obvious difference between the process by which legal documents receive interpretive definition and the process by which rights-based ethical theories receive such definition: in the latter case, there is no formal institution like the judicial system that is charged with the task.

When presenting an ethical theory for our consideration, philosophers typically devote considerable time to the task of showing what the theory entails in specific cases. John Stuart Mill, for example, devotes fully one-quarter of his famous book *On Liberty* to this task (3). Such interpretive definition is meager compared to the rich definition that, for example, the U.S. Constitution has received at the hands of the Supreme Court; however, it does provide some basis for answering questions about the intended application of the theory to specific cases. The preliminary definition provided by a theory's author is refined and enriched over time as the theory is applied to specific cases. Successive applications of the theory serve to define what the theory is presumed to entail regarding specific cases. In a manner similar to case law, previous applications of the theory serve as guides to subsequent applications. Thus, for example, in deciding whether the Highway Beautification Act mentioned earlier is acceptable on libertarian grounds, libertarians would probably compare this statute to various nuisance laws (e.g., prohibiting or regulating eyesores or offensive smells) that they find acceptable. They might note that the latter serve to guarantee the reasonably unfettered enjoyment of one's own property (for example, one does not have to put up with the neighbor's jackhammer while watching *The David Letterman Show*), a claimed right that libertarians have traditionally wished to protect. The

Highway Beautification Act, they might argue, seems instead to have been intended to guarantee motorists' enjoyment of other people's property. The statute restricts an advertising company from erecting large billboards on farmer Jones's property, seemingly because the billboards might interfere with motorists' enjoyment of the farmer's property, a claimed right that libertarians would not wish to recognize! Proponents might argue that, on the contrary, the statute *is* consistent with libertarian support for nuisance laws. The statute, they might argue, is intended to protect the public's right to enjoy something that belongs to it, that is, the public highway. The statute prohibits activities on adjacent properties, that is, creating and maintaining eyesores (e.g., billboards, unfenced junkyards), that would unreasonably interfere with the exercise of this right. Whatever libertarians would decide here, the thing to note is that the application of libertarian theory to this particular statute is guided by previous interpretive decisions. A decision about the present case must find a place within the web of previous decisions that is at once coherent and compatible with those previous decisions.

The need for rights-based ethical theories to receive interpretive definition represents a significant weakness of rights-based policy evaluation. In the absence of formal institutions to provide such definition, the entailments of these theories for specific cases often remain rather poorly defined. There will often be disputes over precisely what these theories entail for specific cases, yet the theories themselves provide no formal mechanism for resolving such disputes. In the absence of any such mechanism, disputes are resolved in one of two ways: either by the application of consequentialist considerations or by the exercise of political power. Resolutions of either sort undermine the claim of rights-based ethical theories to provide the basis for an ethical evaluation of public policy. Resolutions of the first sort push policy evaluation in a utilitarian direction: the entailments of rights-based theories for specific cases are determined by assessing the expected performance of policies sanctioned by one or another interpretive definition of these theories. Thus, for example, one might resolve a dispute over what libertarian theory entailed regarding the acceptability of the Highway Beautification Act by assessing the impact of the statute. If the benefits outweighed the costs, one might conclude that libertarian theory entailed the acceptability of the statute; otherwise, it would not. The effect of resolving interpretive disputes in this way would be to treat rights-based theories as a form of rule utilitarianism discussed in Chapter 3.

Resolutions of the second sort may deprive rights-based evaluations of any claim to moral legitimacy. Talk of rights can easily become little more than political rhetoric that attempts to rationalize the actions of a particular individual, group, or institution. Thus, for example, politicians are often unwilling to disclose politically sensitive information about the sources of their campaign funds. They attempt to give their unwillingness an air of moral respectability by appealing to a right of privacy that they and their contributors are claimed to enjoy.

Even in cases where the theory's entailments are reasonably well defined, rights-based policy evaluation tends to be conservative in nature, favoring public policies that protect the status quo. The reason should be clear: The theory's application to new cases is constrained by its previous application to other cases. Rights-based theories provide no rationale for radical departures from their established interpretive definitions.

Rights-based evaluation also tends to be biased in favor of the individual. It favors policies that protect the claimed rights of individuals affected by the policies, even in cases where this protection can be secured only at some cost to the public welfare. Thus, for example, rights-based evaluation endorses policies intended to guarantee the right to a fair trial even when these guarantees are expensive to implement (e.g., when the courts provide legal counsel for indigent defendants). Whether one counts this bias as a virtue or a defect of rights-based evaluation depends a lot on how one views the present balance in our society between the rights (and obligations) of the individual and the rights (and obligations) of society. Those who think that the balance is tipped too much in favor of the individual will count the bias as a defect, while those who think that the balance is tipped too much in favor of society will count it as a virtue.

Utilitarian (Performance-focused) Evaluation

Public policy is basically a mechanism for distributing and redistributing social goods (e.g, wealth, health, self-respect) and evils (e.g., pollution, disease, crime). Utilitarians or consequentialists propose to evaluate public policies in terms of the goods and evils that they effect. (In this book we use the terms *utilitarian* and *consequentialist* interchangeably.) Unlike rights-based evaluations, which ask simply whether the policy under evaluation is ethically acceptable, consequentialist evaluations typically, though not always, ask whether the policy is, ethically speaking, the best of the available alternatives. For this reason, utilitarianism typically, though not always, requires a comparative evaluation of alternative policies. The utilitarian ethical theories described in Chapter 3 provide the framework for these comparative evaluations. Some of the special problems associated with utilitarianism deserve examination, but first we need to understand the structure and methodology of such evaluations.

Utilitarian or consequentialist theories, we will recall from Chapter 3, consist of a *scope* (specifying what the theory counts as relevant consequences of the action or policy being evaluated), an *axiology* (specifying how the relevant consequences are to be valued), and a *decision rule* (specifying how the values of these consequences are to be aggregated in order to determine an aggregate value for the action or policy being evaluated). Utilitarian evaluations of a policy, or set of policy alternatives, are evaluations with respect to a particular specification of scope, axiology, and decision rule. Once these three parameters are fixed, utilitarian evaluations proceed as follows: (i) the consequences of the policy (or policies) under evaluation that the chosen scope counts as relevant are identified; (ii) these consequences are then valued by means of the chosen axiology; and (iii) the values of these consequences are aggregated and the policy (or policies) assessed using the chosen decision rule. Because the overall assessment of a policy can vary dramatically with a change in any one of these three parameters, sharp disagreements in policy evaluation need not reflect differences in the basic type of evaluation chosen, namely, rights-based or utilitarian; they might instead reflect differences in the choice of one or more of these parameters.

Performance-focused evaluation of public policy has in recent years come to be dominated by so-called **cost-benefit analysis** (hereafter referred to by its usual acronym *CBA*), which proposes to evaluate policies in terms of their attendant social costs and benefits. Since the turn of the century, Congress has required certain federal agencies to consider the costs and benefits of their proposed projects. In the Flood Control Act of 1936, Congress went even further and required the Corps of Engineers to be guided in its projects by a net benefit constraint. Federal statutes passed in the 1960s and 1970s, notably in the environmental and natural resources areas, significantly expanded the scope of federal policies that required CBA justification. Then, in an attempt to promote the efficient use of federal monies, first President Jimmy Carter and then President Ronald Reagan mandated, by Executive Order, the use of CBA by all departments and agencies within the executive branch.

Cost-benefit analyses fall into one of three basic types, depending upon whether the social costs and benefits are quantified and/or monetized. (To say that benefits and costs are *quantified* is to say that they are expressed in terms of measurable units, in other words, lives, acres, miles, dollars; to say that they are *monetized* is to say that they are expressed quantitatively in terms of their monetary value, typically in dollars.) *Informal cost-benefit analysis* provides a systematic assessment of the social costs and benefits of alternative policies but neither quantifies nor monetizes these costs and benefits. *Quantitative cost-benefit analysis* provides a quantified but not necessarily monetized assessment of these costs and benefits. *Monetized* (or *formal*) *cost-benefit analysis* provides a monetized (and hence also quantified) assessment of these costs and benefits. In our discussion, we shall focus on the last form since it is the paradigm of CBA for proponents and critics alike. Moreover, monetized CBA closely approximates the utility calculus that nineteenth-century utilitarians such as Bentham and Mill envisioned.

To describe CBA as providing a systematic assessment of the social costs and benefits of alternative policies is to leave unspecified the scope, axiology, and decision rule of any evaluation procedure that incorporates CBA. There will be as many different procedures of this sort as there are combinations of these three parameters. So rather than think of CBA as a particular kind of utilitarian evaluation, it is probably better to think of it as an analytical assessment of costs and benefits that many different kinds of utilitarian evaluation can incorporate. The distinction between these two ways of thinking about CBA is important, for many of the criticisms that have been leveled against

CBA are leveled more correctly against features of consequentialist evaluations that have nothing in particular to do with CBA, such as their choice of axiology or decision rule.

In principle, utilitarian evaluations that incorporate CBA could take as their scope *all* consequences, direct or indirect, tangible or intangible, that accrue (or would accrue) from the implementation of the policy being evaluated. In practice, however, such evaluations take as their scope only such consequences as their chosen axiologies—typically a preference axiology (see Chapter 3)—are able and prepared to value. Thus, for example, an environmental policy's impact on the aesthetics of an area will be included in the scope of such evaluations only to the extent that these aesthetic impacts are the object of human preferences that are either satisfied or frustrated.

Policy consequences can be usefully represented by means of the matrix in Table 4–1. Under a preference axiology, a policy consequence is counted as a **benefit** if it represents an increase in preference satisfaction, or as a **cost** if it represents a decrease in preference satisfaction (because it represents the utilization of a resource that cannot then be used to satisfy other preferences).

The social costs of goods and services necessary to implement and maintain a policy constitute its direct costs; the social benefits of the immediate products, services, or averted losses from the policy constitute its direct benefits. All other social costs and benefits attributable to the policy are termed indirect. Costs and benefits are tangible just in case they are valued (priced) in the marketplace, for example, the retail price of heating oil; otherwise, they are intangible, for example, the value of an unpolluted sunset over New York City.

Direct tangible costs and benefits are, of course, the most easily measured. Indirect costs and benefits, whether tangible or intangible, and intangible costs and benefits are sometimes quite difficult to measure; at least, they are the costs and benefits of a policy over which there is most likely to be disagreement. The reason should be clear. In the case of indirect costs and benefits, there may be considerable uncertainty and hence disagreement regarding just what the indirect consequences of the policy will be. Policy impact on complex, interdependent social systems is often very hard to predict with any accuracy; there are often unexpected (and unintended) side effects. Thus, for example, few could have anticipated the myriad indirect benefits from the U.S. space program (e.g., satellite communications, the ultralight-weight thermal blankets that are handed out to runners after the New York City Marathon). Nor did Congress (or environmentalists, for that matter) anticipate one of the indirect costs of the Marine Mammals Protection Act. Passage of this act has had the intended effect of increasing California seal populations dramatically over the last decade, but it also has had the unanticipated effect of significantly increasing the local population of great white sharks, the seal's natural predator. Great whites, it turns out, also enjoy that favorite delicacy of cannibals, so-called long pig, with the consequence that

Table 4–1 Types of Cost and Benefit

	Tangible	*Intangible*
Direct	**Market costs** of implementing a policy • Cost of new equipment needed for compliance with a regulation • Government budget outlays for policy **Market benefits** of implementing a policy • Increase in revenues from tourism	**Nonmarket costs** of implementing a policy • Stress and inconvenience associated with changing rules and expectations **Nonmarket benefits** of implementing a policy • Improved air or water quality
Indirect	**Market costs** that are secondary or tertiary effects of a policy • Unemployment associated with gradual decline of an industry **Market benefits** that are secondary or tertiary effects of policy • Growth in sales of goods that substitute for a regulated good	**Nonmarket costs** that are secondary or tertiary effects of a policy • Political tension associated with a change in the ownership of righs and privileges **Nonmarket benefits** that are secondary or tertiary effects of a policy • Social harmony resulting from resolution of conflicts

one of the impacts of this act has been an increase in the number of deaths and injuries from shark attacks.

Intangible costs and benefits pose a quite different problem. The problem is not one of identifying these costs and benefits but of placing a dollar value on them. Monetized CBAs permit comparative evaluations of policies based on their aggregate utility. The aggregation of a policy's costs and benefits, as well as the comparability of alternative policies, requires commensurability in the measurement of all costs and benefits. The dollar value of goods and services that are traded in markets is easily ascertained. It is simply the market price. The dollar value of goods and services that are not traded in markets—the intangibles—is not so easily ascertained. There is no market, for example, in aesthetically pristine vistas or in a spouse's companionship, so if we are to ascertain the dollar value of such goods, we will have to use indirect means. One such means is **shadow pricing**, whereby one attempts to determine the value of the good or service by means of the market price of similar goods that are traded in markets. Shadow pricing assumes that the value of the intangible good is reflected in the price of other goods that are either similar to it or incorporate the intangible good into the price of another good. For example, the value of an aesthetically pristine vista might be assessed by comparing the price of a house with access to such a vista with the value of houses that are of similar size and quality but do not have vistas. It is the house, not the vista, that has a market price, but the higher market value of the house with a vista is assumed to include the shadow price of the vista. As might be expected, shadow pricing becomes much less reliable and less compelling as the similarities between the marketed and nonmarketed good become more attenuated: the role of the analyst's judgment in adjusting the market price of the marketed good with which the nonmarketed good is being compared becomes dominant. The difficulties become obvious if we imagine trying to shadow price a spouse's companionship. What is the relevantly similar tangible good with which spousal companionship is to be compared; is it the "escort" provided by what is euphemistically known as an *escort service?*

A second means of assessing the value of nonmarket goods is **travel cost**. Here the cost of gaining access to an intangible good is used as a substitute for the value of the good. This method is most effective for recreational goods such as parks, lakes, or wildlife that attract recreational users such as hunters, fishers, birdwatchers, and photographers. Each user will spend money to travel to the good each time it is used. The value of the good can be approximated by measuring how much people spend traveling to it. For example, the value of the pristine vista can be assessed by finding out who has taken the trouble to see or photograph it, how far he or she has come, and how much was spent to make the trip. Travel cost is conceptually similar to shadow pricing in that the value of the intangible good is derived from actual monetary expenditures that have been made to gain access to the good.

Policy analysts have increasingly turned to a third means of pricing intangibles, **willingness to pay**. As the name suggests, this approach proposes to price intangible goods and services by determining what someone would be willing to pay for them. Thus, for example, if you want to determine the value to consumers of produce that is free of pesticide residues, you would undertake to determine their willingness to pay for such produce, perhaps by running experiments in food stores where you actually offer such produce for sale at different premiums. If, to take a second example, you want to determine the value to certain workers of a risk-free workplace, you might devise various schemes to ascertain the wage that workers would be willing to forego in order to decrease health and safety risks by a given amount. Or perhaps you might look at union contracts to see how much in additional wages premium union workers required to undertake tasks that carry a known increased risk. (If workers demanded an added $0.50 per hour before performing a job known to carry an increased annual risk of dying of 1 chance in 1,000, then assuming that a worker works 1,800 hours per year, we might conclude that this worker values his life at $900,000.)

The foregoing methods for monetizing intangible goods calculate their value using the actual market prices of tangible goods as a basis. They assume that the value of intangibles is reflected in prices that people are actually willing to pay for similar goods or for goods that are indirectly related to the intangible good. A fourth method of assessing the values of intangibles is called **contingent valuation**, whereby people are simply asked how much they would pay for the good if they could purchase it directly. Here, for example, people would be surveyed to find out how much they would pay to enjoy or preserve a pristine vista. This method seems simple, but it may not be reliable unless cost-benefit analysts use sophisticated survey techniques. For example, the design of the survey must guard against the tendency of people to overstate the amount they would pay for a good if they know that they will not actually have to pay for it.

Once the various costs and benefits attendant to a policy have been identified and appropriately valued, these values must be aggregated to determine the aggregate value (*utility*) of the policy. Aggregating costs and benefits is not simply a matter of adding the benefits and then subtracting the costs. In the first place, costs and benefits are typically distributed over time. Thus, for example, a soil conservation project requiring the construction of various soil erosion structures (e.g., dams, hedgerows) will incur most of its costs up front, but its benefits will be spread across the life of the project and may in fact begin only some years after most of the costs are incurred. Second, money itself has time value. A dollar today is worth more than a dollar next year and much more than a dollar ten years from today. In order to aggregate the costs and benefits of a policy, one must first *discount* them to their present value, that is, determine the value of each at the present moment in time. This is done by multiplying each cost and benefit by an appropriate discount factor (DF)

$$DF = \frac{1}{(1 + i)^t}$$

where t is the year in which the cost or benefit is incurred and i is the so-called rate of social discount (the **discount rate**, for short). If, for example, the discount rate were 6 percent, then a $100 benefit paid next year would have a present value of $94.34. The same benefit paid ten years from now would have a present value of only $55.83. Once a policy's costs and benefits have been monetized and discounted to their present value, they can be aggregated (summed) to obtain the net aggregate value of the policy. This value can then be compared with similarly derived aggregate values for alternative policies and ethically the best (or acceptable) policy chosen from among the alternatives using some decision rule, the choice of which is in no way dictated by a cost-benefit analysis.

Before turning to the question of how a decision rule is used to choose among alternative policies, we should take a moment to appreciate how difficult it is to carry out a credible monetized cost-benefit analysis. In the first place, there is the difficult task of predicting the consequences of a policy, especially when these consequences will be realized far into the future. (No one anticipated the increase in shark attacks that has been a consequence of the Marine Mammals Protection Act.) In some cases, it may be difficult even to ascertain whether certain consequences are to be counted as benefits or as costs. There will be the admittedly difficult task of pricing indirect and intangible costs and benefits, but even pricing the direct tangible costs and benefits of a policy will not be the relatively straightforward task one might imagine. CBA, we have seen, proposes to take simulated and real market values as the measure of these costs and benefits. Yet critics of CBA have been quick to point out that real market values would provide an accurate measure of social costs and benefits *only if* such markets were perfect in the sense that there was (i) *perfect knowledge*, that is, buyers and sellers in the market have all relevant information, (ii) *perfect mobility*, that is, there is no problem getting goods to people who want them, (iii) *no externalities*, that is, all social costs of production are borne by the market, and (iv) *perfect competition*, that is, there are no monopolies pricing their products at higher than the marginal social cost of production. But real markets are never perfect; hence, if market values are to be used as a measure of social costs and benefits, they will have to be adjusted to compensate for imperfections. Thus, for example, when doing a cost-benefit analysis of nuclear power, it is necessary to recognize and compensate for the significant externalities in the form of government subsidies to the nuclear power industry. The difficulties posed by market imperfections are not insurmountable; however, they do complicate assessment of a policy's social costs and benefits. These difficulties become even more acute if the policy itself is likely to have a significant impact on markets, since in order to price the policy's costs and benefits it will be necessary to predict these impacts accurately, something that has proved extremely hard to do.

Determining the proper rate at which to discount benefits and costs is difficult but important. The outcomes of CBA tend to be very sensitive to the choice of discount rate. A study of the projects authorized by Congress in 1962, for example, reveals that whereas only 9 percent had cost/benefit ratios of less than unity on an assumed discount rate of 4 percent (policies with ratios of less than unity are net losers), 64 percent of these policies had cost/benefit ratios of less than unity on an assumed discount rate of 6 percent [see Fox and Herfindahl in Williams (6)]. The controversy surrounding the choice of discount rate focuses both on what theoretical discount rate to use and on how to modify this rate to reflect market imperfections, notably taxes and risk. Analysts generally agree that the discount rate should reflect the opportunity cost (i.e., the cost measured in terms of opportunities foregone) of taking money out of the private sector and investing it in the public sector, but there is little agreement about how to determine this cost.

In light of the difficulty of developing a monetized CBA for a policy, not to mention the attendant cost (and time), it is hardly surprising that policy analysts have often been willing to settle for something less by way of a CBA. The goal of CBA, after all, is to facilitate the evaluation of public policies. In many cases, achieving this goal will not require a monetized analysis of all costs and benefits in order to evaluate a number of policy alternatives. Sometimes it will be enough to monetize the costs and benefits that can be easily monetized, to quantify those that can be easily quantified, and simply to identify others that can be neither monetized nor quantified. Consequentialist policy evaluation, in short, does not always need formal CBA, even if policy makers have increasingly sought the reassurance that having a CBA of their policies seems to bring.

Policy Choice Using Utilitarian Evaluation

The foregoing problems not withstanding, CBA provides a very useful technique for identifying, and in some cases quantifying and monetizing, the social costs and benefits associated with public policies. In itself, however, CBA does not provide a complete assessment of policies for the simple reason that it does not provide any guidance on how policies having these costs and benefits should be evaluated. In other words, merely knowing the social costs and benefits of a policy does not tell us how to use this knowledge to evaluate policies. Evaluation becomes possible only with the specification of a *decision rule* that provides such guidance. The mistaken assumption that CBA does provide such an evaluation procedure can be traced to the fact that CBAs often include an evaluation of the policy or policies under analysis based upon a decision rule that is never explicitly stated. In this section we shall examine the employment of two decision rules introduced in Chapter 3: the *utilitarian maxim*, which instructs policy makers to select the policy that maximizes the benefit, and the *Kaldor-Hicks (net benefit) criterion*, which establishes a less rigorous criterion for policy acceptability. Most consequentialist evaluation of public policy is guided by one of these two rules.

The *classical utilitarian maxim* ("the greatest good for the greatest number"), we will recall, counts as ethically best the policy that maximizes net aggregate utility. In principle, this maxim would seem to be incompatible with the notion that public policies should aim to secure a broad range of social goods, such as national defense, public health, economic stability, and food security, inasmuch as it would direct us to choose between those various goods. In practice, however, the maxim does not have this effect since it typically is employed in choosing one among a set of policies, each of which aims to secure roughly the same social goods.

The utilitarian maxim, like any utility-maximizing rule, presumes that alternative policies can be rank-ordered from best to worst; however, in the absence of a formal, monetized CBA, effecting such a rank ordering is often very difficult. The Kaldor-Hicks criterion avoids this difficulty. It counts as ethically acceptable any policy that produces more benefits than costs. The criterion, it should be noted, evaluates a policy in terms of its acceptability, not in terms of its being the best of a number of alternatives. It is not a maximizing rule. As such it does not presume that policy alternatives can be rank-ordered. Use of the Kaldor-Hicks criterion is particularly appropriate when we are being asked to evaluate policies that have very different aims and outcomes. It is especially useful in evaluating alternative policies when we are unable (or unwilling) to rank-order the alternatives so as to be able to apply the utilitarian maxim.

It is, we noted in Chapter 3, compatible with the Kaldor-Hicks criterion that acceptable public policies could provide a net social benefit while nonetheless incurring significant social costs, perhaps even causing serious harm to some. The Pareto principle would have us count as unacceptable any policy that made anyone worse off; however, this seems an unrealistically stringent criterion. It would, for example, count as unacceptable most environmental legislation because that legislation typically makes some individuals or corporations, such as polluters, worse off. The simple fact is that social good is often, perhaps invariably, accomplished only at someone's expense. An alternative to the Pareto principle, the pure Pareto improvement criterion, recognizes this fact but attempts to preserve the spirit of the Pareto principle by counting as ethically acceptable only those policies that actually compensate losers for their losses. Obviously, such compensation will be possible only if the benefits outweigh the costs, since only then could losers be compensated fully for their losses.

The pure Pareto improvement criterion requires that losers be compensated for their losses. But many public policies would appear to be ethically quite acceptable even though they do not satisfy the criterion. Changes in the U.S. Tax Code or in Federal Reserve monetary policies, for example, often result in big losses for some, but we do not consider these policies unacceptable on those grounds alone. In some cases, compensation seems not only unnecessary but even ethically unacceptable. We do not, for example, think that public policies that put crack dealers out of business should include provisions that compensate them for any losses they incur as a consequence of these policies! In other cases, there would be nothing unacceptable about compensating losers. It is just impractical; the cost to society of compensating losers would simply be too great. In still other cases, such as when the state condemns a piece of property to build a highway, compensation seems not only appropriate but ethically obligatory.

The general point here is that compensation is not always required, indeed not always appropriate. Thus, a decision criterion such as the pure Pareto improvement criterion that counts as acceptable only those policies that provide compensation is on shaky ground. At best, it might claim to be the appropriate decision criterion to use in cases where compensation was required. In such cases, the criterion would tell us not to accept any policies that did not produce benefits sufficient to fund such compensation.

Confronted with cases in which compensation is either not required, not feasible, or inappropriate, some policy analysts acknowledge that acceptable policies do not actually have to compensate losers; it is enough, they say, that policies generate sufficient benefits that losers could, in principle, be fully compensated. This criterion, sometimes called the potential Pareto improvement criterion, is equivalent to the Kaldor-Hicks criterion. Policies satisfying the criterion produce an outcome that is called a *potential Pareto improvement*; that is, they produce an outcome that results in a net benefit. When combined with either of the previously stated decision rules, CBA can be seen to provide two different sorts of ethical foundation for public policy, depending upon how the combination is used. Used one way, it provides a procedure for ethical policy making. A person or groups with decision-making authority can commission a CBA for each of several available policy options and then select one of these options by applying the chosen decision rule. Used the other way, it provides a supporting argument or rationale for (or against) a given policy. Parties to a policy debate can commission and use a CBA to bolster their arguments for (or against) a given policy. Both uses of consequential policy evaluation occur routinely in the policy process.

Objections to Utilitarian Evaluations

These two applications of consequentialist evaluation provoke different sorts of criticism. The use of such evaluation as a supporting argument often arouses controversy over the methods used to value goods. If there are interests that are already mobilized in support of a particular policy, opposing interests have reason to scrutinize carefully the arguments for that policy. Since the methods for deciding which effects to include and how to quantify or monetize them are themselves controversial, opposing groups can often find judgments and assumptions that might have been made differently. Alternative interpretations of scope and axiology (e.g., of shadow prices, travel cost, willingness to pay, or contingent valuation) might favor different policies. As such, debates about analytic judgments can easily become politicized. Philosophically, such disputes represent a "family quarrel" among consequentialists since all parties have accepted the general pattern of evaluating a policy in terms of its consequences.

The use of consequentialist evaluation as a procedure for policy choice can lead to the sorts of family disputes described earlier, but it can also raise deeper, more philosophical issues. Such procedures presume, in a way that the use of utilitarian evaluation in supporting argument does not, that utilitarian ethical theories provide an entirely sufficient basis for the ethical evaluation of proposed public policies. Critics of utilitarian approaches to policy choice have challenged this presumption on a number of grounds, most notably on grounds having to do with *allocative efficiency*.

Utilitarianism has been criticized both for being overly preoccupied and for being insufficiently concerned with the efficient allocation of community resources. Critics who think that these procedures are insufficiently concerned with allocative efficiency point out that a public policy may satisfy one or another of the Pareto improvement criteria (including the Kaldor-Hicks criterion), yet may not be the best policy available. There may be another policy that offers even greater net benefits. A similar criticism can be raised against evaluation procedures that employ the utilitarian maxim, which enjoins us to choose the policy among some antecedently specified set of policies that maximizes social utility. There may be a policy, not included among the set of alternatives being evaluated, that offers even greater net benefits. The point of these criticisms is this: If one of the important goals of public policy is to maximize social good through the efficient use of always limited community resources, then a policy may satisfy one of these various decision rules, yet may not achieve this goal. Evaluation procedures should, these critics argue, provide policy makers with some means of determining what would constitute an efficient allocation of community resources.

A form of policy analysis called **marginal utility analysis** is said to offer just such a means, especially in those policy situations where providing the first few units of the good in question is less expensive than providing subsequent units. For example, reduction of food-borne risk is a good. It may be easy to provide some reduction in risk by requiring sanitary facilities for preparing and handling food, but greater reductions of risk may be accomplished only at considerable expense. At some point, the benefit of further reducing food-borne risk may be outweighed by the cost of doing so. In the language of economics, this is the point beyond which the **marginal social benefit** no longer outweighs the **marginal social cost**. An efficient food safety policy would be one in which the marginal benefits equal the marginal costs. A policy committed to producing a higher reduction of risk would have a lower aggregate utility (i.e., would provide a lower net benefit to society) since every incremental increase in the social cost of regulating food-borne risk would return less social benefit than what was invested. By the same token, a policy allowing a higher level of food-borne risk would also have a lower aggregate utility, since any incremental increase in investment that does not go beyond the point where marginal costs equal marginal benefits would return more social benefit than was invested.

Informal analogues of marginal utility analysis are common in our everyday lives, when, for example, we have to decide how much time to spend getting ready for a date, how much to study for an exam, or how much insurance protection to purchase. In each such case, we examine in a very informal way marginal costs and benefits in order to determine what would constitute an efficient expenditure of personal resources (e.g., money, time, patience). Such analyses can be useful in determining both whether a given public policy makes efficient use of public resources and what sorts of changes would improve the policy's efficiency. If the marginal costs to society of a policy exceed its marginal benefits, then the policy is inefficient because it siphons off resources that could be used more effectively elsewhere. The policy's efficiency would be improved by cutting its costs, even though these cuts would result in fewer benefits. If, on the other hand, the marginal benefits exceed the marginal costs, then once again the policy is inefficient, but in this case because resources that are being used elsewhere could be used more effectively here. In this case, the policy's efficiency would be improved by investing more resources in the policy. Such investment would return more by way of social benefits than its social costs (provided, of course, that the investment did not push us over the point where marginal benefits just equal marginal costs).

Most utilitarians would concede that (i) public policy should endeavor to use community resources in an efficient fashion, (ii) policies judged acceptable by the Kaldor-Hicks criterion or the utilitarian maxim may be inefficient, and (iii) marginal utility analysis provides a useful evaluation procedure for developing policies that maximize allocative efficiency. But they would also be quick to point out that public policy is practiced in the real world where available policy alternatives are limited by real-world contingencies, most notably by political feasibility. Pareto improvement criteria, like the utilitarian maxim, provide a decision rule for evaluating—and, in the case of the maxim, choosing between—available policy alternatives. They are not intended to provide a technique for determining what would constitute the ideal (i.e., efficient) policy. Knowledge of the ideal might be helpful when formulating policy; however, it does not eliminate the need for criteria by which actually available policies can be evaluated, and this is what these criteria and the maxim provide. Use of Pareto improvement criteria and the utilitarian maxim does not guarantee an efficient public policy; however, it does guarantee that our policy decisions will move us in that direction since the implementation of policies that satisfy one or another of these decision rules will result in improved efficiency (provided, of course, that the assessment of the policy's costs and benefits is correct).

Far more critics have objected to consequentialist evaluation procedures on the grounds that they are *overly* concerned with allocative efficiency than have objected on the grounds that they are not sufficiently concerned with it. These critics note that the historical record offers little support for the supposition that allocative efficiency should be the goal of public policy. In the United States at least, public policy historically has exhibited little regard for efficiency considerations, stressing individual rights instead. Most of the regulatory policies enacted in this century (e.g., in the areas of environmental protection, occupational safety, food safety) can hardly be justified on efficiency grounds; indeed, some of this legislation explicitly prohibits federal agencies from appealing to efficiency considerations when administering and enforcing the provisions of this legislation (for further discussion, see Chapters 5 and 6).

The general question of when allocative efficiency is and is not an appropriate norm for public policy is large and difficult. Many philosophers and economists have investigated this question in the last decade, and it is not possible to summarize the full scope of that debate in this chapter. Perhaps the most comprehensive criticism is one that was noted years ago by Frank Knight (2) and has recently been argued forcefully by economist Daniel Bromley (1). Bromley notes that welfare economists have understood Pareto improvement (an increase in efficiency) in terms of voluntary exchange. We may assume that people would not agree to an exchange if they did not see it as being in their mutual interest, so exchange makes at least one person better off and no one worse off. However, people may voluntarily exchange only the goods that they own or control. As such, the structure of rights, particularly property rights, establishes preconditions for exchange. Allocative efficiency is defined only in terms of voluntary exchange (or willingness to pay) under a given structure. If there are sharp differences between two different structures, between two different configurations of property rights, the trades and exchanges that people would be willing to make might be quite different. Bromley concludes that efficiency is a poor criterion for evaluating significant changes in structure.

Another way to express Bromley's point is to say that preference utilitarianism provides no basis for comparing policies that change the existing pattern of rights and privileges with the policies of the status quo. The preferences that people have now are the result of status quo rights and privileges; who can say how preferences would have been formed under a different system? Even if one accepts the force of this criticism (and not all economists or utilitarian philosophers do), there are at least two responses that might follow. One is to revert to rights theory or to virtue theory as a source for understanding public policy. Those who advocate this view understand structure as constitutional in the sense that individuals' tastes and preferences are constituted by (or conditioned upon) existing rights and privileges. Public policy then becomes divided into constitutional issues, understood as those issues that have an impact upon the shape and content of people's preferences, as well as relatively minor changes in structure that are presumed to be close enough to the status quo to permit an application of efficiency rules.

An alternative strategy maintains the framework of utilitarian theory and undertakes the difficult task of comparing the **intrinsic value** of goods, the value that goods have without regard to a given structure of rights and privileges. Hedonic axiology aims at intrinsic values, but some forms of intrinsic value may have little bearing upon pleasure and pain. Amartya Sen (4, 5) has written extensively on this approach. In addition, environmental philosophers and other applied ethicists who have written on the value of wildlife, of natural settings, or of freedom and autonomy have understood themselves to be doing research on intrinsic value. In this book, we have left open the question of whether values being discussed are intrinsic or whether they are **exchange values**, that is, values determined solely by the exchanges people make under a given set of property rules. Distinguishing between these two types of value will be very important for someone who wishes to apply utilitarian philosophy to constitutional issues.

Yet another way to approach the philosophical problem here is to criticize allocative efficiency as being insufficiently concerned with equity or fairness. John Rawls's *A Theory of Justice* (discussed in Chapter 3) contains a detailed discussion of why utilitarian decision rules are inadequate tools for evaluating the most basic public rules and policies of a society. Rawls analyzes the decision rules discussed here, along with several others, and concludes that all are deficient in that they permit extremely inequitable distributions of wealth. A simple thought experiment can illustrate the problem. Suppose that an average farm owner currently makes $50,000 per year from a farming operation, the full-time workers employed on the farm make $15,000 per year, and the seasonal migrant workers make $5,000. A new policy is proposed that will change the outcome so that the owner will make $500,000 per year, while the full-time workers will make $20,000 per year. For argument, let us assume that all other costs and benefits (to the environment, health, and consumers, for example, as well as to the migrant laborers) remain the same. How would a utilitarian evaluate such a policy?

It does not take formal cost-benefit analysis to conclude that any kind of utilitarian is likely to evaluate this policy favorably compared to the status quo. Although real policy proposals always involve more complex assessment of costs and benefits, there are reasons to object even to this idealized case. The owner is receiving a tenfold increase in income, while the full-time workers are receiving only $33\frac{1}{3}$ percent more. The migrants receive nothing. The owner's increase represents a change of economic status from middle income to upper income. The extra $5,000 that the full-time workers get will surely be welcomed, but it is still far below the average family income (about $35,000) in the United States. The migrants remain among the poorest of the poor. Those who feel that there is a problem with this policy are likely to object to it by saying that it is inequitable or unfair. Perhaps policies that improve total social utility (or make Pareto improvements) by benefiting those who are already comparatively well off should be rejected.

Two points should be noted before leaving this example. The first is that the concern for equity might well be accommodated within the framework of consequentialism. One could argue that a drastic change in relative incomes itself produces undesirable consequences (envy, distortions of political power) that may themselves outweigh the benefits. One may also argue that equality of wealth tends, over the long run, to produce desirable social consequences, such as social stability and even economic growth. Rawls made such arguments in *A Theory of Justice*, and some have interpreted his difference principle (choose so as to benefit the worst-off group) as a decision rule that could substitute for the optimizing rules discussed in Chapter 3.

The second point is that if one modifies utilitarian theory to make it more responsive to equity, doing so simply underscores why efficiency is not the supreme criterion for evaluating public policy. Equity, along with concern for civil liberties and opportunity rights, may be among those criteria that must be applied to policy at a constitutional level, that is, at the level of determining an acceptable range of policies, prior to the specification and implementation of any particular administrative decision. Efficiency may be an appropriate decision criterion about how to administer regulations. But if equity and rights are taken to establish parameters for efficiency evaluation, alternatives that propose different rules for establishing equity and rights are neither more nor less efficient than one another. Each simply establishes the ground rules for measuring efficiency in a different way. Efficiency is a criterion for evaluating public policy that has limited applicability at best.

Both strategies identify an area within the policy arena for which allocative efficiency is the proper goal. Some proponents of the efficiency doctrine argue that efficiency is the appropriate goal of distributive and regulatory policy, that questions of equity and welfare should be addressed by redistributive policy (see Chapter 2 for the definitions of these three types of policy). Others argue that efficiency is the appropriate goal of the policy process only after considerations of equity have been addressed, typically by deciding who are to be the beneficiaries and who are to bear the costs of a policy. Thus, for example, once we decide that a certain amount of public funds is to be expended on health care for the poor, it becomes entirely appropriate to invoke efficiency considerations in determining the exact nature of the health care to be provided. No matter how proponents propose to define the proper domain of efficiency considerations, their proposals preserve a role for efficiency considerations only at the price of conceding that efficiency is not the sole goal of public policy. This concession has practical as well as philosophical import. Claims to the effect that efficiency considerations should be decisive, even relevant, in the evaluation of a proposed policy always will be open to challenge. Whatever the truth about these matters, the deep philosophical differences that separate consequentialists from their critics can be expected to find expression in public debate about particular public policies, just as do the equally deep differences that separate proponents of rights-based ethical theories from their critics. Consequentialists and rights-based theorists alike can expect to find themselves called upon in policy disputes to defend their evaluative framework against the charge that its basic assumptions are flawed.

Accommodating Rights and Consequences: A Mixed Mode of Policy Evaluation

Both rights-based and consequentialist ethical theories succeed in capturing important aspects of what individuals living in a pluralistic society like our own would intuitively take to constitute the ideal social contract. Rights-based theories capture the guarantees of individual liberties, and perhaps of well-being, that such a contract must incorporate (or at least entail) if it is to accord proper importance to the individual as the fundamental entity of ethical consideration. Rights-based theories uphold, in a way that consequentialist theories do not, the fundamental idea that a consensus for the social contract must be founded on the presumption that each individual contractor should benefit from the contract. Contractors would have little reason to consent to a contract that appeared unable or unlikely to satisfy this presumption. Consequentialist theories, for their part, capture the important insight that the benefits of public action are rarely distributed uniformly across society; rather, these benefits typically are secured only at a cost to some members of society. Contractors would presumably understand this fact about public action and therefore might be expected to endorse a contract that, as in consequentialist theory, evaluated public action in terms of its aggregate utility rather than in terms of its utility for specific individuals, provided that it did not impose undue hardships on particular individuals.

The weaknesses of both rights-based and consequentialist theories are as salient as their strengths. Rights-based theories offer no decision rule for choosing among alternative policies consistent with the rights postulated by a theory; from the rights-based perspective, one such policy is as good as the next. In adopting such a perspective, rights-based theories fail to capture an important aspect of the social contract, namely, the intent to maximally benefit parties to the contract. Consequentialist theories offer a particular expression of this intent; however, they do so by neglecting the guarantees of individual liberties and well-being that are captured by rights-based theories. Consequentialists often try to assuage worries regarding this matter by arguing that public action that maximizes aggregate benefit typically, though admittedly not always, will preserve the individual liberties and well-being that rights-based theories propose to guarantee. But proponents of rights-based theories are unlikely to be reassured, since it is precisely in situations where consequentialist-based action would not preserve individual liberties and well-being that the guarantees provided by rights-based theories are needed.

Faced with these two sorts of ethical theory, which are complementary in their strengths but seriously defective in their weaknesses, contractors might well decide to endorse a social contract that incorporates both the guarantees of rights-based theory and the utility-maximizing scheme of consequentialist theory. Concretely, the provisions of the two sorts of theory could be ordered in their application so that the consequentialist calculus of costs and benefits was applied only to those policy alternatives that satisfied the acceptability constraints of the rights-based theory. Put in other terms, policies consistent with the individual rights and protection postulated by rights-based theory would define the set of alternative policies from which the consequentialist calculus would choose a best policy. A social contract based upon such a mixed theory would not be satisfied with evaluating policies simply with respect to their minimal ethical acceptability, but neither would policies or practices that violated basic liberties and protection (e.g., slavery, child labor) be candidates for possible consequentialist justification.

American political institutions are structured roughly along the lines described here. The use of consequentialist evaluation schemes is not mandated constitutionally, but neither is it prohibited, provided that no constitutionally protected rights are infringed. Specific uses can therefore be mandated by executive order or legislative statute, provided, of course, that they do not conflict with any specific constitutional provisions. Thus, for example, the Executive Order mentioned previously requires the cost-benefit analysis of all new regulatory policies prior to implementation. Constitutionally guaranteed protection of individual liberties such as freedom of religion and assembly and due process clearly restricts the use of consequentialist evaluation schemes such as CBA; so too, do the provisions of many administrative regulations or statutory laws. Sometimes these restrictions are explicit; at other times, they are only implicit. Such restrictions obviously circumscribe the scope of the Executive Order mandating the use of CBA. Thus, for example, the Occupational Safety and Health Act of 1970 directs the Occupational Safety and Health Administration (OSHA) to establish permanent standards regulating occupational safety and health hazards that "most adequately assure, to the extent feasible, on the basis of the best available evidence, that no employee will suffer material impairment of health or functional capacity even if such employee has regular exposure to the hazard dealt with by such standard for the period of his working life" [Sec. 6(b)(4)]. In *American Textile Manufacturers Institute v. Donovan* (1981), the Supreme Court held that in the absence of an explicit provision in the act permitting the use of cost-benefit analysis to set exposure standards, such use by OSHA was not permitted. The statute was held to be unconditional in the protection that it intended OSHA to afford workers' health and safety.

Accommodating Ethical Plurality: A Rationale for Procedural Theory

In a society that is pluralistic in its ethical commitments (both in the sense that different segments of society endorse different ethical theories and in the sense that individuals endorse different ethical theories, depending on the particular issue at hand), there is great potential for ethical conflict regarding both the goals of public policy and the means of reaching those goals. The possibilities of conflict are innumerable, and cases of actual conflict are extremely common. And yet the very possibility of public policy in a pluralistic society based on the notion of government by consent presumes some mechanism for the resolution of these conflicts. The obvious question, then, is: How within the context of public life, and more specifically within the policy process, do we resolve conflicts between these basic ethical stances?

Short of an exercise of political power in which the more powerful simply impose their will on the political process, there is basically only one way to resolve such conflicts: *Parties to the conflict must consent to a procedure the outcome of which all agree to accept as fair and binding.* The strategy here is a common one: Children draw lots to see who gets the last piece of cake; football teams flip a coin to see who gets the option of kicking or receiving; labor and management sometimes settle labor disputes through binding arbitration. The procedures by which policy conflicts are resolved differ only in the fact that these procedures are more highly institutionalized. There are established, often complex and elaborate mechanisms for resolving such conflicts. The precise character of these mechanisms is not important here (some are described in later chapters); however, obviously these mechanisms differ significantly with regard to both the institutional context and the nature of the conflict. Within the executive branch of government, for example, policy conflicts that cannot be resolved through informal negotiation are generally resolved by executive decision, whereas in the legislative branch, they are typically resolved by vote; constitutional issues are resolved by judicial test. Policy conflicts that cannot be resolved in any of these ways, perhaps because political institutions lack the will to do so, are sometimes resolved by public referendum.

What is crucial to the success of these various procedures of conflict resolution is the willingness of parties to the dispute to abide by an unfavorable outcome. Parties must value the procedure as a means for conflict resolution more than they value a favorable outcome to the conflict. Otherwise, none can be expected to consent to the procedures, much less abide by their outcomes. In a pluralistic society where the social contract that binds us together as a society is largely procedural rather than substantive, the social contract itself may be threatened by an unwillingness to abide by the outcomes of these procedures.

Summary

This chapter has discussed how and where in the policy process ethics bears upon public policy. Public debate over policy, at least in this society, is conducted largely in ethical terms, that is, it makes explicit reference to rights, obligations, equity, and fairness. Ethics bears on policy in that ethical values provide *criteria for ethically acceptable policy.* And because in a pluralistic, democratic society like our own ethical acceptability is very often a precondition for political acceptability, ethical values provide criteria for politically acceptable policy as well. Evaluations of policy acceptability tend in our society to be either *structure-focused* or *performance-focused*, depending upon the substantive ethical theory that provides the basis for the evaluation. Rights-based evaluations are structure-focused. They seek to determine whether a policy's structure is consistent with the specification of acceptable configurations of rights (and obligations) provided by an antecedently adopted rights-based ethical theory. Any policy structure that is consistent with the specification is ethically acceptable. Consequentialist evaluations, by contrast, are performance-focused. They seek to determine whether the policy under evaluation has the best social consequences of any available policy option or at least satisfies certain Pareto improvement criteria. The right policy is one that maximizes social utility or satisfies certain performance criteria. Performance-focused evaluations are always relative to some antecedent specification of scope, axiology, and decision rule that provides guidance on how consequences are to be identified, valued, and assessed. In recent years, performance-focused evaluation has come to be dominated by *cost-benefit analysis* (*CBA*), which proposes to provide a quantified, monetized assessment of the social costs and benefits of policy. The reliance on CBA often has been a source of controversy, principally because of the practical difficulty of assessing indirect and intangible costs and benefits. Consequentialist evaluations have been criticized more generally for their preoccupation with allocative efficiency to the neglect of considerations of equity and fairness. Rights-based evaluations, for their part, have been criticized for being overly preoccupied with the rights of individuals to the neglect of general social well-being.

Because evaluations of policy acceptability often will be based on different substantive ethical theories, there often will be competing views as to which policy option is correct or legitimate. Ideally, one would hope that differences of opinion would be resolved by rational discussion and debate, including the presentation of evidence as well as argument. In fact, this ideal is difficult to achieve in practice. Rights-based theorists emphasize structure and place little stock in arguments that emphasize consequences. Utilitarians take the opposite view. There is a tendency for the arguments of one group never to engage truly the concerns of others. This inability to resolve rationally such substantive disagreements explains the important role played by procedural ethical theory: when we find ourselves unable to reach a consensus on substantive issues, we must resort to procedural solutions as a means of policy making.

The open-ended nature of ethical debate over substantive policy issues is exploited by special interests, too. Individuals or groups with interests at stake may find it easy to be persuaded by the philosophical position that supports policies most consistent with their interests; and, of course, some interest groups care little about ethics at all, adopting philosophical rhetoric when it gives them an advantage to do so. In actual instances of problem identification, policy formulation and adoption, and program implementation and evaluation, ethics bears upon policy through the political process, where arguments appealing to ethical values are just one force among many attempting to influence policy. Although any one view of the social contract might provide criteria for evaluating or choosing a policy, the multiple views of the social contract and the complexity of the political process preclude such a straightforward application of ethics in most cases. The following chapters take up specific policies and topics related to food and agriculture. Traditionally, philosophers writing on such topics would present an argument for one policy option or for certain criteria that should be used in evaluating several options. One begins to get a sense of ethical conflict over policy only after reading the works of several different philosophers who take roles as advocates in the policy process. But people who have no training in philosophy or ethical theory also make arguments that rely upon alternative interpretations of the social contract. The following chapters emphasize philosophical arguments made by key actors in the political process. In most instances, their vantage point on a policy problem has given them a particular insight on the problem that leads them to formulate their arguments in a particular way. In many of the cases to be examined, key actors differ with one another over the points of conflict that have been outlined in this chapter: rights versus consequences, noninterference versus opportunity rights, or ways of quantifying and ranking consequences. Yet, in some cases, the philosophical issues become apparent only after careful analysis. The case chapters that follow illustrate the philosophical conflicts that are embedded in policy disputes but leave the construction of arguments or criteria for evaluating policy to others.

Readers of this book should be able to identify groups of key actors in each policy dispute and should, particularly with the help of the supplementary readings listed at the end of each chapter, be able to construct philosophical arguments that articulate and support the viewpoints that each of the key actors might take. We hope that a better understanding of all parties' points of view will help our readers to form more sensitive and responsible views of their own, but we do not provide instruction as to how that should be done. To do so would have undercut the primary objective: to provide a model with extended examples of how ethics bears on the policy process.

Key Terms

benefit	marginal social benefit
contingent valuation	marginal social cost
cost	marginal utility analysis
cost-benefit analysis	moral agents
discount rate	shadow pricing
exchange value	travel cost
intrinsic value	willingness to pay

References

1. Bromley, Daniel. 1989. *Economic Interests and Institutions.* New York: Basil Blackwell.
2. Knight, Frank. 1935. *The Ethics of Competition.* London: George Allen & Unwin.
3. Mill, John Stuart. 1859. *On Liberty.* Reprinted 1978. E. Rapaport, ed. Indianapolis: Hackett.
4. Sen, Amartya Kumar. 1985. "Well-being, Agency and Freedom: The Dewey Lectures, 1984." *Journal of Philosophy* 82:169–221.
5. ———. 1987. *On Ethics and Economics.* New York: Basil Blackwell.
6. Williams, Deborah Lee. 1979. "Benefit-Cost Analysis in Natural Resources Decisionmaking." *Natural Resource Lawyer* 7:761–796.

Suggestions for Further Reading

The material in this chapter linking ethics to public policy analysis is being published here for the first time. Readers wishing more information on this linkage should turn back to the suggested readings for Chapters 2 and 3. Those who wish to explore the suggestion that there should be more emphasis upon conduct in public affairs may wish to examine Alasdair MacIntyre's *After Virtue* (Notre Dame, Ind.: University of Notre Dame Press, 1981), the book that has spawned the resurgence of virtue ethics. Martha Nussbaum provides a different view on virtue ethics in *The Fragility of Goodness* (Cambridge: Cambridge University Press, 1986). A more traditional argument for stressing conduct can be found in Patrick Devlin, *The Enforcement of Morals* (Oxford: Oxford University Press, 1965).

Public choice theorists have come to stress conduct through an entirely different route. Beginning with James Buchanan and Gordon Tullock's *The Calculus of Consent* (Ann Arbor: University of Michigan Press, 1962), public choice has emerged as a subdiscipline that examines incentives created by the structure of public policy. Typically, public choice theorists have maintained the welfare economist's interest in policy performance, but Buchanan himself has written on the ethics of conduct in a manner that is quite consistent with the points raised in this book. See James Buchanan, *The Ethics and Economics of Constitutional Order* (Ann Arbor: University of Michigan Press, 1991). Buchanan's interest in constitutional choice links the assessment of conduct to another topic discussed in this chapter, the limitations of efficiency criteria. In addition to Buchanan and the cited works by Knight and Bromley, readers may consult Allen Buchanan's *Ethics, Efficiency and the Market* (Totowa, N.J.: Rowman and Allanheld, 1985), as well as Allan Schmid's book discussed in Chapter 2.

The idea that John Rawls should be read as a consequentialist, rather than as an egalitarian or a rights theorist, has also been widely discussed. Many early readers of *A Theory of Justice* assumed that the difference principle was to be understood as a consequentialist decision rule. This discussion has been collected by Norman Daniels in a book entitled *Reading Rawls* (New York: Basic Books, 1975), but papers in *Consequentialism and Its Critics*, ed. Samuel Scheffler (Oxford: Oxford University Press, 1988) are also relevant. Thomas Pogge's book *Realizing Rawls* (Ithaca, N.Y.: Cornell University Press, 1989) makes a good statement of the case against interpreting Rawls as a consequentialist in the usual sense.

Much of this chapter focuses on the use of CBA, a topic much discussed by both philosophers and economists. Readers are encouraged to consult the references for this chapter. A good, high-level introduction to the issues can be found in a National Research Council report *Cost-Benefit Analysis* (Washington, D.C.: National Research Council, 1958). Now classic works on the subject include E. J. Mishan, *Cost-Benefit Analysis* (Boston: G. Allen & Unwin, 1982), and Allan Randall, *Resource Economics* (New York: Wiley, 1987).

Mark Sagoff, *Risk-Benefit Analysis in Decisions Concerning Public Safety and Health* (Dubuque, Iowa: Kendall/Hunt, 1985) provides a philosophical critique. Paul Portney has edited a volume of papers, *Public Policies for Environmental Protection* (Washington, D.C.: Resources for the Future, 1990), that illustrate how economists use CBA in the analysis of environmental policy. Though CBA is not subjected to any philosophical review in Portney's book, it is the (sometimes implicit) basis for analyzing a series of public policies in air and water pollution, toxic substances and hazardous waste.

5

Food Safety Policy

Human concern about harm from hazards in food dates back to ancient times, but the role of government in controlling exposure to food hazards has expanded with the development of markets. When households were largely self-sufficient in food production, the role of government was very limited. The more expanded role of government today began with the emergence of national and international food markets. For example, in the United States, more foods began to be mass-produced and marketed nationwide in the 1860s following the Civil War. This led to concerns about how foods would be handled, processed, and packaged by a large number of people the food consumer had never met (8). These concerns have been fueled over the years by reports of unsafe food production practices and outbreaks of food poisoning. For example, at the turn of the century, the publication of *The Jungle* by Upton Sinclair (12) described unsanitary and dangerous conditions in U.S. meatpacking plants that horrified the public and led to national and international demands for expanded government programs on food safety. Today government plays an active role in guarding the safety of the food supply.

A series of recent food scares have focused public attention on the issue of food safety policy. They include Alar in apples, cyanide poisoning of Chilean grapes, contamination of watermelons with the pesticide alicarb, contamination of chicken and milk with the pesticide heptachlor, and several outbreaks of illness from bacterial contamination of milk, meat, chicken, and eggs. These events have prompted a host of questions about existing U.S. food safety policy.

The purpose of this chapter is examine these questions and to see how answers to them depend on philosophical orientation. First, we provide some background on the types of hazards that create food safety problems and the forces that cause these hazards to change over time. Next, we examine the question of the meaning of safety. Then we examine philosophical justification for the role of government in making choices about safety and what form government action should take. After examining current food safety policies, four case studies are presented, raising questions about what level of safety government should ensure, how certain government should be before establishing that safety level, how much the safety level should be enforced, and what level of government, national or international, should decide what the safety standards should be.

Types of Food Hazards

In the modern food system, potential **hazards** in food may originate at any point along the complex route food takes from plant and animal breeding and production of raw foods, through their processing and packaging into commodities, to their final consumption as a meal. **Food contaminants** such as bacteria, viruses, fungi, mycotoxins, parasites, pesticides, animal drugs, and other chemicals such as lead may enter food as by-products of food production, processing, cooking, handling, packaging, transport, or storage, causing harm when, because of human ignorance, accidents, or negligence, too much is present in food. Raw, unprocessed foods are made up of thousands of different **natural food constituents** such as proteins, fats, carbohydrates, and minerals, some of which are potentially harmful when too much is present in food. Food sources, such as fisheries, may become polluted, resulting in **environmental contaminants** in food. Finally, **food additives** such as flavors, texturizers, colors, and preservatives can increase the taste, appeal, and shelf life of food, but too much or the wrong kind can harm health.

Microbial hazards have always been the most serious of these food safety concerns. Some bacteria (*Salmonella, Campylobacter,* and *Listeria monocytogenes*) and parasites (*Trichinella spiralis* and *Toxoplasma gondii*) are contaminants of livestock, eggs, milk, mollusks, shellfish, or finfish. Other bacteria (*Shigella* and *Staphylococcus aureus*) are more likely to be introduced by food handlers during processing. Viruses, for example hepatitis, are more likely to enter food processing plants through contaminated water or infected food handlers. Bacteria and fungi can multiply during food storage, whereas parasites and viruses do not.

While modern sanitation controls such as milk pasteurization, animal disease control, irradiation, and high-temperature processing have substantially reduced many microbial hazards, reported cases have increased for some common diseases, such as salmonellosis. A joint study by the Centers for Disease Control and the Carter Center at Emory University estimates that 6.5 million Americans become ill with foodborne disease annually. The four most important bacterial contaminants, *Campylobacter, Salmonella, Staphylococcus,* and miscellaneous enteric organisms, each cause more than 9,000 estimated deaths annually in the United States. In addition, chronic diseases such as central nervous system disorders, heart complications, blood poisoning, and kidney disease occasionally result from common bacterial and parasitic diseases. Technical literature on food safety is reviewed by Roberts and van Ravenswaay (11).

The increase in reported cases of foodborne disease caused by microorganisms is partly due to greater diligence by public health agencies but also to changes in food consumption and production patterns. More food is being prepared and/or eaten away from home. While microbial hazards occur in both food consumed at and away from home, a greater percentage of cases of illness results from food eaten away from home. New convenience foods such as precooked entrees for reheating at home or in restaurants pose new food hazards. Vacuum packaging hinders the growth of spoilage bacteria but may permit the growth of *Clostridium botulinum* at temperatures found in most commercial and home refrigerators. Also, precooked foods may be minimally heated, which eliminates the traditional last line of defense—thorough cooking immediately before eating. The widespread use of microwave ovens exacerbates this problem since they often have cold spots where bacterial pathogens and parasites may not be killed. The increasing diversity of the American diet, with food imported from many countries with different microbial contaminants, also adds to the potential for microbial contamination.

Changes in Food Hazards

As national and international markets for food commodities have grown, the demand for large, stable supplies of commodities has increased. To meet this demand, wide-scale use of synthetic chemicals in agriculture began after World War II. Fertilizers were used to boost crop yields. Pesticides and animal drugs were developed to control insects, diseases, funguses, rodents, and other pests that spoil food. For example, herbicides control weeds that reduce yields, and insecticides control insects before and after the harvest. Fungicides kill molds and viruses that infect plants and spoil fruits, vegetables, and grains during storage. Antibiotics and sulfa drugs help livestock fight disease and grow bigger and faster. Hormones help to regulate or promote the growth of plants and animals. These agricultural chemicals produced huge increases in crop yields and reduced food prices. However, by the 1960s, concerns about the effects of pesticides on the environment and their potential to cause cancer surfaced with the publication of Rachel Carson's *Silent Spring* (1). Concerns also arose about the potential effects of animal drugs on the development of resistant strains of bacteria, allergic reactions in sensitive humans, and cancer.

This chemical revolution in food production is being quickly overtaken by a revolution in genetic engineering. Throughout human history, plant and animal breeders have encouraged the genetic expression of useful plant and animal traits, thus altering the natural constituents present in raw foods. However, genetic selection has been limited by the reproductive process, which limits breeding across species. Modern genetic engineering essentially eliminates this constraint, making greater genetic alteration of plants and animals possible. For example, toxins produced by *Bacillus thurengensis*, or *bt*, can kill certain insects. The gene that enables *bt* to do this is now being inserted into potatoes, cotton, and other plants so that they can produce their own pesticides. This breakthrough promises great environmental gains, but it also raises concerns about how to prevent potential harm from new "natural" food constituents.

Modern food processing methods have also contributed to a more plentiful, reliable, appealing, and convenient food supply, but some of these methods have potentially harmful as well as beneficial effects. For example, modern canning methods have substantially reduced problems from spoilage and bacterial contamination, but the lead solder used to seal cans creates some lead contamination of food, raising concerns about harmful effects on the brain (3). Similarly, nitrite is an effective way to prevent food poisoning from certain bacteria in pork products, but it has been found to be a carcinogen. Saccharin enables diabetic and overweight individuals to enjoy sweetened foods without the harmful effects of sugar on insulin and calorie regulation, but has been found to be carcinogenic (6).

The wide-scale use of industrial chemicals has created pollution in our environment that has sometimes jeopardized our food supply. For example, fish from the Great Lakes have been found to contain polychlorinated biphenyls, raising concerns about the effects on the development of fetuses in utero (9). Traces of mercury, a highly toxic heavy metal, have been found in both fresh- and saltwater fish and in wild pheasants. Oyster beds in some rivers have been contaminated with toxic chemicals such as kepone.

Detecting Food Hazards

Until this century, most knowledge of the harmfulness of food hazards was limited to observation of obvious or acute health effects in humans. Modern methods of experimenting with animals in the laboratory have enabled scientists to learn about the less obvious delayed effects of exposure to hazards, as well as the effects of long-term chronic exposure to small levels of hazards. The use of these methods is a very recent development. The basic biology of rats, mice, and other mammals had to be understood before they could be employed as animal models of the mammalian response to microbial and chemical toxins. Not until after World War II were large colonies of these laboratory animals available for experimental work. In many cases, we are just beginning to discover that the levels of certain chemicals and microbes normally present in food are not as harmless as we thought.

Methods for detecting the presence of potential hazards in food and assessing their harmfulness have evolved slowly over the centuries, paralleling the developments of modern science and medicine. The first chemical tests for detecting food chemicals were developed by Robert Boyle and his contemporaries in the 1600s. These and other chemical tests were developed over two centuries, culminating in the first major treatise on food poisons and contaminants published in 1820 by Accum (4). The sensitivity of the methods used to detect the presence of food hazards has vastly improved over the past several decades. It is now often possible to detect levels of chemical contaminants in parts per billion and, in some cases, in parts per trillion or quadrillion.

The development of new knowledge about chronic effects of food hazards and sensitive detection methods has raised a whole new set of policy issues by causing us to rethink the meaning of *safe*. As toxicologists point out, "The dose makes the poison." That is, some levels of exposure to potential hazards cause no harm, so a safe level of exposure to potentially hazardous chemicals and microbes may be established. However, the case is not always so clear-cut for especially virulent microbes or for cancer-causing chemicals. For example, the question of whether any exposure to a carcinogenic compound is safe is still unsettled. Current law says no, but when compounds can be measured in parts per billion, the wisdom of this way of dealing with scientific uncertainty can be questioned. Is there a potential hazard when a chemical or microbe is present in an amount equivalent to one molecule in an Olympic-sized swimming pool? At what point shall we deem something unsafe when such tiny amounts of hazard exposure can be measured? Is the term *safe* even meaningful if our ability to measure it keeps improving?

The Meaning of Safety

For a person to exist in a state of perfect physical safety means there is no chance of experiencing bodily harm. Obviously, this is not the human condition. The human body ages and, through the activities of living, is exposed to many hazards, both natural and human-made, causing illness, injury, disability, or death. To exist in a state of some physical danger or **risk** causes alarm and concern, regardless of whether we ultimately suffer harm. How much alarm and concern a person experiences depends on the probability of bodily harm and the seriousness of the harm anticipated. Thus, a high probability of a particular harm is more alarming than a low probability of that same harm. The seriousness of harm depends on its immediacy, severity, duration, and reversibility, as well as its timing during the life cycle. For example, an immediate, severe, lengthy, or irreversible harm to a child is more serious than a mild, brief, and reversible harm to a mature adult (2, 10).

The seriousness of the bodily harms people experience can be mitigated by human action. For example, remedies have been developed that reduce the severity of harm (e.g., antihistamines for allergies), reduce the duration of harm (e.g., antibiotics for infectious disease), or reverse the harm (e.g., surgery). In the remainder of the analysis, we will assume that policies regarding the development and distribution of remedies are a fixed part of *structure* and are not at issue. However, it is important to recognize that the availability of remedies affects preferences for managing hazards in the human environment. Since individuals may not have equal access to remedies due to lack of income or allergic sensitivity to certain treatments (e.g., antibiotics), preferences for policies to manage hazards may differ among individuals. Similarly, the availability of remedies may change over time due to investments in research, so preferences for policies for managing hazards may change over time. For example, antibiotics for infectious diseases have decreased mortality from these diseases, making them substantially less dreadful.

The risk or danger posed to an individual by a particular hazard depends on the hazard's potential harmfulness, on the individual's susceptibility to harm, and on the extent of the individual's **exposure** to the hazard. Very harmful hazards cause immediate death or very severe, lengthy, or irreversible illness or injury with very little, infrequent, or brief bodily exposure. Less harmful hazards produce only mild illness or slight injury after only very great, frequent, or lengthy bodily exposure. Some people may be more susceptible to harm from some hazards, depending on their underlying state of health, maturity, or sensitivity to the hazard. The extent of the individual's exposure to hazards depends on their presence in this individual's environment as well as on choices the individual makes about preventing exposure to hazards.

The potential harmfulness of a particular hazard under particular conditions of human exposure is a fixed variable, a part of the *situation*. For example, certain forms of bacteria and certain types of chemicals tend to cause certain types of bodily harm in otherwise healthy individuals at particular levels of exposure. The harmfulness of different hazards varies, so preferences may vary about the way different hazards are managed. For example, people may wish to have stricter management of more harmful hazards. Later we will examine the role that information about harmfulness plays in policy choice.

Human susceptibility to harm will be taken to be a fixed factor, although human actions can in fact change this variable over time. For example, vaccinations can create immunity to some bacterial hazards, and proper nutrition and exercise can provide resistance to disease. While policies that diminish susceptibility to harm can have important consequences for food safety, we shall not consider these policies to be a part of the structure of food safety policy. However, it is important to realize that individuals vary in terms of their susceptibility to harm. For example, some individuals are highly allergic to some food ingredients, additives, and contaminants. Consequently, the variability in susceptibility across humans should be important in analyzing food safety policy. It is also important to realize that, like changes in the development of remedies, changes in human susceptibility over time can change policy preferences for hazard control.

Human exposure to a hazard can be reduced by either reducing bodily contact with hazards already present in the environment or reducing the formation or presence of hazards in the environment. In the analysis that follows, we will consider policies affecting actions (i.e., conduct) to reduce exposure to foodborne hazards as the structural alternatives at issue. Policies that affect exposure to nonfood hazards will be taken as a given part of *structure*. However, it is important to realize that policies that reduce human exposure to other hazards will affect preferences for policies that control exposure to foodborne hazards. For example, policies that have improved general sanitation and drinking water safety, along with policies that have increased remedies and vaccinations for infectious diseases, have increased life expectancies. Longer life means increased chances for developing degenerative diseases such as cancer and heart disease, thus changing preferences for avoiding exposure to hazards that have been shown to contribute to these diseases (smoking, fat and cholesterol, pesticide residues, and the like). Also, individuals may differ in the extent of their exposure to other hazards, thus affecting their preferences for reducing exposure to foodborne hazards.

To summarize the analysis so far, we have narrowed the scope of our inquiry to the problem of bodily harm from exposure to hazards through eating food. A condition of perfect safety would exist only if the probability of bodily harm were zero, which would require no exposure to hazards in food. Foods containing hazards that cause any type of bodily harm would, by definition, be unsafe, creating a condition of risk. Since such foods exist or may be produced, safety would require either completely eliminating bodily contact with any hazards already present in food (e.g., discarding all contaminated food) or completely eliminating the formation or presence of hazards in food (e.g., sanitation to eliminate harmful levels of bacterial growth; pasteurization or thorough cooking to kill bacteria).

The Role of Information

Before we can act to eliminate exposure to foodborne hazards, we have to have knowledge of (i) the harmfulness of hazards and either (ii) their presence or absence in food or (iii) how to eliminate their formation or presence in food. Knowledge of harmfulness is necessary to comprehend that something is a hazard and a cause for concern. Knowledge of whether hazards are present or absent is necessary to avoid consuming food that contains a hazard. Knowledge of how to eliminate the formation or presence of hazards in food is necessary to avoid the situation of having hazards in food in the first place.

The human situation, however, is one of imperfect knowledge. We are not knowledgeable about every hazard in food. Our ability to detect such hazards is not perfect. Our ability to limit the presence of every known hazard in food is not completely foolproof. It is costly to develop these types of information. Furthermore, new hazards develop, routes of exposure to old hazards change, and new methods for reducing or preventing exposure need to be developed. Consequently, information becomes outdated and needs to be replaced. As we shall see, one set of food safety policy issues focuses on our knowledge of hazards in food. In particular, questions arise about who should produce this information, how much should be produced, who should get the information, and who should decide what to do with it.

Even if information about a hazard was perfect, we would still have the problem of deciding how to act on it for two reasons. First, reducing exposure to hazards has costs because you either have to throw out the contaminated food or spend resources preventing the formation or presence of hazards in food. Second, some hazards are useful as well as harmful. For example, synthetic pesticides may be the only effective alternative for controlling pest damage to some types of crops grown in certain locations, but they may also be carcinogenic. Consequently, perfect safety might theoretically be possible but not practical. Thus, a second set of food safety policy issues involves how much safety we want.

Food Safety and Public Policy

We have an extensive set of laws at the local, state, federal, and international levels addressing food safety. What is it that justifies this collective action to affect the supply of food safety? (The fact that some people become sick from food hazards does not in itself provide sufficient justification.) What forms should government action take? How much government action is best?

Human exposure to a food hazard depends on how much and how often the hazard is present in particular foods and on how much and how often those particular foods are consumed. Food producers determine how much and how often a potential hazard is present in particular foods. Food consumers decide how much and how often to eat those foods. In today's society, food producers and food consumers are frequently not the same individuals. If they were, it would mean that all individuals were completely self-sufficient, breeding their own plants and animals; raising their own crops, livestock, poultry, and fish; harvesting, preserving, packaging, and storing their own food; and preparing and serving their own meals. In this case, the individuals would be completely responsible for preventing their exposure to food hazards. On the other hand, few individuals purchase all their own food in the form of completely ready-to-eat meals from others, and few producers engage in all the stages of food production. Rather, a chain of exchange relationships exists between suppliers and purchasers. Government is also a key actor at several places along the chain of exchange relationships.

Let us examine this structure as if there were no government involvement. To simplify the analysis, let us assume that no individual produces food for personal consumption but acquires it from others who perform all the stages of food production, and that there are many consumers and many producers. Consumers consent to giving producers some form of payment in exchange for a particular type of food. Producers consent to provide this food in exchange for the payment. The arrangement is a type of contract, and the structure is pure bargained exchange.

As discussed in Chapter 3, procedural theories hold that agreed-upon contracts are just so long as they are based upon consent. For consent to be meaningful, certain conditions must be met. In particular, consent must be freely given by competent and informed individuals (5). The condition that consent be freely given is met under this structure unless all the consumers or all the producers form a single union. If they did this, coercion would exist because, with only a single customer or only a single supplier, the threat of receiving no income or no food would exist. However, we will assume that this type of anticompetitive behavior does not exist. The condition that consent be given by competent individuals would also presumably hold for most consumers except children and the mentally disabled. However, while we might want to decide collectively to bar such individuals from making consumption or production decisions, this is true of many goods, not just food. Thus, the fact that some consumers or producers might be incompetent does not justify a particular food safety role for government, although it may justify a more general policy on the role of these individuals in society. The condition that consent be given by informed individuals requires that both consumer and producer understand the terms of the contract and their likely consequences. This condition would not be met if information is withheld from either party or if either party lacks prior knowledge or skills necessary to interpret the information. We shall argue that these two conditions are not met with respect to the information relevant to preventing exposure to food hazards, thus providing justification for government involvement.

Justifying Government Involvement

For consumers to be able to make perfectly informed decisions about food purchases, they need to know if the food contains hazards. It is unreasonable to assume that consumers possess either ability to sense the presence of most food hazards or knowledge of their potential harmfulness. The ordinary human senses are unable to determine for certain what ingredients were used and how they were processed, let alone detect harmful natural constituents, contaminants, or additives. Even if they could be detected, the consumer, unless specially trained, would lack knowledge of their potential harmfulness and, thus, an understanding of the consequences of exposure to them. The question then is whether the producer would possess all the information and knowledge needed to judge whether hazards are present and how harmful they are, and whether he or she would provide this knowledge to the consumer.

For certain types of hazards, we would expect producers not only to provide information but to act to eliminate consumer exposure to the hazard. This occurs when consumers can detect food hazards after experience with the good. That is, although they may not be able to tell if a producer's food is safe prior to eating it, they can tell after eating it. This occurs when hazards cause immediate harm (i.e., are present in food at acutely toxic levels), and the consumer can, through experience, determine the cause of the harm. Producers would have an incentive to prevent consumer exposure to such hazards because their reputation for producing a safe product would be jeopardized. Consumers would learn about the harm and, in order to avoid exposure themselves, would stop buying the product. As the news spread, consumers would become extremely cautious about who they dealt with, making it more difficult and costly for scrupulous suppliers to establish a reputation.

Because the producer has a strong incentive in this situation to produce a safe product, we have an instance of what was called *hypothetical consent* in Chapter 3. That is, the situation with acutely toxic hazards under the bargained exchange structure does not result in a fully informed consumer, but rather in a consumer who, if fully informed, would be likely to consent to the terms of the exchange. Thus, a role for government is not justified in this instance. Note, however, that under this structure, food producers would always have to worry about the possibility of unscrupulous competitors or muckrakers trying to disparage their products. Consequently, producers might desire some form of protection from government against product disparagement, though this is true for a much larger class of products and product characteristics than just food and safety. (Such laws have in fact been developed.)

Unfortunately, many hazards in foods cannot be detected by experience because the harm they produce is either sufficiently delayed in time that the consumer cannot be certain of its cause, or because the consumer obtains foods for a single meal from a sufficiently large number of different sellers to be uncertain of its source. Thus, the consumer cannot rely on his or her ability to detect some hazards ex ante or ex post and cannot verify the safety claims of the producer. In this situation, producers have little incentive to inform consumers of the presence of such hazards in food because it would reduce demand for their product. Producers also have little incentive to prevent such hazards from occurring in food because they would not be able to recover the costs of doing so since consumers would not be able to detect the safety improvement. Scrupulous producers who feel it is their moral duty to produce the safer product would be higher-cost producers than unscrupulous producers and would be driven from the market since consumers could not tell the safety difference between their products and could only see the difference in their price. Consequently, the condition of hypothetical consent does not obtain, and a need for some kind of protection of the consumer in this contract exists. However, the case for *government* to provide this protection is still not complete.

Before pursuing this argument, however, we should point out that one of the least intrusive forms of government involvement in ensuring hypothetical consent would be a system of liability and negligence law with private enforcement by individuals or class action suits. Under this structure, individuals who could prove they had been harmed would be permitted to collect damages, including court costs and attorney's fees, from unscrupulous or negligent sellers. This structure would create greater incentives for sellers not to be unscrupulous or negligent about the safety of their product for any of the hazards where consumers knew they experienced harm. However, for food hazards with substantially delayed effects or for which proof is hard to establish, liability and negligence laws would have little impact. Some consumers would continue to suffer foodborne disease or would reduce their consumption of suspect food products. The cost to suppliers of establishing product reliability would still be high.

To pursue the argument for other forms of government protection, let us construct a hypothetical structure that would completely remedy the problem of consent in the case of hazards that consumers cannot detect ex ante or ex post. Such a structure would require sellers, at their own expense, to submit their products for premarket inspection to a warranty agency controlled by the community of food consumers or their designated representatives. The agency would develop information on the harmfulness of every chemical and microbe in food, test all foods for these hazards, and then give the food a safety rating on a readily understood scale such as "no chance of harm," "negligible risk of harm," and so on. The seller would then be able to advertise the safety rating to potential customers. However, there would have to be a way of preventing forged guarantees, such as policing for and punishing forgeries, to ensure that the guarantees provided consumers with reliable information. Further, sellers who wanted to stay in business would need to be able to pass on the cost of the guarantee to buyers. Since the cost of the premarket evaluation and forgery enforcement system would be passed along to the purchaser, this structure would increase the price of food products to households while improving information accuracy about their potential harmfulness. Also, safe products would cost more than risky products, the price reflecting the costs of preventing the presence or formation of the hazard in food.

Note that this structure does not require a role for government action. The warranty agency is a private entity set up by some enterprising consumers on behalf of other consumers. The structure also has some very nice properties in addition to informed consent. It gives consumers the freedom to choose how much income they are willing to trade for safety, although egalitarians would object to having this freedom if income is distributed among consumers unequally. It is not coercive to producers since it permits them to choose the level of safety they prefer to produce, as well as whether or not to produce food. However, most individuals familiar with the science and technology of food safety would point out that this type of warranty is not feasible. Consumers would not be able to afford it. First, it would be prohibitively costly to inspect every food, or even a sample from every batch of food, at every production facility unless the number of facilities was substantially reduced. Second, it would be prohibitively costly to inspect every sample for every known hazard. Third, it would be prohibitively costly to develop information on every kind of harm that every imaginable hazard might produce. Fourth, it would be extraordinarily difficult for the consumer representatives to reach agreement on the definition of each of the safety rating categories. (For example, should safety be defined in terms of safety for the most sensitive individual or the average individual?)

Let us set aside the question of whether it is infeasible to produce precise warranty information for the moment and assume that it is. Under this condition, would people prefer a single private warranty agency or some other provider? One objection to the single private warranty agency is the problem of monopoly. If there were only one warranty agency, it could charge the highest possible price, regardless of how much it cost to produce the warranty. Neither consumers nor producers would want this to happen, especially since food is a basic human necessity. On the other hand, if there were several warranty agencies, prices would drop, but consumers would not be able to tell which warranties were trustworthy for the same reasons that they would not be able to trust the safety claims of food producers in the first place. Furthermore, development of information about the harmfulness of food hazards is a nonrival good. Competition among several agencies producing such information would add unnecessarily to costs. Thus it would appear that we have provided the justification for a government that is representative of the people to provide the warranty service.

Note, however, that the justification for some form of consumer protection in this situation could be made on grounds other than procedural theory alone. For example, libertarian notions of negative rights would justify consumer protection on the grounds that people should be free from bodily harm from others. Egalitarian theories would stress the positive right of the individual to safety. Utilitarians might argue that the benefits of providing safer food outweigh the costs.

Current Food Safety Policies

Existing food safety laws are a compromise on many of the features of this ideal structure for the cost reasons outlined previously. As we shall see, the compromise is different for different food hazards because the costs of providing safety guarantees vary by type of hazard.

As pointed out, the unregulated market fails to produce information on the harmfulness of hazards and the amount of them in foods. However, the reason for this performance outcome is different for the two forms of information. Information about the harmfulness of hazards suffers from the public goods problem, i.e., the general difficulty of establishing an efficient market for nonrival, nonexcludable goods. Exposure information suffers from the problem of information asymmetry. These problems are different for different food hazards. In the case of providing information on the harmfulness of a hazard, the public goods problem is greater for naturally occurring contaminants than for human-made ones. The primary reason is that a single responsible party cannot be identified in the case of a naturally occurring toxin, making cost-sharing rules arbitrary. Consequently, two methods have been used to ensure the supply of information on harmfulness: government-required private research and publicly sponsored research. In the case of human-made contaminants (e.g., pesticides, animal drugs, environmental contaminants, and food additives), the private party that manufactures the potential food contaminant is required to produce the information before introducing the substance into the food supply. However, for naturally occurring toxins produced by bacteria or fungi, where there is no one responsible party, publicly provided research is necessary.

In the case of providing information on exposure, the information asymmetry problem is greater for hazards that are more difficult and costly to detect. For example, potential hazards that are added in known amounts to food—such as food additives—require little new information to determine their presence; thus, their presence in food can be labeled with relatively little cost. Food contaminants and environmental contaminants, by contrast, occur more randomly, requiring expensive testing to determine their presence and thus making labeling much more costly. In this case, it may be much less costly to restrict their occurrence in the food system. This can be done by specifying food production practices (e.g., sanitary measures and rules for the use of chemicals) or by establishing allowable levels of contaminants in foods. The latter alternative allows producers a greater range of choice of production methods, whereas the former may in some cases be less costly to enforce. (The cost depends on how easy it is to observe a particular production practice.)

Even in those cases where exposure can be labeled with relatively little information cost, a consumer would still require information on the harmfulness of the hazard. This requirement would not only mean that many foods would have to be accompanied by a booklet, it would also mean that consumers would have to be very sophisticated in their scientific training. However, consumers' costs of processing this information are reduced if the government prescreens the information to determine a safe level of exposure.

Current federal regulations in the United States require safety testing of human-made substances added to food or used in food production. This requirement produces the information needed to decide if there is a safe level of exposure and, if so, what that level is, given food consumption patterns. Exposure to these substances is mainly controlled by limiting how much and what substances are permitted in foods rather than by influencing food consumption choices through labeling. To label every food product for microbial and chemical contaminants, each food item would have to be tested for literally hundreds of substances at several points in the production process. This still would not indicate contamination at the site of final preparation. Testing methods are nonexistent for many contaminants, and few tests are rapid enough for results to be available before food spoils. Even if tests were available and affordable so that each consumer could test foods just prior to consumption, the task of determining the safe level of each substance and communicating this information to consumers remains. Finally, the enormous number of decisions made by consumers in a supermarket is likely to cause information overload, and consumers may prefer to have regulators make safety decisions for them.

The regulatory tools most often used by the U.S. Food and Drug Administration (FDA), the U.S. Department of Agriculture's Food Safety and Inspection Service (FSIS), and the Environmental Protection Agency (EPA) are tolerances, food manufacturing process standards, and registrations for food technologies such as pesticides and animal drugs. *Tolerances* are legal limits on the amount of a substance that will be tolerated or allowed in a commercially sold food. *Food manufacturing process standards* include sanitation and construction requirements for packing plants, food processing establishments, groceries, and restaurants. *Registrations* state how, when, and where a substance such as a pesticide or animal drug may be used in food production. Today the establishment of tolerances, process standards, and registrations is a lengthy process. For example, a new animal drug may have to undergo years of specific types of safety testing. Field studies for demonstrating residues under prescribed conditions of use must be conducted. Further tests are needed to determine what happens to residues of compounds during food processing.

Once safety standards are set, some mechanism for enforcing them is needed. This requires an inspection system for testing foods, observing the premises of food producing establishments, and prescribing penalties when violations are detected. Because inspection is extremely costly, it is usually done on a sampling basis with a penalty for noncompliance. The sampling rate determines the probability of being caught in noncompliance. This probability, coupled with the penalty imposed for noncompliance, creates an expected cost for violating the law. The higher the expected cost of violation, the more violations that are deterred.

An exception to the reliance on policies that seek only to influence the amount of substances in food occurs when substances are added to foods in known amounts. This is the case for colors, flavors, preservatives, artificial sweeteners, and other food additives. In this instance, the presence of additives can be indicated accurately on the label, and consumers can make their own choices about consuming them. However, government still plays an important role in ensuring that what is added is safe, or at least poses small health risks, and that the label is informative. Another notable exception is telling consumers to cook pork well, rather than inspecting for the parasite that causes trichinosis.

Food Safety and Public Controversy

Policy choices regarding particular food hazards represent decisions as to whether the government will provide consumers with a safety warranty for their food. These choices are often controversial, usually because the warranty can be provided only at some cost. One controversy is over **zero risk**, a concept that implies the unachievable goal of perfect safety. The first case to be presented illustrates how zero risk criteria are embedded in existing policy structures for food safety. The controversy that was probably most visible to members of the public in the 1980s was over Alar, the second case to be discussed. The ethical issue here concerned **uncertainty**, the problem that arises when scientific data are incapable of settling questions about the probability of harm. One view is that regulation is not appropriate until scientists are relatively sure about their knowledge; another is that uncertainty should prompt regulatory action. The issue of **enforcement**, of how government resources should be allocated to ensure compliance with regulations, is raised in the third case on animal drug residues. Finally, the question of **jurisdiction**, of who will regulate, is raised in a fourth case that examines food safety and international trade.

<hr>

CASE 1

Zero Risk versus Negligible Risk: The Case of Pesticide Residues

To protect consumers' health, the U.S. EPA registers the use of pesticides and sets tolerances on the level of residues that may be present in food. These tolerances are enforced by the FDA and, in the case of meat and poultry, by the FSIS. Today it takes many years for a new pesticide to go through all the tests needed to determine its safety to workers, the environment, and food consumers. Beginning in 1978, the Federal Insecticide, Fungicide, and Rodenticide Act (FIFRA) imposed new requirements on what must be known about the chronic toxicity and presence of food residues of pesticides before the EPA can approve their use on specific crops. Consequently, pesticides introduced in the last decade have faced tougher scrutiny than ever.

However, many widely used pesticides and plant growth regulators currently on the market were approved for use prior to these new data requirements and at a time when little was known about their potential to cause cancer. As new toxicity data have become available on these older pesticides, the EPA has sometimes had to revise its risk assessments and to reconsider whether the pesticide should be reregistered or banned. Despite the new evidence that some widely used pesticides pose cancer risks, most toxicologists do not view pesticide residues as a serious health risk. They claim that the level of pesticide residues typically present in food poses at most only a negligible risk. However, pubic reaction to the new risk assessments has been very negative. It is the public reaction, rather than scientific concerns about health risks, that has primarily triggered the public policy controversy over pesticide residues in food.

Currently, pesticide residues on raw commodities are regulated using a risk-benefit approach, whereas residues on processed foods are subject to the Delaney Clause or *zero cancer risk* standard. Some have argued that residues on raw commodities should also be subject to the Delaney Clause. Others argue that residues on both raw and processed food should be regulated using a *negligible risk* standard such as no more than a "one in a million lifetime risk" of cancer. A study by the National Academy of Sciences published in 1987 recommended that the latter policy alternative be adopted on the grounds that while the Delaney Clause would eliminate 100 percent of the risk from pesticides but would require a ban on 90 percent of fungicides, a negligible risk standard would eliminate 98 percent of the risk with only a few fungicides banned (7). Their policy recommendation was subsequently adopted by the EPA. However, several environmental groups challenged this interpretation of the Delaney Clause in the courts and won. It is now up to Congress to decide whether it is better to have a negligible risk standard or to retain the Delaney Clause.

CASE 2

How Certain Do We Have to Be? The Case of Alar

Alar is a trade name for the growth regulator daminozide, which is manufactured by Uniroyal. Daminozide regulates fruit set, size, coloring, and ripening. It is used primarily on apples and sometimes on cherries, nectarines, peaches, concord grapes, and peanuts. Daminozide was originally registered for use on apples in 1963. Tolerances of 30 parts per million (ppm) were established for its residues on fresh and processed apple products (e.g., juice and applesauce). In July 1984, the EPA announced that it would re-examine its risk assessment on Alar because of new scientific evidence that daminozide and its derivative, UDMH, might be carcinogens. This evidence consisted of chronic toxicity studies carried out in the 1970s that indicated that high doses of daminozide and UDMH caused cancer in laboratory mice and rats. Thus began the long public controversy over whether Alar should be banned for use in agriculture.

Over the next year, the EPA reviewed the studies. In August 1985, the EPA announced that it had estimated the lifetime risk of consuming foods with Alar residues as one extra cancer death per 10,000 individuals. Because some of the Alar and UDMH residues occurred in processed apple products such as juice, the Delaney Clause appeared to be applicable. Consequently, the EPA recommended a ban on Alar to its Scientific Advisory Panel (SAP). The proposed ban was subsequently criticized as being economically burdensome by the fruit industry and scientifically invalid by the members of the SAP.

In January 1986, after meeting with groups representing industry, consumers, and government, the EPA announced that instead of a ban, it would require Uniroyal to conduct new studies on the carcinogenicity of daminozide. Meanwhile, the EPA would lower the tolerance for daminozide to 20 ppm. The reason given for this action was that the SAP had found that the existing studies were too flawed to conclude whether there was a cancer risk from daminozide or UDMH.

The EPA's decision not to ban daminozide resulted in a flurry of actions by state governments, consumer groups, and industry in 1986 and 1987. The states of Massachusetts, New York, and Maine petitioned the EPA to prohibit further use of daminozide and sought to set their own safety standards. Ralph Nader filed a lawsuit appealing the EPA's decision not to ban it. The largest supermarket chains and food processors announced a boycott of apples produced with Alar. Apple growers responded by announcing a voluntary ban on its use. In early 1988, NutriClean, an independent laboratory in Oakland, California, announced that it had detected residues of daminozide ranging from 0.58 to 2.52 ppm in apples advertised as "Alar free" at some supermarket stores in California. This event stirred months of debate over whether the food industry was in fact working to ensure a voluntary ban on daminozide.

On February 1, 1989, the EPA announced that preliminary results from the studies it had requested from Uniroyal indicated that Alar posed an unacceptable cancer risk. Consequently, the EPA stated that it anticipated a ban on Alar when the tests were complete in 18 months. The next day, the EPA announced that it had asked Uniroyal to voluntarily suspend sales of Alar. Uniroyal declined to do so until there was scientific evidence of a cancer risk.

In the following days, consumer groups criticized the EPA for failing to ban Alar. Then, on February 26, CBS's *60 Minutes* aired a program focusing on Alar and findings of the Natural Resources Defense Council (NRDC) on cancer risks to children from Alar and other pesticides in food. The NRDC formally released its report, "Intolerable Risk," the next day. The NRDC estimated lifetime excess cancer risks from Alar of 2.4 per 10,000 persons. This estimate was an order of magnitude greater than the EPA's revised estimate of 3.5 cancers per 100,000 persons but similar to the EPA's earlier risk estimate.

The NRDC heavily publicized the findings of its study. Selected employees of the NRDC appeared on talk shows and were interviewed by the press. The actress Meryl Streep was asked and agreed to serve as a spokesperson to spur creation of local chapters of a new group—Mothers and Others for Pesticide Limits.

On March 2, the EPA responded to the increasing controversy by requesting Congress to grant it emergency suspension authority for removing dangerous pesticides from the market, but the request was later refused. Throughout March, NRDC representatives presented their report on TV shows such as *Phil Donahue* and NBC's morning news program. On March 13, traces of cyanide were reported to have been found in grapes imported from Chile by the FDA. The major news and women's magazines all subsequently featured articles on food safety and pesticide residues in food.

In April and May 1989, supermarket chains began their own residue testing for widely used pesticides. More stores began to offer organic produce as well. The Washington State apple industry announced that its growers would voluntarily stop using Alar by the fall of 1989. The EPA continued to state that it would seek to ban Alar by the fall of 1991. The *60 Minutes* show ran another report on Alar, criticizing supermarkets that claimed to sell Alar-free fruits when tests showed them to have residues.

Finally, following a move in the U.S. Senate to consider a proposal to ban Alar, Uniroyal decided to halt sales of Alar in June 1989. The EPA stated that it still intended to seek a ban on Alar, but with Uniroyal's voluntary ban in place, the publicity and public controversy over Alar died down. However, controversy continued to rage in the apple industry following heavy sales losses. The apple industry estimated that it had lost $100 million in sales, apple juice companies claimed losses of up to 90 percent of sales, and apple growers claimed that they were near bankruptcy. Other fruit and vegetable growers began to worry about what might happen in their markets. The apple industry charged that *60 Minutes*'s reports were inaccurate and heavily criticized the actions of the NRDC in publicizing its study on Alar. The apple industry felt that it had been singled out and began discussing the possibility of a product disparagement lawsuit against *60 Minutes* and the NRDC. In the fall of 1990, Washington State apple growers filed suit against CBS and the NRDC.

The Alar case shows the extent of public alarm and the damage that can occur when there is uncertainty about the hazards to which people might be exposed. How certain should the government be before it bans widely used and beneficial food production practices? Should the law be changed to give the EPA the emergency authority to cancel the registration of pesticides on a temporary basis before definitive data are in, or should the agency have to go through the process of complete testing first?

The Alar case also raises the question of the most appropriate forums for resolving uncertainty about hazards. By reporting on the possible hazards from Alar, the news media and the NRDC provided people the opportunity to avoid a possible hazard, but at great financial harm to food producers. Should the news media be permitted to report this, or should the forum of debate over potential hazards, foodborne or otherwise, be limited to experts?

CASE 3

How Much Should the Law Be Enforced?
The Case of Animal Drug Residues

Animal drugs are used both therapeutically and subtherapeutically in livestock production. Both uses lower the costs of producing meat, dairy, and other products derived from livestock. Therapeutic uses of animal drugs cure sick animals such as dairy cows with mastitis or calves with scours.

Subtherapeutic uses improve animal growth. For example, low doses of antibiotics and sulfa drugs added to livestock feed have been shown to increase weight gain and the efficiency of animals in converting feed to muscle gain or milk output. Animal drugs now under development promise to increase the leanness of pork and to reduce significantly the cost of producing milk.

To protect consumers' health, the FDA registers the use of animal drugs and sets tolerances on the level of residues that may be present in meat and dairy products. The tolerances are enforced by the Food Safety and Inspection Service. New animal drugs must undergo extensive safety testing. However, like many pesticides, many animal drugs now on the market were registered for use many years ago. Many of the old safety evaluations are now considered outdated and inadequate. As new data becomes available, the toxic potency of many drugs widely used to promote weight gain and disease control in livestock may come into question. For example, the safety of sulfa drugs—which are widely used in swine and veal production—is seriously being questioned. While it has long been recognized that some sensitive individuals are allergic to sulfa drugs, recent studies by the National Center for Toxicological Research indicate that sulfamethazine may be a carcinogen. Based on preliminary risk assessments, the FDA has warned that it will ban sulfamethazine use as well as subtherapeutic uses of antibiotics in livestock feed.

Adequate or timely detection methods do not exist for approximately 70 percent of the animal drug residues in meat, milk, and eggs that the U.S. Department of Agriculture is responsible for monitoring (13). Currently, progress is being sought in developing tests for detecting their presence in food. The FSIS has made considerable progress in developing tests for detecting antibiotic and sulfa drug residues; however, drug residues above the legal tolerance limit may occur when the cost to producers of complying with the law exceeds the expected cost of violating it. The cost of compliance depends on the cost to the producer of using the next best alternative to drugs. The expected cost of violating the law is a function of the probability that a violation is detected times the size of the penalty imposed on the violator.

Continuing residue problems with antibiotics and sulfa drugs in swine and veal calves in the United States reflect the fact that the cost of violating is often much smaller than the cost of compliance. For example, in the 1980s, the FSIS found violation rates of 5 percent or more for antibiotic and sulfa drugs in veal calves. Despite large increases in the rate at which the FSIS sampled calves at slaughter, no statistically significant change in the violation rate occurred—primarily because the penalty for being caught was much smaller than the benefit of drug use in calves (14).

These problems raise the issue of how much enforcement government should produce. If food safety laws are on the books but violations occur, are government food safety standards trustworthy? Is perfect enforcement required or is something less than perfect enforcement desirable?

CASE 4

What Jurisdictional Boundary Should Rule?
The Case of International versus National Interests

Increased international trade in commodities since World War II led to conflicts in how different countries addressed food safety issues. To harmonize divergent food safety standards, the Food and Agricultural Organization (FAO) and the World Health Organization (WHO) jointly established the Codex Alimentarius Commission in 1962. The Codex establishes international food safety standards such as maximum residue limits (MRL) for residue concentrations on raw agricultural commodities. Under the Uruguay Round of the General Agreement on Tariffs and Trade (GATT) negotiations, harmonization of international food safety standards has been recognized as a basic principle that furthers the GATT objective of reducing nontariff barriers to trade. Thus, international trade considerations are becoming increasingly important in the development of food safety policy in the United States.

In many cases, the rules established by the Codex may be quite different from those established by individual countries in terms of food identity standards, food processing and production methods, animal and plant health and quarantine, maximum residue tolerance levels, and methods of analyzing, sampling, and penalizing in the enforcement process. For example, the United States has accepted only approximately 29 percent of the Codex standards for pesticide residues. Thirty-seven percent of Codex standards are less strict than U.S. standards. Thirty-five percent of Codex pesticide residue standards are stricter than U.S. standards. If the Delaney Clause were applied to both raw and processed food in the United States, the percentage of Codex pesticide residue standards that are not as strict as U.S. standards would increase. However, U.S. policy stated in the GATT talks is that harmonization of health and sanitary measures should be recognized as a basic principle furthering the objectives of GATT. Extension of the Delaney Clause to raw foods would seem inconsistent with this policy on international trade.

From both an ethical and an economic perspective, it is not necessarily evident that harmonization of food safety standards makes sense. For example, consumers in different countries may have very different ethical philosophies about the appropriate role of government in food safety, as well as different preferences for safety and different exposures to food hazards, and thus may desire a different level of safety than the international standard. Likewise, different countries are likely to face different costs in complying with international standards, so having one international standard would shift the comparative advantage in the production of different commodities. Since little is known about differences between countries in terms of ethical philosophies, consumer preferences, and costs of compliance, the question of the ethical desirability of international standards is still very much unexplored.

Summary

Hazards in food can arise from food contaminants, natural food constituents, environmental contaminants, and food additives. The first laws for government regulation of food safety were passed in the first half of the twentieth century. They were based upon the assumptions that hazards in food would produce observable symptoms and that the causes of injury could be identified unambiguously. Scientists have dramatically improved their ability to identify the presence of hazardous substances in all four categories since World War II. Arguably, some of these substances can now be identified at levels so low that a food consumer's risk of injury is negligible.

Food safety is understood primarily in terms of the probability of consumers experiencing harm, but the immediacy, severity, duration, reversibility, and timing of potential harm also influence the seriousness of a safety concern. The probability of harm is determined by a variety of biological factors, as well as by the level or frequency of exposure to the hazardous substance. People who have knowledge about the presence and potential hazard of a substance can reduce the probability of harm through appropriate conduct, so information is crucial. Food producers, however, may or may not have incentives to provide consumers with sufficient information.

The case for public policies to regulate food safety follows from the fact that consumers may lack enough information to avoid important hazards without some government intervention. A procedural justification for food safety policy would stress the role of consent. It would be ethical for consumers to be exposed to risk in eating a food provided that criteria for consent have been fulfilled. Government then takes the role of either requiring that information be provided on a label so that consumers may express actual consent through their food purchase, or of regulating the presence of hazards in foods so that criteria of hypothetical consent (consumers would consent if they had the same information that the regulatory agency has) can be satisfied.

Given a general ethical philosophy for regulation of food, a number of problems still arise in the attempt to formulate policy. Four problems that plague existing food policy are zero risk criteria, uncertainty, enforcement, and jurisdiction.

Key Terms

enforcement

environmental contaminants

exposure

food additives

food contaminants

hazards

jurisdiction

natural food constituents

risk

uncertainty

zero risk

References

1. Carson, Rachel. 1962. *Silent Spring*. Boston: Houghton Mifflin.
2. Fischhoff, B., et al. 1978. "How Safe Is Safe Enough? A Psychometric Study of Attitudes Towards Technological Risks and Benefits," *Policy Sciences* 9:127–152.
3. Groth, Edward, III. 1986. "Lead in Canned Food," *Agriculture and Human Values* 3(1&2):91–145.
4. Hutt, Peter B., and Peter B. Hutt, II. 1984. "A History of Government Regulation of Adulteration and Misbranding of Food," *Food Drug Cosmetic Law Journal* 39:2–73.
5. Johnson, Deborah. 1986. "Ethical Dimensions of Acceptable Risk in Food Safety," *Agriculture and Human Values* 3(1&2):171–179.
6. Merrill, Richard A., and Michael A. Taylor. 1986. "Saccharin," *Agriculture and Human Values* 3(1&2):33–73.
7. National Research Council. 1987. *Regulating Pesticides in Food*. Washington, D.C.: National Academy Press.
8. Okun, Mitchell. 1986. *Fair Play in the Marketplace: The First Battle for Pure Food and Drugs*. Dekalb: Northern Illinois University Press.
9. Office of Technology Assessment, U.S. Congress. 1979. *Environmental Contaminants in Food*. Washington, D.C.: U.S. Government Printing Office.
10. Rescher, Nicholas. 1983. *Risk: A Philosophical Introduction to the Theory of Risk Evaluation and Management*. New York: University Press of America.
11. Roberts, Tanya, and Eileen van Ravenswaay. 1989. "Effects of New Scientific Knowledge on Food Safety Policy," *Agriculture and Food Policy Review*. USDA-ERS Agricultural Economics Report No. 620. Washington, D.C.: 315–322.
12. Sinclair, Upton. 1906. *The Jungle*. New York: New American Library.
13. U.S. Congress. Committee on Government Operations. 1985. *Human Food Safety and the Regulation of Animal Drugs*. Washington, D.C.: U.S. Government Printing Office.
14. van Ravenswaay, Eileen O., and Sharon A. Bylenga. 1991. "Enforcing Food Safety Standards: A Case Study of Antibiotic and Sulfa Drug Residues in Veal," *Journal of Agribusiness* 9(1):39–54.

Suggestions for Further Reading

Problems in food safety policy relate generally to the expanding literature on risk, risk perception, and risk management. An anthology entitled *Readings in Risk*, ed. Theodore S. Glickman and Michael Gough (Washington, D.C.: Resources for the Future, 1990), collects many of the seminal papers. An anthology entitled *Acceptable Evidence: Science and Values in Risk Management*, ed. Deborah Mayo and Rachelle Hollander (Oxford: Oxford University Press, 1991), includes useful original essays by people such as Paul Slovic, Sheila Jasanoff, and Roger Kasperson. Kristin Shrader-Frechette's *Risk and Rationality* (Berkeley: University of California Press, 1991) is a book-length treatment of philosophical problems in the assessment and management of risk.

Readers wishing a philosophical treatment of risk issues in food safety should consult the cited paper by Deborah Johnson and, for a contrasting view, Henry Shue's "Food Additives and 'Minority Rights': Carcinogens and Children," in *Agriculture and Human Values* 3 (1 & 2):191–200. Tanya Roberts and Eileen vanRavenswaay provide an overview of issues in "The Economics of Safeguarding the U.S. Food Supply," USDA-ERS Agriculture Information Bulletin No. 566 (Washington, D.C.: USDA). Julie Caswell's collection on *The Economics of Food Safety* (New York: Elsevier, 1991) is also recommended. Paul Thompson discusses ethical issues related to communicating with the general public about food safety in "Risk: Ethical Issues and Values," in *Agricultural Biotechnology, Food Safety and Nutritional Quality for the Consumer* (Ithaca, N.Y.: National Agricultural Biotechnology Council, 1991). For additional information on the international dimensions of food safety policy, see Alexander Nemajobsky and Terence Centner's "Pesticide Residues in Food: The Delaney Clause and Global Harmonization of Pesticide Standards," in *Agribusiness: An International Journal* 7(3):178–196.

CHAPTER | 6

Agriculture, Natural Resources, and the Environment

Agrarian writers throughout American history repeatedly have praised farmers' stewardship of the land: Farmers might violently wrest their fields from the forest and prairie, the bounty of their crops from the furrowed soil; however, they lovingly protect the land from which this bounty springs. Yet even the briefest survey of our nation's history reveals that the reality does not accord with this agrarian myth of good stewardship. Whether it is the eroded badlands of Oklahoma, the dust bowl era immortalized in Steinbeck's *The Grapes of Wrath* (10), the massive destruction of hundreds of thousands of acres of wetlands in the San Joaquin Valley of California, the depletion of the Ogallala aquifer of the High Plains, the fertilizer-induced eutrophication of the Chesapeake Bay, or the salination and siltation of the Colorado River in Arizona, the conclusion is inescapable: American farmers have not always been good stewards of the land. American farming practices, like many farming practices elsewhere in the world, have been and continue to be environmentally destructive. The most notable of these destructive effects have been (i) *environmental contamination* (pesticides, fertilizers, siltation, salination, animal waste, etc.), (ii) *habitat destruction* (for example, draining of wetlands, deforestation), and (iii) *resource depletion* (soil erosion, water depletion, and the like).

The agrarian myth of good stewardship makes it very difficult to formulate, much less implement, an effective public policy to deal with these destructive environmental impacts. Public policy, we have seen, is developed only in response to a perceived need for policy, but the agrarian myth of good stewardship implies that there is no need for such policy. Production agriculture is often exempted from statutes that might otherwise serve to ameliorate environmentally destructive agricultural practices.

This chapter focuses on the basic philosophical and ethical issues surrounding public policy initiatives intended to prevent or at least mitigate these destructive impacts. The issues to be examined are ones that arise largely because these initiatives conflict with certain goals of, and economic constraints on, agricultural production. We address these issues in a discussion of two case studies that illustrate these conflicts.

CASE 1

Irrigation Drainwater Contamination in the San Joaquin Valley

The west side of the San Joaquin Valley in central California is an extremely fertile agricultural area, supplying one-fourth of the table food in the United States (see Figure 6–1). Such high productivity on these once arid lands is the result of a sophisticated water collection, transfer, and distribution system, financed largely by public funds, that brings great volumes of irrigation water from dams located in mountains many miles to the north and west. The water that makes this agricultural production possible also makes possible the extensive agriculture-related businesses that are such important contributors to the regional and state economies.

The San Joaquin Valley is a critical habitat not only for humans but also for millions of migratory waterfowl. The valley is a major stopover on the Pacific Flyway that connects Canada and Mexico. Fully one-fifth of North America's waterfowl winter in the San Joaquin Valley. California once had 5 million acres of wetland that supported untold millions of migratory waterfowl. Today it has only 450,000 acres. In the San Joaquin Valley only 6 percent of its original 1.25 million acres of wetland remain. Most migratory waterfowl in the Valley now live on "reservations," specifically on national wildlife refuges and private duck-hunting preserves.

Life on the reservation turns out to be little better for birds than for the American Indians. In spring 1983, U.S. Fish and Wildlife Service (FWS) field biologists discovered unusually high numbers (in excess of 20 percent) of deformed chicks and dead embryos among newborn waterfowl, including coots, greves, stilts, and ducks, at the Kesterson National Wildlife Refuge. They also observed unusually high mortality rates among adult birds. The FWS identified selenium poisoning as the cause; it identified the agricultural drainwaters that fed the Refuge as the source of this contamination. What began as an environmental issue that pitted waterfowl against farmers quickly broadened, however, into a public health issue when the U.S. Geological Survey measured selenium concentrations in the Kesterson Reservoir and adjacent surfacewaters of 84 to 4,200 parts per billion (ppb), well above the federal EPA's standard for drinking water of 10 ppb. Health authorities warned the public not to eat fish and waterfowl taken from the area.

When news of these discoveries surfaced in the local press, farmers soon found themselves caught up in a political controversy that threatened the

Figure 6–1 The San Joaquin Valley of California

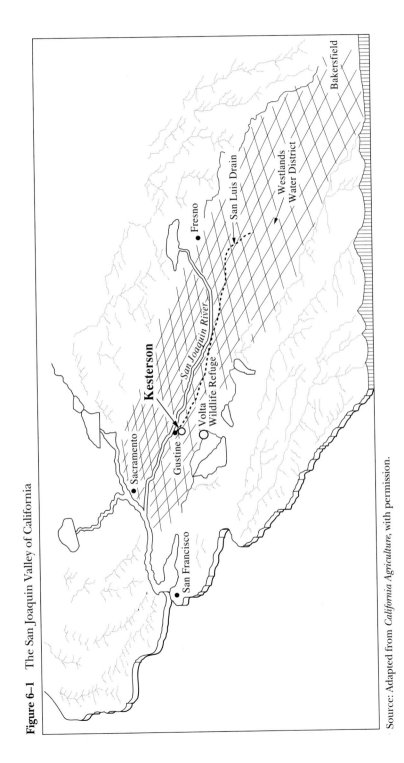

Source: Adapted from *California Agriculture*, with permission.

133

very future of irrigated farming in the western San Joaquin Valley. This controversy is the subject of the present case study. We begin by reviewing the events, public policies, and agricultural practices that led to the environmental calamity and the ensuing controversy.

Historical Background of the San Joaquin Case

Irrigated farming in the western part of the San Joaquin Valley began in the 1860s with the construction of an irrigation canal that drew water from the adjacent San Joaquin River. Development of the turbine pump in the 1920s allowed major growth of irrigated farming in the region. The really significant expansion occurred as a result of the massive, publicly funded Central Valley Project (CVP) begun by the U.S. Bureau of Reclamation (USBR) in the 1930s. The CVP brings irrigation water to the western part of the San Joaquin Valley by canal from Shasta Dam on the Sacramento River, some 300 miles to the north. The portion of the valley with which we will be concerned, the 600,000-acre Westlands Water District, which is located in the western part of the valley, receives about 1.2 million acre-feet per year (i.e., enough water each year to cover this 937-square-mile area 2 feet deep).

Irrigation causes a gradual accumulation in the soil of salts and other minerals that are toxic to plants. If these salts and minerals are allowed to accumulate, they will soon depress and eventually destroy the irrigated farmland's agricultural productivity. Provision must therefore be made for leaching these salts and minerals from the root zone of crops. This is accomplished by applying sufficient water to the soil (much more water than is required for optimal plant growth) to ensure that water percolation through the root zone leaches away these undesirable salts and minerals (see Figure 6–2).

The San Joaquin Valley is underlain by an impermeable clay lens some 10 to 40 feet below ground surface that holds these leachate-rich waters close to the surface. Provision must therefore be made for draining these leachwaters from below the fields. This is accomplished by means of subsurface drainage systems (see Figure 6–2). For many decades, leachwaters were drained back into the San Joaquin River; however, with the dramatic expansion of irrigated farming in the 1950s, it became apparent that an alternative way of disposing of drainwaters would have to be found. In 1960, Congress authorized the construction of the 280-mile Valley Master Drain, to run from Bakersfield in the south to the Delta in the north, where drainwaters would be discharged into rivers feeding San Francisco Bay. Before the project could be completed, the State of California informed the U.S. government of its inability to participate financially in the project. Public support for the project had waned. Farmers had reneged on their agreement with the state to pay a share of the construction and operating costs, and there was growing concern in the Delta/San Francisco Bay area regarding the environmental impact of the drainwaters on the Delta region and Bay. By 1975, when federal appropriations for the project finally ran out, the USBR had constructed an 85-mile segment of the drain (the so-called San Luis Drain) that terminated

Figure 6–2   The Need for On-Farm Drainage

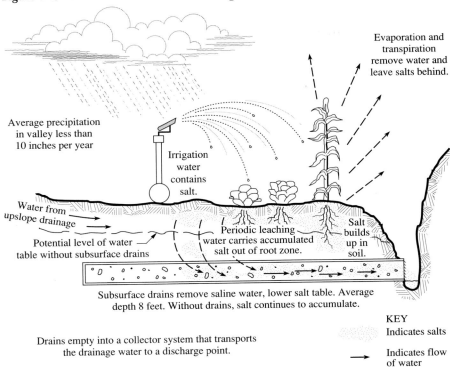

Source: U.S. Bureau of Reclamation, "Drainage and Salt Disposal," Information Bulletin 1, San Luis Unit, Central Valley Project, Calif (Sacremento, January 1984).

in the Kesterson Reservoir. This reservoir, which was intended to provide temporary storage for drainwater being moved north through the master drain, would now serve as the terminal evaporation pond for drainwater collected by the completed San Luis Drain.

In 1972, the Kesterson Reservoir began receiving surface runoff from adjacent irrigation farms. The reservoir's 1,200 acres of ponds and 4,700 acres of grasslands quickly attracted numerous waterfowl. Kesterson seemed to be a cost-effectiveness expert's dream come true: built with one purpose in mind, the reservoir would now serve a second. Kesterson was soon incorporated into the National Wildlife Refuge System, administered by the FWS.

In early 1981, Kesterson began receiving, via the San Luis Drain, subsurface drainwater from some 42,000 acres of irrigated farmland. In June 1981, the FWS first detected high levels of selenium at Kesterson. This naturally occurring nonmetallic mineral, which is essential to animal diets in very small concentrations but extremely toxic in high concentrations, was apparently being leached from the soil (11). The selenium contamination was revealed to the public only in May 1983, when rumors began to circulate in the local press about the high incidence of death and deformity among waterfowl at the Reservoir. In December 1983, the USBR assured an uneasy public that it would find a solution to the selenium contamination problem in the ten years before the proposed (but then unfunded) drain was completed. By summer 1984, the FWS found birds no longer nesting at Kesterson; many adult birds were found dead. The FWS instituted hazing efforts, using noise-makers, to scare remaining waterfowl away from Kesterson. Selenium contamination, it discovered, was not restricted to the Kesterson National Wildlife Refuge. The 77,000 acres of wetlands adjacent to the refuge, representing one-fourth of the prime wetland habitat for the Pacific Flyway, were also found to be contaminated. In November, a respected environmental group, the Bay Institute, revealed that selenium had been found in assays of striped bass taken from both the San Joaquin River and San Francisco Bay.

In January 1985, the U.S. Department of Interior officially notified the State Water Resources Control Board (SWRCB) of the high levels of selenium found in waterfowl and fish in the Kesterson Reservoir and adjacent wetlands. The SWRCB responded by ordering the USBR to produce a plan to clean up Kesterson within three years. It ordered the adjacent Grasslands Water District, which represented local irrigation farmers, to develop a plan to reduce the high levels of selenium in the district's wetlands caused by subsurface effluent from upslope irrigated farming. In March, the Interior Department, citing international treaty obligations to both Canada and Mexico, took the unprecedented (and completely unexpected) action of ordering the immediate closure of Kesterson to irrigation drainwater and the complete cutoff of irrigation water to the 42,000 acres of irrigated farmland that were drained to Kesterson. Faced with the immediate prospect of financial ruin, irrigation farmers (represented by the local water districts), who had until then been unwilling even to meet with state and federal officials concerning the Kesterson problem, entered into intense negotiations aimed at finding a solution. In the following month, the Interior Department agreed to resume providing irrigation water to the 42,000 acres, but only on the condition that the farmers agree to a phased reduction of drainage flows into the San Luis Drain, beginning in September 1985. All collectors for the Drain were to be plugged by July 1986. The agreement had succeeded in shifting the onus of finding a solution to the drainwater problem to the farmers whose irrigation practices had generated the problem. In June 1986, the USBR completed the plugging of collectors to the San Luis Drain and issued an environmental impact statement detailing three different proposals for cleaning up the Kesterson Reservoir over a three- to five-year period. In March 1987, the SWRCB rejected all but the most comprehensive of these proposals, a plan that called for on-site disposal of contaminated soil and materials. The SWRCB ordered the USBR both to complete the cleanup within three years and to mitigate the loss of the Kesterson Reservoir to wildlife by providing cleanwater flows to the adjacent grasslands and various national wildlife refuges in the area. The USBR complied with the board's order, cleaning up Kesterson at a cost to taxpayers of many millions of dollars.

The USBR's cleanup of Kesterson left unresolved the problem of what to do with the agricultural drainwater that was the source of the problem. The possible solutions to the problem were limited: (i) discharge the untreated drainwater into the Delta (as per the original USBR plan) or perhaps directly into the Pacific; (ii) develop a technology for removing selenium, salts, and other contaminants from drainwater; (iii) take the cropland responsible for drainwater contamination out of production; or (iv) prohibit off-farm disposal of drainwaters and strictly enforce all existing environmental statutes, but otherwise do nothing, leaving farmers to fend for themselves as best they could. Each of these solutions had obvious drawbacks. There were, for example, no discharge points for untreated drainwater that were environmentally safe, politically acceptable, and economically feasible; no one wanted the farmers' problem in his or her backyard. A technology for removing drainwater contaminants was not presently available. Taking cropland out of production would entail significant losses both to the affected farmers and to their communities.

In April and May 1985, the local and regional press began to carry an increasing number of articles suggesting that perhaps the best solution to drainwater problems in the San Joaquin Valley might be to let affected farmers sell their irrigation water allotments and then go out of irrigated farming. This solution might have gained favor had the press not also begun to carry reports suggesting that the problem was much more extensive than was first thought. It seemingly affected the entire San Joaquin Valley, rather than only the western part. The potential economic losses were staggering.

For its part, the Westlands Water District, representing the farmers on the affected 42,000 acres, first proposed to build a series of its own evaporation ponds on poor land to the south and pump drainwater there for disposal; however, the plan was soon abandoned as being too costly to implement. Instead, and in the interim until a satisfactory solution could be found, farmers would construct their own on-farm evaporation ponds. In addition, they would implement various wildlife protection measures at these ponds that would discourage waterfowl from using the ponds. Clearly these on-farm ponds were not a long-term solution; they simply moved a portion of the original problem into each farmer's backyard. The Westlands Water District therefore took the unprecedented step of joining with the Environmental Defense Fund to find a viable long-term solution to the problem, one that would develop both a technology for removing contaminants from agricultural drainwaters and farming practices that would reduce the volume of drainwater that required treatment. This research is still underway; however, technologies that exploit the bioaccumulation of selenium in the food chain seem especially promising. Algaes that bioaccumulate the selenium contaminants are grown in the evaporation ponds; the matured plants are periodically harvested and then disposed of in toxic waste dumps.

Ethical Justification for Public Intervention

The contamination of the Kesterson Reservoir and surrounding grasslands, along with the attendant harm to migratory waterfowl and the potential threat to public health, set in motion a series of events that resulted in the U.S. Secretary of the Interior ordering the closure of the drains that fed the Reservoir. The announced rationale for the Secretary's action was international treaty obligations; however, it seems clear that such action would have been undertaken even in the absence of an international treaty. The actions of farmers in discharging selenium-contaminated drainwater into the Reservoir provided clear legal justification for public action; indeed, certain public agencies (notably, the FWS, USBR, EPA, SWRCB, and the State Department of Health) were legally obligated to act. But what, we might ask, was the *ethical* justification for public action? Why should the government have gotten involved?

The answer to this question begins by noting some facts. A number of producers—irrigation farmers, as it happens—had for many years employed production practices that produced, among other things, an effluent by-product toxic to both humans and wildlife. The policy structure in place at that time allowed farmers to externalize the costs associated with the environmental impact of irrigation despite the known risk to wildlife and other human beings. The fact that these producers happened to be farmers normally would not be thought to confer a special ethical privilege to act in a fashion that puts the general public and wildlife at risk, nor is it the case that risks were accepted in exchange for vitally needed commodities. One-half of the affected acreage in the valley, for example, is planted in cotton, a surplus crop that the U.S. government pays farmers not to produce. Indeed, over the past several years, about 10 percent of the acreage has been fallowed under the U.S. government's Payment-in-Kind Program. What is more, the cost of the water that these farmers use to irrigate their fields (and on one-half of which they produce a surplus crop) is heavily subsidized by federal and state governments. The USBR itself estimates that farmers in the Westlands region pay only about 15 percent of the actual water project costs. Nor can these farmers present themselves as impoverished or deprived of economic opportunity. The farms in question are not the moderate-sized family farms whose economic plight has received public attention in recent years. In 1985, the 42,000 acres served by the now plugged Westlands drainage system contained only fifty-three farming operations, eight of which exceeded 1,280 acres, with annual gross revenues averaging about $750,000. In many cases, the owners of these operations have major operations elsewhere in the valley, state, or nation. The size of these operations has for decades been a source of controversy. The Reclamation Act of 1902, which created the federal programs that provide federally subsidized water to farmers in the arid Southwest, limited to 160 acres the amount of private land in single ownership eligible to receive water from a reclamation project. Farmers in California, however, have been quite successful in circumventing these acreage limitations.

The reasons for changing the existing policy structure will differ, depending upon whether one adopts a rights-based or a utilitarian perspective.

Those who adopt a rights-based perspective will argue that public action is generally appropriate, sometimes even mandatory, to prevent one person from harming another. They may even argue that this rationale encompasses harm done to wildlife and the environment. They will argue further that the present case is just such a case: the farmers' action in discharging contaminated drainwater violates the noninterference rights of waterfowl and potentially violates the human right to health. Those who adopt a utilitarian perspective will argue that public action regulating or prohibiting the action of individuals is warranted in cases where the social costs of the action outweigh its social benefits. They will argue further that the present case is just such a case: the social costs of the farmers' current farming practices (i.e., the cost to society imposed by the discharge of these drainwaters) outweigh the benefits (i.e., the agricultural production that depends on these practices), especially when one factors in taxpayer subsidies of water and surplus commodities.

While rights-based theorists and utilitarians would be unlikely to disagree on the justifiability of public action, they might well disagree about what sort of action was appropriate. For rights-based theorists, the appropriate public action would secure the right of the general public (and perhaps of waterfowl) not to be harmed by these farmers' actions; public action would force farmers to desist from actions that were harmful to waterfowl and potentially harmful to human health. For utilitarians, the appropriate public action would seek to modify the existing structure to ensure that these farmers' actions no longer imposed a net social cost on society. If these utilitarians were free-market theorists, they would probably regard this case as an instance of market failure. They would view the contaminated drainwater as a cost of agricultural production that farmers had improperly externalized. For them, the appropriate public action would be to force these farmers to internalize this externality, thus ensuring that their production costs would reflect the true social costs. One way of doing this might be to levy an effluent tax on these farmers; such a tax, if fixed at the right level, would force farmers to shoulder the social costs of their discharge of contaminated drainwaters while permitting such discharges. Rights-based theorists would undoubtedly find such a solution unacceptable since, far from securing the public's right not to be harmed, it would in effect offer farmers a license to inflict harm, provided that they were able to afford the license.

Rights-based theorists and utilitarians often agree on the need for public action but disagree about the appropriate action to be taken. Yet successful policy making obviously accommodates to this fact of political life, because our political institutions are generally able to settle upon a course of public action acceptable to both rights-based theorists and utilitarians.

Crafting Acceptable Public Action: Where Ethics Fits In

Acceptable public action aimed at solving the environmental problems in the Kesterson case will have to satisfy certain minimal conditions or constraints.

In particular, it will have to be (i) *legal* (i.e., it must be consistent with applicable federal and state laws), (ii) *politically viable* (i.e., it must have whatever political support is necessary to ensure the adoption, funding, and implementation of the solution), (iii) *enforceable* (i.e., there must be the means to ensure compliance sufficient to guarantee implementation), (iv) *cost effective* (i.e., the costs must be reasonable compared with the costs of alternative solutions), (v) *technologically feasible* (i.e., the technology needed to implement the solution must exist), (vi) *environmentally sound* (i.e., the solution must protect wildlife and preserve critical habitats; it must restore and protect water quality in the local area, but without simply transporting the problem elsewhere), and (vii) *ethically defensible* (i.e., the solution must be generally perceived as ethically defensible).

The short-term solution imposed by the Secretary of the Interior, closing the drains that fed the Kesterson Reservoir, satisfies these constraints surprisingly well. The farmers were no longer able to export their contaminated drainwater and were forced to comply with state laws regarding the storage, treatment, and disposal of a toxic substance (which include provisions intended both to protect wildlife and to prevent contamination of groundwater). Thus this action shifted the onus (and the cost) of finding a long-term solution to the farmers themselves. The circumstances that justified public intervention had been largely addressed. From the perspective of rights-based theorists, the threat to waterfowl and public health had been diminished considerably. From the perspective of utilitarians, the previously externalized social costs of the contaminated drainwater were now internalized, with the consequence that these costs would now have to be included in farmers' costs of production. (Farmers would have to develop technology for treating drainwater, would have to set aside some of their land for this purpose, and might even have to accept decreased agricultural production.) The market would determine whether irrigated farming in the valley was a viable business enterprise when these costs were internalized. There would still remain the problems of (i) controlling subsurface migration of drainwater into the Kesterson Reservoir and adjacent grasslands from upslope farms and (ii) preventing waterfowl from using the on-farm evaporation ponds that farmers were likely to construct; however, state and federal agencies had statutory authority to handle these problems.

Goals of Agricultural Production: Productivity versus Stewardship

The Kesterson case is one in which the viewpoint of public officials charged with formulating and administering policy is relatively easy to illustrate. It is also one in which farmers, by first opposing and then delaying regulatory reform, may appear to be acting with almost total disregard for the social contract. There are, however, several reasons why farmers might have felt justified in their actions. One is the general rationale that individuals are always justified in pursuing their interests up to the limit of the law. Such a rationale may be broadly supported by libertarian noninterference rights, but in specific cases like Kesterson, the harm done to others undercuts the rationale considerably. Besides lacking a firm ethical foundation, pursuing their interests up to the limit of the law was almost certainly not in the long-term interests of farmers in the San Joaquin Valley. The considerable public ill will that their intransigence provoked seems bound to damage their ongoing fight to maintain their allotment of publicly subsidized irrigation water in the face of ever-increasing water demand for municipal and industrial uses.

A more respectable justification of the farmers' actions can be found perhaps in a rationale that stresses agricultural productivity rather than environmental stewardship. For many decades, two goals have dominated both production agriculture and the public policy concerned with production agriculture: *maximal production* and *productivity*. Production has to do with output (e.g., bushels of corn, hundredweights of beef); productivity is efficiency of production and refers to the ratio between the value of a farmer's output, measured, for example, in the dollar value of product, and the value of the inputs necessary to produce this output, measured in similar terms. Public policy has aimed to maximize production and productivity consistent with economic stability, and farmers generally have acted in a way that maximizes their individual production and productivity given the economic and policy constraints under which they operate. Farmers in the Kesterson case may have felt justified in their actions so long as they pursued goals of maximal production and high productivity. Public policy has endorsed these two goals because, so long as they remain consistent with economic stability, achievement of these goals helps to ensure the provision of adequate food and fiber at an affordable cost to consumers, minimal commitment of human resources to farming (thus freeing this labor for more productive utilization elsewhere in the economy), independence from foreign producers (national food security), and a supply of competitively priced export commodities. Such goals might be justified in the language of rights or of consequences. Farmers, for their part, have worked to achieve these goals because increases in production and productivity generally result in greater profits, at least in the short run.

Critics of U.S. farm policy who are concerned with environmental protection often argue that these two goals are responsible both for the crisis in contemporary agriculture (e.g., surplus commodities, depressed farm prices) and for the destructive environmental impacts of American agriculture. These critics argue that an enlightened agricultural policy that recognized goals other than maximal production and productivity could both alleviate the farm crisis and mitigate destructive environmental impacts. Such criticisms provide the basis for a diagnosis of the underlying causes of environmentally destructive agricultural practices such as those illustrated by the Kesterson case. A particular interpretation of the economic forces that undermine the profitability of farm operations and eventually result in environmental damage is central to this diagnosis.

A basic tenet of agricultural economics states that demand for agricultural products is largely inelastic; demand for products does not change substantially with moderate fluctuations in price. This implies that increased farm production should be accompanied by lower farm prices. Farmers wishing to increase the profitability of their operations must therefore increase their productivity (efficiency). Increased productivity promises both to increase the profit margin on farmers' current production (i.e., they can produce the same output for less input) and to enable them to capture market share from farmers who are less productive (i.e., if they can produce goods more cheaply than their competitors, they may be able to increase production profitably since they can underprice their less efficient competitors and still make a profit).

Farmers understand these facts of economic life and continually struggle to increase their productivity. Often they are able to increase profits by externalizing some of their costs of production or by adopting more productive farming technologies. Both sorts of action may lead to environmental damage. The costs that farmers are generally in a position to externalize are those having to do either with the utilization of natural resource inputs to agricultural production (e.g., soil, habitat, water) or with the disposal of unmarketable by-products (e.g., animal waste, pesticide contamination, siltation, salination). Externalizations of the first sort result in resource depletion, externalizations of the second sort in environmental contamination. Thus, for example, ranchers may overstock their pastures in an attempt to increase productivity, eventually destroying the productivity of the land.

The path that leads from the adoption of more productive technologies to environmental damage is more indirect. Farmers generally adopt these new technologies (e.g., more powerful tractors, hybrids) if they can afford them since failure to adopt technologies that others adopt will typically undermine the profitability of their operations and may eventually force them out of business. Yet adoption of these more productive technologies often fails to increase profitability. In the past fifty years productivity-enhancing technologies have been capital intensive: they cost money, which often must be borrowed. Some have required expansion of farming operations in order to achieve the economies of scale that will enable a farmer to recoup the costs of adoption, and even where they do not require such expansion, the technology must enable the farmer to increase production enough to cover these costs. Because many other farmers are also adopting this more productive technology and also planning to pay its costs through increased production, significant overproduction results. Because of the inelasticity of demand for agricultural goods, prices fall, with the result that profitability remains basically unchanged or in some cases actually decreases. From the farmers' perspective, the best that can be said for the adopted technology is that it has kept farmers in business by allowing them to preserve market share, something that farmers who fail to adopt the technology may be unable to do. Farmers who have assumed significant debt in order to finance this technology find themselves in an especially vulnerable position. Any number of unforeseen events, such as drought or increasing interest rates, may push them over the edge into bankruptcy. But even if farmers with significant debt loads manage to avoid such catastrophic eventualities, they are still in trouble. Their debts limit their ability to qualify for subsequent loans and hence to adopt future technologies; the cost of servicing their debts effectively decreases their productivity. Debt creates a short-term constraint on farmers' decisions. They must be able to service debt or there will be no long term.

One strategy available to farmers who find themselves in this bind is to adopt farming practices that, while not sustainable over the long run, do result in short-term increases in productivity. They increase production by deferring fallowing schedules and bringing marginal, perhaps highly erodible, land into production; they increase the stocking levels on their pasturelands; they fail to ensure the proper treatment of animal waste. Caught in this productivity bind, these farmers find good stewardship of the environment an obligation that they cannot afford to honor.

To the extent that producers see themselves as serving the social goals of maximal production and high productivity, the constraints that may lead them to neglect environmental stewardship may not seem ethically important. For environmental groups, however, the emphasis upon production and productivity is one of the primary causes of environmental problems. While farmers may see themselves making ethically justifiable choices under a set of legitimate constraints, environmentalists see farmers as externalizing (i.e., failing to count) costs to the environment and to future generations in their production decisions. This conflict might be analyzed as a philosophical dispute over scope and axiology. Farmers pursue a commercial goal (profitability) that is consistent with and ethically legitimated by the social goals of production and productivity. But environmentalists think that the argument that justifies these goals has left out some important consequences.

CASE 2

Water Rights in the Edwards Aquifer: The Texas Water War

Fights over water are stuff of which many a Western movie has been made. And rightly so, for the American West is virtually by definition that part of the country (west of the 100th meridian) where water is an exceedingly scarce, precious resource. The history of the settlement of the American West is itself a history of our nation's attempt to water this water-starved region, largely through a series of water projects whose magnitude dwarfs any public works projects previously attempted. Yet despite these projects, and sometimes even because of them, water remains a scarce resource in the

West. Fights over water continue unabated, but with this important difference: instead of being pitted against one another, farmers and ranchers increasingly find themselves pitted against municipal and industrial interests,
on the one hand, and environmental interests, on the other. The current
battle over the Edwards Aquifer is such a case.

The Edwards Aquifer skirts the southern extremity of the large Edwards
Plateau in southwest Texas, extending some 250 miles from Brackettville
near the Rio Grande to Temple some 80 miles north of Austin (see Figure
6–3). The disputed region of the aquifer stretches some 175 miles from
Brackettville in the west to Kyle in the east, and underlies five counties
(Uvalde, Medina, Bexar, Comal, and Hays). In this region the Edwards is a
large, porous limestone formation some 400 to 700 feet thick and 10 to 30
miles wide, bounded on the north by the Balcones Escarpment that defines
the Edwards Plateau and on the south by a bad-water line that marks the
southernmost extent of freshwater in the aquifer. The Edwards is the major,
indeed virtually the sole, source of water for this five-county region, which includes the city of San Antonio. Secondary aquifers contribute little to the
five-county area served by the Edwards. Low average annual rainfalls (22 to
30 inches west of San Antonio, 30 to 34 inches east of San Antonio) and high
average annual reservoir evaporation rates (35 to 55 inches) severely limit
natural surfacewater sources. San Antonio has the dubious distinction of being the largest city in the United States that is completely dependent on
groundwater for its water supply.

Water use in Uvalde and Medina counties (west of San Antonio) is largely
for irrigation, in Bexar County (which includes San Antonio) for municipal
and industrial uses, and in Comal and Hays counties (east of San Antonio)
for springflow at Comal Springs and San Marcos Springs.

Impetus for a Groundwater Management Policy

The fight over water in the Edwards Aquifer was occasioned by the development of a proposed groundwater management policy championed by the
City of San Antonio, supported by Comal and Hays counties, but rejected by
Uvalde and Medina counties. The impetus for a regional groundwater management plan becomes clear if one compares the projected water demand
over the next fifty years with the average annual recharge of the Edwards
Aquifer. Water demand projections predict that in the absence of a management plan, annual groundwater withdrawals can be expected to exceed the
average annual recharge by 2015. The projected deficits become all the more
significant when one realizes that the projected demand does not include
the estimated 150,000 acre-feet per year in springflows necessary to serve
spring-related and downstream users. If one includes this springflow, *current*
withdrawals already exceed the average annual recharge of the aquifer. A severe drought of the sort that struck the region in the 1950s would probably
leave the Comal and San Marcos springs dry.

Figure 6–3 The Edwards Aquifer

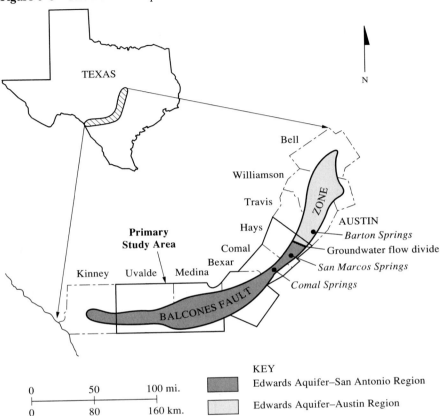

Source: Senger, R. K. and Charles Kreitler, 1984. "Hydrogeology of Edwards Aquifer," Report of Investigation No. 141. Bureau of Economic Geology, University of Texas at Austin, Austin, Texas.

Accompanying the projected increase in water demand during the period from 1980 to 2040 is a significant shift in the nature of the demand: agricultural water use is projected to remain constant or to decrease during the period, while municipal and industrial use is projected to increase from 270,000 acre-feet per year to 760,000 acre-feet per year. The increase and the shift in water demand are attributable almost entirely to a projected population increase in Bexar County (where San Antonio is located) from 1.36 million in 1980 to 3.29 million in 2040.

The expected consequences of significant, long-term overdrafting of the aquifer would be these:

1. Water elevations throughout the aquifer would decrease.

2. Springflows at Comal and San Marcos springs would cease entirely.

In addition:

3. Some wells on the northern edge of the aquifer would cease producing water entirely.
4. The bad-water line on the southern edge of the aquifer would migrate north.

Declining water elevations would increase pumping costs for users. Decreasing springflows would adversely affect both spring-related tourist economies in San Marcos and New Braunfels and downstream irrigation farmers who depend on streamflows. Environmental impacts, including harm to such endangered species as the San Marcos salamander, the San Marcos *Gambusia* (mosquito fish), and the fountain darter (a near relative of the snail darter, made famous in the landmark *TVA v. Hill* case) also would be significant.

One possible further consequence of these harmful effects could be litigation brought against the City of San Antonio by any number of other users of Edwards water. Texas law has traditionally treated groundwater as subject to *free capture;* that is, a landowner has the right to drill a well and pump unlimited amounts of water on his or her land for any beneficial use, regardless of its impact on others. National trends, however, especially in the West, favor a more equitable distribution of water resources to all users; moreover, the presumed rationale of Texas law, namely, the inability to ascertain with any certainty the impact of groundwater withdrawals, is undercut by the rather detailed knowledge of the Edwards Aquifer (i.e., there is a good argument to be made for treating the Edwards in the same manner as surfacewater, for which a right of free capture is not recognized). Such litigation could very well overturn the doctrine of free capture, find the City of San Antonio liable for the harmful effects of its dramatic growth, and put limits on the city's presently unfettered utilization of the aquifer.

Proposed Groundwater Management Plan

Faced with the possibility of such litigation, not to mention the prospect that limited access to groundwater resources might curtail growth and development, the City of San Antonio became a strong advocate of a proposed Regional Water Resources Plan (4), developed by the city and the regional Edwards Underground Water District, that would (i) cap annual groundwater withdrawals from the aquifer at a level that will ensure adequate springflows at Comal and San Marcos springs and (ii) make up for the resulting shortfall in groundwater supply to the city by a combination of conservation, reuse, and surfacewater projects (e.g., new reservoirs).

The proposed plan is quite complex; however, it has three basic features that are pertinent here: (i) the plan would implement a groundwater withdrawal policy that would abolish the current right of free capture and replace it with vested water rights, according to which current users would receive a deeded right to a certain quantity of water (based on current water usage); (ii) it would finance the costs of the surfacewater projects for the city by a combination of well permit fees levied against new users, well pumpage fees levied against all users, water rates and hook-up fees levied against all municipal and industrial users, and sales taxes levied across the entire region; and (iii) it would establish a market in water rights that would allow landowners, especially irrigation farmers, to sell their rights.

Viewpoints of Affected Parties

Public support varies dramatically across the five-county region that the aquifer underlies. Residents of Bexar, Comal, and Hays counties generally support the plan. They are not enthusiastic about the taxes and user fees necessary to fund the surfacewater projects; however, the plan guarantees Bexar County (and the City of San Antonio) a water supply sufficient to sustain continued urban growth and development and Comal and Hays counties springflows sufficient to sustain their spring-related industries. Residents of agriculture-dependent Uvalde and Medina counties in the west, by contrast, have been vociferous critics of the plan, viewing it as a thinly disguised attempt by the City of San Antonio, with the connivance of the two eastern counties, to deny them their rights and steal their water.

Proponents of the plan have criticized as emotional the response of the two western counties. San Antonio lobbyist Steve Stagner has likened the farm community's response to the plan to its response to gun control: "You can have my water when you peel my cold, dead hand off my pump" (2). The source of this emotion is not hard to find (or understand). Water demand in Uvalde and Medina counties (principally for irrigation) has been relatively constant at about 110,000 acre-feet per year over the last several years and is projected to remain so or even to decrease over the next fifty years. Water demand in Bexar County, by contrast, is projected to triple during the same time period from 200,000 to 600,000 acre-feet per year. Residents of these western counties wonder why they should be expected to bear any of San Antonio's growth and development costs. They argue that under the proposed plan, not only would they have to shoulder some of the cost of San Antonio's surfacewater projects, but they would also have to shoulder significant costs imposed by the plan's water rights scheme.

Farmers currently irrigating their lands would not suffer. Their rights to irrigation water would be vested in the deeds to those lands (in the amount of 1.5 acre-feet per year per acre under irrigation); indeed, the proposed water rights marketing scheme conceivably could provide them with a windfall if they were willing to sell their water rights (a point to which we will return shortly). Owners of land that is irrigable but not presently irrigated, however, would not fare so well. They would be able to irrigate their land at some future time only if they paid a withdrawal fee equal to the prevailing cost of conserving an equivalent amount of water elsewhere in the region. Moreover, if the average annual withdrawal for irrigation was at the time in excess of 200,000 acre-feet per year (for accounting purposes, water rights sold by irrigation farmers to municipal and industrial users would be counted as part of this 200,000 acre-feet per year), then would-be irrigators would have to purchase water rights at prevailing market prices, something the authors of the plan assume (probably correctly) that these landowners could not do profitably. In effect, then, owners of land that is irrigable but not currently irrigated would be required under the proposed plan to forfeit a valuable opportunity right that accounts for an unspecified but arguably significant percentage of current land values. Forfeiture of this opportunity right, these landowners argue, would depress their land values, causing them considerable financial losses. Loss of land value, they argue, would in turn decrease the tax base upon which county and local governments depend, causing significant harm to local communities.

The proposed groundwater management plan includes a water rights market scheme according to which irrigation farmers in the two western counties would be permitted to sell their vested water rights to other users, notably municipal and industrial users. The scheme has generally been viewed in the western counties as a sop to irrigation farmers inasmuch as it promises them substantial windfalls should they ever decide to sell their water rights. In fact, the scheme occupies a more central role in the management plan than most have realized. Authors of the plan explicitly introduced the market scheme as a means by which water rights eventually will be transferred from agricultural users in the western counties to municipal and industrial users in San Antonio. Irrigation farmers would have substantial inducement to sell their water rights. Over the next fifty years, irrigation of farm land is predicted to increase net annual farm return an estimated $105 per acre in Uvalde County. During this same period, the annual cost for debt service and maintenance and operating costs for the surfacewater projects proposed in the plan for the City of San Antonio are estimated at $600 to $1,000 per acre-foot. The proposal to vest irrigation farmers with a salable right to 1.5 acre-feet per year for each acre of land under irrigation implies that the net annual value of this right to the irrigation farmer should not exceed $70 per acre-foot, which is far less than its value to the City of San Antonio. The magnitude of this difference makes it exceedingly unlikely that these water rights would not be sold to the City of San Antonio, since by buying these rights the city would be able to avoid the costs of the surfacewater projects that these purchased rights to groundwater would replace.

The proposed plan does not address the economic impact on the western counties of this anticipated sale and transfer of water rights. An economic analysis conducted by researchers at Texas A&M University, however, estimates the total net economic impact of irrigation in Uvalde County at approximately $23 million, or about 5 percent of total county economic activity (6). The sectors of the local economy most severely affected would include households, finance, insurance, real estate, utilities, and retail services (most notably farming-related retail services). There is little reason to believe that the proceeds from the sale of water rights would or even could be productively reinvested in the local economy of these counties. It is the plan's generally insouciant attitude regarding the impact of its provisions on the western counties that gives credence to the suspicion on the part of many that the entire policy is a scheme on San Antonio's part to steal these counties' water.

Water Politics

Political activity in the wake of the plan's publication in July 1988 was intense. Opposition groups sprang up immediately in the two western counties. These groups' first act was to petition the county governments to put the counties' continued membership in the Edwards Underground Water District to a public referendum. (The Edwards Underground Water District's Board of Governors had previously approved the plan, with only the six representatives from Medina and Uvalde counties dissenting. The enabling state legislation that authorized the formation of the Water District contained provisions that permitted a county to withdraw from the district.) The vote for secession was overwhelming in both counties.

The secession of the western counties in January 1989 threw the entire issue into the state legislature. Proponents of the plan, led by legislative representatives from the City of San Antonio, introduced legislation that would grant the Texas Water Commission (TWC) authority to set pumping limits in the aquifer. Opposition groups from the western counties mounted an intense lobbying effort to defeat the legislation. Their lobbying effort found strong support from the Texas Farm Bureau and other farm groups concerned that loss of the right of free capture in the Edwards might set a statewide precedent. This coalition of farm groups, aided by the seeming unwillingness (perhaps fiscal inability) of the City of San Antonio to commit itself to the needed surfacewater projects, was sufficient to defeat the proposed legislation.

The dispute then moved into the federal courts. In summer 1989, when the region was suffering a severe drought that threatened to dry up the Comal and San Marcos springs, the Guadalupe-Blanco River Authority (which represents springflow-dependent farming and business interests) and the Sierra Club filed a notice of intent to sue in federal court under the Endangered Species Act. At the same time, the U.S. Fish and Wildlife Service, which is charged with enforcement of this act, reportedly began planning for a possible federalization of the aquifer in the event that pumping restrictions were necessary to ensure adequate springflow to protect endangered species. The Guadalupe-Blanco River Authority also initiated legal action at the state level to have the aquifer declared an underground river, thereby giving the State of Texas authority to protect downstream interests and to allocate pumping rights. Heavy rains throughout the entire Edwards region during 1989–1990 broke the drought and temporarily kept the dispute out of the courts; however, when the legislative initiatives failed, the Guadalupe-Blanco River Authority (GBRA) and the Sierra Club filed suit, seeking regulatory protection of a number of endangered species, including not only such springflow-dependent species as the San Marcos salamander, the San Marcos *Gambusia,* and the fountain darter, but also several species that live underground in the aquifer itself. Named as defendants in the suit are all users—including the City of San Antonio and irrigation farmers in the western counties—who pump water from the aquifer, as well as the U.S. Fish and Wildlife Service.

In an unexpected move on April 16, 1992, the Texas Water Commission declared the Edwards an underground stream. Then, under its statutory authority to regulate withdrawals from Texas streams, the TWC temporarily banned all well drilling in the aquifer (except for livestock and domestic uses) and announced its intention to regulate all withdrawals from the aquifer. The TWC proposed to determine how much water is available on an annual basis from the aquifer and then allocate rights to this water to "riparians." Environmentalists and springflow-dependent interests in the eastern counties hailed the TWC's action; they believe that it guarantees that aquifer-fed springs will not run dry as a result of aquifer overdrafting. Agricultural interests in the western counties, and indeed throughout the state, criticized the action as an illegal invasion of well-established property rights, notably the right of free capture. The City of San Antonio, which was on record as opposing the underground stream designation, expressed concern over the impact of TWC regulations on future growth and development; it is particularly concerned that these regulations might force the city to undertake controversial (and expensive) surfacewater projects. The TWC's actions will not be the last battle in this ongoing water war: Several different groups have challenged the TWC's action; at the same time, suits brought by the GBRA and the Sierra Club on behalf of endangered springflow-dependent species continue to work their way through the federal courts.

The Ethical Issues

The ethical issues posed by the overdrafting of the Edwards Aquifer are reasonably clear, even if their proper resolution is not. Traditional users of the aquifer, including both irrigation farmers in the western counties and springflow-dependent users in the eastern counties, find their continued use of the aquifer challenged by the ever-increasing water demand of San Antonio's municipal and industrial users. Given that the Edwards Aquifer is incapable of satisfying the water demands of all current and future users, both human and nonhuman, there are two basic ethical issues to be resolved here: (i) What would constitute a proper allocation of the aquifer's water among these users (measured, for example, in acre-feet per year)? (ii) What are the respective obligations of each of the users (measured, for example, in tax liability) to undertake and fund surfacewater projects and conservation programs that would help alleviate the current and projected scarcity of water?

The respective stances adopted by the various user groups on these issues are predictable. As regards the first issue, residents of the western counties claim a historically exercised, basically libertarian noninterference right, embodied in the traditional legal right of free capture, to make use of such amounts of groundwater as they can capture and reasonably use. It is unclear whether they recognize the unqualified extension of this right to other users, notably the City of San Antonio. When the probable consequences of the city's exercise of this claimed right are pointed out (increased pumping costs in the western counties, decreased springflow in the eastern counties), they invariably emphasize the historical priority of their right to Edwards water. As regards the second issue, residents of the western counties acknowledge no obligation to help fund the surfacewater projects and conservation programs necessary to sustain the City of San Antonio's continued growth and development. They regard these programs as a cost of growth and development that city residents and businesses should shoulder themselves. Residents of the western counties do acknowledge an obligation to make wise use of the water that they withdraw from the aquifer, but they have not yet been willing to endorse any conservation regulations (e.g., on irrigation practices) that might promote such wise use.

San Antonio, not surprisingly, has a different perspective on both issues. While not denying its legal right of free capture, it has rested its claims to Edwards water on a utilitarian argument. The city's water needs are said to give it a compelling claim, especially when one considers the relative efficiency of municipal and industrial uses compared to alternative, notably agricultural, uses. In other words, municipal and industrial uses of the water provide the greatest good for the greatest number; they make the most efficient use of a scarce resource. As regards the second issue, the city emphasizes the aggregate benefit to the region of its continued growth and development, arguing that in light of this benefit the region should be willing to underwrite some of the costs of securing this benefit.

Springflow-dependent interests in the eastern counties, for their part, emphasize their historical dependence on and continuing need for aquifer-fed springflow. These interests argue that they have a right, an entitlement, to continued springflow that is justified on what are in effect egalitarian grounds by this historical dependence and continuing need. Because this claimed entitlement does not rest on a well-established legal property right such as the right of free capture, springflow-dependent interests also emphasize the deleterious environmental impacts, especially on endangered species, of diminished springflows. They argue that aquifer users have an obligation to preserve endangered species that further supports their claimed right to adequate springflows. Springflow-dependent interests find support for the claim that we have such preservationist obligations in the fact that we, as a nation, have given this obligation legal recognition in the form of the federal Endangered Species Act. As regards the second issue, springflow-dependent interests have recognized no obligation on their part to help San Antonio fund the development of surfacewater and conservation programs necessary to support the city's growth and development; however, they acknowledge that any politically viable solution to the problem that protects their interests may demand their participation in and contribution to such programs.

It is hardly surprising that users in the western counties should adopt a basically libertarian stance in this dispute, the City of San Antonio a utilitarian stance, and springflow-dependent interests in the eastern counties an egalitarian stance. These are the obvious ethical stances for each party to adopt, given its interests and the economic and legal circumstances in which it finds itself. Some will be tempted to see in each of these stances simply an attempt on the part of each party to wrap its particular self-interest in a cloak of ethical respectability. While it is certainly true that each party's ethical stance is self-serving, it is also true that these stances do in fact serve to justify the policy positions that the respective parties advocate. Each stance provides a justification for its proponent that any ethically acceptable solution to this dispute must consider. There is a well-established noninterference right of free capture, even if this right should in this case give way to more compelling considerations of general social welfare; there is a compelling efficiency argument for allocating more water to municipal and industrial users, even if such an argument should not in this case override considerations of historical right and equity; and there is a good case to be made for the claim that springflow-dependent users are entitled to a share of the aquifer's water, even if this entitlement should not in this case insulate these users from sacrifice. The difficult question is how to craft an aquifer use policy that adjudicates in an ethically acceptable manner these competing claims for this resource. Clearly the first step is to acknowledge and understand the ethical basis of each party's claim.

Arguably, the most significant shortcoming of the original Regional Water Resources Plan was its failure to address the ethical issues that surrounded the plan. The authors of the plan conceded that "the issue of 'who pays and how much' has been at the heart of the difficulty in developing a regional water plan for many years" (4, p. 34), yet it is precisely this issue that the plan failed to address. There is considerable detail regarding schemes for financing surfacewater projects and conservation programs, but there is no discussion of the central issue of how much each of the affected parties in the region should pay or how much each should sacrifice. There is no evidence to suggest that the authors of the plan took fairness and equity to be major policy considerations. Even the usual platitudes are missing. The authors appear not to have appreciated the extent to which regional support for the plan depended crucially on developing a regional consensus that the plan was both fair and equitable. Perhaps such a consensus was not possible. Yet had the plan attempted to address these issues explicitly and directly, they might have defused much of the hostility of the western counties. Certainly nothing is more likely to create animosity than the failure to recognize and understand the ethical basis of an opponent's position. Such recognition and understanding does not require one to endorse the opponent's position, but it does require one to appreciate that the position in question is one that an ethical person might reasonably endorse.

The Goals of Environmental Policy

In the Kesterson case, environmental groups opposed producers. In the Edwards Aquifer case, development interests in San Antonio might have gotten into a conflict with environmentalists and other springflow-dependent interests in the eastern counties, but the political opposition from irrigation farmers in the western counties gave the city an incentive to reach a compromise with springflow-dependent interests. The rest of this chapter examines how production and development goals can conflict with the preservationist goals of much environmental policy.

Some economists and policy analysts (but certainly not all) believe that environmental policy should be evaluated *only* in terms of efficiency in the allocation of resources necessary to produce wanted goods and services. According to this view, which we shall dub the "doctrine of allocative efficiency," scarce natural resources should be allocated to those who value them most. Those who are willing to pay the most for their use are arguably the people who value them the most. Those who are willing to pay the most for the use of these resources will, it is argued, use them most efficiently or profitably. Specifically, they will use these resources to produce those goods and services for which there is the most pressing demand, that is, those for which consumers are willing to pay the most. The doctrine of **allocative efficiency** is a way of interpreting the utilitarian maxim. It states that resources should go to their most valued use and specifies the optimum in terms of the distribution that is brought about when individuals express their willingness to pay for the use of resources through markets that allow them to purchase these resources.

Proponents of the doctrine of allocative efficiency typically presume that markets offer the appropriate allocative mechanism. Markets will effect an efficient allocation of resources (i.e., get the resources to those willing to pay the most for them), provided that trading in these markets is not distorted or hindered by one or another source of **market failure** such as monopolies, externalities, or free-rider problems. Proponents of this doctrine further assume that government may properly and legitimately intervene in markets to correct such failures since in so doing they maximize the satisfaction of consumer preferences (which they take to be the sole justification for government intervention in markets).

The doctrine of allocative efficiency has sometimes been thought to provide an ethical foundation for industrial or commercial development, such as that associated with the City of San Antonio, and for the increased agricultural productivity desired by California growers. In the United States, both development and production have been guided by market incentives. Developers and producers have found willing buyers for their products and services, and it goes without saying that the developers and producers who produce for a market are willing to sell at the market price. Development and production are paradigmatic examples of transactions that must be presumed to make both the buyer and seller better off.

The idea of market failure has come to be seen more recently as a problem with the ethical argument for development and production. The validity of the argument depends on the assumption that transactions are based on a full accounting of costs and benefits. If there is a third party, in addition to the buyer and seller, affected by the transaction, the fact that the buyer and seller agree on a price does not guarantee an increase in total utility. The third party must also be able to affect the transaction. Resource economists have shown how markets either fail or are missing altogether for many environmental goods that have high exclusion costs. True allocative efficiency is not achieved until the value of these goods is reflected in market prices.

Those who endorse the allocative efficiency doctrine construe environmental quality as a marketable commodity. Environmental problems, including agriculture-related ones, are instances of inefficient allocations of resources, occasioned by market failures of one sort or another. Allen Kneese, a respected resource economist, puts the claim this way:

> The main source of our environmental problems is the inability of market exchange as it is presently structured to allocate environmental resources efficiently—that is, to price their destructive use appropriately. (5, p. 259)

These problems are said to be remedied best by regulatory policies that intervene to correct these market failures, thus establishing a market that can allocate natural resources efficiently. In cases where market failures arise because certain common or unowned assets and externalities are not traded and hence not priced, the government can devise schemes that levy shadow or hypothetical prices in the market for these resources. Thus, for example, irrigation farmers in the San Joaquin Valley might be allowed to purchase pollution permits for the contaminated drainwater that they release into local streams and estuaries. The price for these permits would be set appropriately, and the resulting allocation of resources would be efficient just in case it represents the most (and no more) that anyone else would be willing to pay for these same resources. The cost of the permits would ensure that the market price of these farmers' products would reflect the true social costs of their production.

Conservationism versus Preservationism in Environmental Policy

Not everyone involved in environmental politics is convinced that development, production, and environmental quality can be reconciled by the doctrine of allocative efficiency. Since its inception in the late nineteenth century, the environmental movement in the United States has been shaped by two different, often antagonistic approaches, to environmental protection: **conservation** and **preservation**. The basic issue separating these two approaches is the relevance of efficiency considerations to environmental and natural resource policy. Conservationists have been strong proponents of the doctrine of allocative efficiency. Preservationists, on the other hand, have been equally firm in their rejection of this doctrine. The goal of an enlightened environmental policy, they argue, is not simply, even primarily, the efficient allocation of natural resources. The history and basic tenets of these two approaches that continue to shape the debate over U.S. environmental and natural resource policy are essential components of ethical arguments in agriculture.

The conservation and preservation movements were both a reaction to the post–Civil War influence of large private corporations on federal land policy, which resulted in the waste and destruction of many natural resources. But the same events that led conservationists to embrace the doctrine of allocative efficiency that promoted the efficient development and use of natural resources led preservationists to argue that wilderness areas and wildlife should be preserved from commercial development and exploitation of any sort. Although the two groups occasionally reconciled long enough to fight a mutual enemy, they often found themselves pitted against one another, especially over timber policy. One of the most bitter battles was fought over the Hetch-Hetchy Valley in California. John Muir's Sierra Club had persuaded Congress to incorporate this beautiful valley into Yosemite National Park; however, when the City of San Francisco petitioned the government for permission to build a reservoir in the valley, U.S. Secretary of the Interior James R. Garfield, with the full support of conservationist Gifford Pinchot, then Chief Forester of the newly formed National Forest Service, approved the petition. Preservationists, led by Muir, fought the reservoir for several years but eventually lost. The "Hetch-Hetchy steal" came to symbolize for preservationists the fundamental incompatibility of conservationist and preservationist programs. The event crystallized public support for the creation of the National Park Service, which preempted any management role for the Forest Service within the National Park System. The conviction that preservationist objectives are best served by a formal segregation of public lands according to their intended use has played a major role in public land management since that time. To this day, the National Forest Service is a conservationist agency, while the National Park Service is largely preservationist.

Although preservationism enjoyed rather limited political influence at the turn of the century, it has been a powerful political force during the last thirty years. We need only consider the long list of preservationist legislation enacted by Congress during this period to appreciate the movement's power to shape environmental/natural resource policy: Wilderness Act (1964), Wild and Scenic Rivers Act (1968), National Trails System Act (1968), Bald Eagle Protection Act (1969, 1972), National Environmental Protection Act

(1969), Wild and Free-Roaming Horse and Burro Act (1971), Endangered Species Act (1973), Eastern Wilderness Act (1975), Federal Land Policy Management Act (1976), Surface Mining Control and Reclamation Act (1977), Endangered American Wilderness Act (1978), Public Rangelands Improvement Act (1978), Archeological Resources Protection Act (1979), and Alaska National Interest Lands Conservation Act (1980).

   The point to be made about this preservationist legislation is that it defines a significant part of U.S. environmental policy. The doctrine of allocative efficiency cannot claim to provide the sole justificatory rationale for environmental policy because it cannot justify such preservationist legislation. Some proponents of the efficiency doctrine are willing to bite the bullet and argue that preservationist policy, and hence these acts, are unjustifiable. Pinchot, for example, was quite explicit in his rejection of preservationist rationales for environmental protection:

> The object of our forest policy is not to preserve the forests because they are beautiful . . . or because they are refuges for the wild creatures of the wilderness . . . but . . . the making of prosperous homes. . . . Every other consideration comes as secondary. (3, pp. 41–42)

Nor, Pinchot emphasized, was the conservation movement especially concerned with the welfare of future generations:

> Conservation demands the welfare of this generation first, and afterwards the welfare of the generations to follow. The first principle of conservation is development, the use of the natural resources now existing on this continent for the benefit of the people who live here now. (7, p. 43)

Contemporary proponents of the efficiency doctrine have no more patience than did Pinchot with the suggestion that environmental policy might find its justification in a variety of ethical, cultural, and aesthetic purposes, none of which is reducible to the goal of allocative efficiency. Kneese, for example, is especially critical of suggestions to the effect that what we need is a new morality or a new ethic if we are to avoid despoiling the earth. Such suggestions, he recognizes, emphasize normative goals of, and constraints upon, environmental policy that are incompatible with the singlemindedness of the efficiency doctrine. They are, he claims, "really a call for a new set of values which lays more emphasis on the natural, the tranquil, the beautiful, and the very long run" (9, p. 191). Contemporary proponents of the efficiency doctrine share with their turn-of-the-century counterparts a preoccupation with the welfare of present generations. The cost-benefit analyses that these proponents favor employ, as we have seen (Chapter 4), a social discount rate in order to be able to weigh benefits and costs occurring at different points in time. On any reasonable discount rate, the present value of future damages will almost certainly be outweighed by present benefits if those damages occur sufficiently far in the future. Long-term consequences therefore typically have little impact on the acceptability of present policy.

Allocative Efficiency and Environmental Policy

Some environmental problems do arise, as a result of the failures of markets to reflect in their pricing mechanisms the true social cost of producing the objects traded in those markets. For those problems, resource economists have developed a number of useful schemes for ensuring that markets price those objects at their true social costs. Effluent or emission taxes, for example, effectively internalize a social cost of production that polluters would otherwise succeed in externalizing. Yet in many cases the problems that environmental policy addresses cannot be construed simply as instances of market failure. Occupational safety legislation is a case in point. We prohibit exposure in the workplace to certain toxic substances, not only because markets fail to reflect costs (risks) to workers' health, but also because we believe that a society such as ours should not allow any of us to be exposed to such hazards in the workplace.

The preservationist legislation surveyed earlier is not easily subsumed by the efficiency doctrine. The Endangered Species Act (1973), for example, requires, among other things, that actions authorized, funded, or carried out by federal agencies or departments not jeopardize the continued existence of endangered species or modify their critical habitat. In *TVA v. Hill* (1978), which pitted an endangered snaildarter species against the Tennessee Valley Authority's Tellico Dam, the Supreme Court ruled that this statute did not allow balancing endangered species protection against other objectives, notably economic costs: if a proposed agency action poses a threat to the survival of an endangered species or its habitat, the project must be altered or canceled in order to remove the threat, regardless of the cost. During the five years following passage of the statute, there were only a handful of cases like the Tellico Dam case which led to unresolvable conflict between economic development and protection of endangered species; nevertheless, the statute was amended in 1978 to provide some balance between these two goals. The impact of these amendments on the protection afforded endangered species under the original statute seems to have been minimal. The point to be made in the present context, however, is this: even if the amendments provide a mechanism for balancing economic and preservationist goals, the fact remains that the rationale or justification for preserving endangered species is not (and never was) allocative efficiency. Proponents of the efficiency doctrine urge us to accept that doctrine as the sole acceptable rationale or justification for environmental policy. The historical record, however, indicates that allocative efficiency to date has not been the rationale or justification for much of this nation's environmental policy; rather, such policy has been motivated and directed by a number of different goals, only one of which is allocative efficiency. Proponents of the efficiency doctrine have no choice but to concede the historical facts, but having done so, they might argue that allocative efficiency should be the sole rationale or justification. So much the worse for existing or past policy, they might argue, that it has not recognized the doctrine of allocative efficiency. Paul Portney, a well-known resource economist, expresses this view well:

> Natural resource policy in the "real world" may have nothing to do with economic efficiency whatsoever. In fact, as an attribute of policy design, efficiency is often more noticeable in the breach than the observance. . . . [F]ederal water policy . . . originally was designed to help open up the West. Even though that goal has been accomplished, and even though the perpetuation of those policies often leads to blatant misallocations of water resources, they continue because those who benefit from them are politically effective in arguing their point. (8, p. 7)

There is clearly a sense in which environmental policy, indeed all social policy, is shaped by the preferences of citizens. Virtually all of us would prefer to live in a society where all citizens live, work, and play in a healthy, safe, and aesthetically pleasing environment; most of us would prefer to live in a society that values and adequately prepares for the welfare of our children and for subsequent future generations. Many, if not all, of us would prefer to live in a society that is committed to the preservation of our rich national heritage, including both wildlife and its natural habitat. An enlightened environmental policy would surely aim to satisfy such preferences to the extent possible. These preferences are often not of a sort that could be described as *consumer* preferences, i.e., they are not preferences that can be satisfied in a market (unlike, for example, preferences for certain foods). Rather they are often a species of what might be called *moral* preferences, preferences that we believe that everyone ought to have, whether or not we (and others) express them in our consumer choices. These **moral preferences** might be better characterized as beliefs regarding what our society should be like, how it should be structured, what it should stand for, and what it should value. We have the moral preferences that we do because we hold certain beliefs about what makes society just and good, and being citizens commits us to preferring a society that lives up to these beliefs, at least as far as possible. We may, for example, support mandatory recycling of household solid waste, even though we are not presently recycling these wastes voluntarily and even when studies that show that the costs of recycling exceed the benefits. Our support for this policy may rest on nothing more than the belief that recycling is something that our society ought to do, no matter what the consequences.

The distinction between consumer and moral preferences provides a way of restating criticisms of allocative efficiency that were discussed in Chapter 4. There it was noted that efficiency becomes meaningful only when one assumes a relatively stable structure of rights and privileges. Large changes in the structure redefine property rights, and economic theory has not solved the problem of how to compare the exchanges that people make under one configuration of property rights with those that they make under a radically different structure. Three sets of ideas are available for making what is essentially the same point. In Chapter 2 we distinguished between constitutional choices and conventional policy choices. In Chapter 4 we noted that one can distinguish between exchange and intrinsic value. Here we distinguish between consumer and moral preferences.

All of these distinctions involve the question of when existing patterns of conduct and choice provide decisive information on the ethics of public policy. The criterion of allocative efficiency urges policy makers to be sure that resources go to the use that people currently value most highly. It tells a policy maker to give the people what they want. However, one reason why there is ethical debate about the environment is that at least one segment of the American people wants a policy that will make us better. The environmentalist viewpoint on the Kesterson and Edwards cases illustrates this theme.

In both cases, an existing policy structure gave farmers great discretion in the use of water. Both can be analyzed as cases of market failure, as structures that produce conduct that results in inefficient performance. In both cases, there is a conflict between farmers who feel justified in exercising existing property rights to the limit of the law and those who want to restructure farmers' incentives to provide more efficient use. In both cases, restructuring proposals create markets for water rights, arguably allowing efficient levels of water use or, in the Kesterson case, pollution. In both cases, environmentalists may have had political reasons to support proposals that restructure farmers' incentives, but their ethical concerns extend well beyond a desire for increased efficiency. They want policies that will help present and future generations appreciate the value of waterfowl, of endangered species, or of natural beauty. This reflects a concern for intrinsic rather than exchange values, for moral rather than consumer preferences. Although they may not want a change in the U.S. Constitution, they clearly do want a change in the informal network of rules, practices, and beliefs that shape tastes, conduct, and shared perceptions of reality. In this respect, these cases are quite similar to the conflict between Muir and Pinchot.

If environmental policy aims to change existing consumer preferences or exchange values, then the efficiency doctrine does not provide the correct rationale or justificatory framework for an environmental policy. That doctrine would allocate resources to those willing to pay the most for them; that is to say, it would allocate resources in such a way as to maximize satisfaction of the preferences that we in fact have. The preferences that environmental policy aims to satisfy are those that we think we ought to have; such policy is concerned with intrinsic rather than exchange values. There is no reason to assume that the preferences that we in fact have are the ones that we ought to have; indeed, the mere fact that we need an environmental policy is evidence that our actual preferences are not those we should have. The fundamental ethical problem with the efficiency doctrine, then, is this: *It attempts to answer the question of what public policies we ought to prefer by appealing to a doctrine that takes our actual preferences as normatively correct.* This is a position of moral conservatism that no one, not even political conservatives, should endorse, since it tells us that we ought to do only what in fact we want to do, whatever that happens to be.

Preservationist environmental policies are more consistent with rights-based ethical theories than with utilitarianist ones. Rights-based theories begin with the assumption that rational persons would prefer not to live in a state of nature in which people are free to act in any way they wish in pursuit of pure self-interest. Rather, rational persons would prefer to live in a civil society in which everyone, including themselves, is prevented from acting on preferences that involve harm or injustice to others. Rights-based theories, like utilitarian theories, accept self-interested consumer preferences as given (i.e., it is a fact that people have them), but they do not assume that such preferences are therefore good. Nor do they assume that public policy should promote the satisfaction of those preferences. Indeed, it is the proper role of government to frustrate certain preferences of its citizenry.

The egalitarian's original position probably provides more support for including environmental preservationist goals in the social contract than does the libertarian's state of nature. As shown in Chapter 3, the state of nature supports the case for noninterference rights. One could make a strong libertarian argument that pollution that harms others violates noninterference rights, but the case for more positive duties to promote stewardship and ecological integrity would be more difficult. The original position asks us to define the structures of our public policy under the assumption that we do not know what position we will occupy. If this is interpreted to mean that someone in the original position does not know whether he or she is a member of the present generation or of future ones, it becomes plausible to think that contractors in the original position would endorse policies that preserve the natural world. Future generations will surely have as much to observe, appreciate, and learn from a preserved natural environment as do present generations. Activities that permanently alter landscapes and ecosystems will be acceptable only to the extent that they are truly necessary to support vital functions. While providing for food security would qualify as vital, the convenience and variety of the typical American diet might not.

In the original position, contractors can also ask each other about the opportunities that are necessary for a rewarding life. Although income and education are the most frequently mentioned opportunities, the opportunity to experience nature also may qualify. Americans have long believed that the experience of nature is an essential part of personal development in at least two different ways. First, the sights, sounds, and smells of the natural world are thought to educate the senses. That is, the ability to discern the signs of nature—from animal tracks to a ring around the moon—is thought to be a mark of adulthood. Second, the experience of working in nature, be it farming, hunting, or gathering berries, is thought to cultivate an understanding and appreciation of humanity's place in the cosmos and of individual human purpose. If citizenship requires that people have knowledge and understanding of the workings of nature, then we will want to design a society that will continue to produce people with the experience that engenders such understanding.

The prisoner's dilemma does not offer preservationist policies the same kind of support. The prisoner's dilemma is a situation in which less than optimal choices are made because prisoners cannot rely on one another. They cannot, without help, make the bargain that they would choose. They are experiencing a market failure. The arguments from the state of nature and the original position state stronger philosophical positions in that they stipulate rights and social goals that *ought* to be secured and sought, even if people at a given moment in history do not happen to want them. It is, of course, arguable whether the preservationist goals of environmental policy have the moral force of obligations. Utilitarians would deny that they do. We cannot address this issue here; rather, we can only recognize that utilitarians and rights-based theorists will disagree on this issue, with the consequence that most utilitarians are conservationists rather than preservationists.

Arguments that raise constitutional or intrinsic values in environmental policy typically do not address the economic considerations that invariably must shape a policy. The difficulty of measuring trade-offs from large changes in structure does not mean that they do not exist. How then do economic considerations enter? A recent survey describing and summarizing a number of public opinion polls on environmental issues provides some interesting suggestions about how the public would answer this question (1). Most of those surveyed describe themselves as environmentalists. They consider environmental protection very important, despite the fact that they assume both that such protection is probably costly and that they will be the ones who will end up footing the bill. Few of these respondents agree with the proposition that we should pursue environmental protection goals without regard to cost; however, they are very reluctant to answer questions about their willingness to pay for environmental protection. Asked how much they are willing to pay for a clean environment, approximately 20 percent claim to be willing to pay at least $5 per month and another 20 percent claim to be willing to pay $1 to $5 per month, but almost half of those surveyed simply did not answer the question. Their responses to other questions indicate that they wanted to see the financial burden for environmental protection placed on those directly responsible for the problems, even though they explicitly acknowledge that these costs will eventually be passed on to them. What seems to be important to these respondents is that responsibility for environmental degradation be assigned to specific individuals or entities such as corporations or government agencies even if the costs of environmental protection end up being more widely distributed. The responses further suggest that while respondents recognize that the levels of environmental protection actually achieved will be determined significantly by the costs of environmental protection, they do not think that the goals themselves should be based on such considerations. Economic considerations are thought to be relevant primarily in determining the extent to which and the rate at which we are able to achieve the goals we set. Allocative efficiency emerges as only one of many social goals that environmental policy should aim to advance. This book provides no final solution to the problem of evaluating the economics of environmental choice. Future study and debate will be improved, however, by recognizing the philosophical issues that must be joined.

Summary

The Kesterson and Edwards cases illustrate conflicts of interest in the resolution of environmental problems facing agriculture. Environmental impacts of agriculture are of three kinds: environmental contamination, habitat destruction, and resource depletion. Belief in farmer stewardship of natural resources has produced public policies that rely upon farmers' willingness to control these impacts voluntarily. The two cases illustrate situations in which voluntary stewardship does not appear to have been enough. The Kesterson case illustrates contamination; the Edwards case is an example of resource depletion. Habitat destruction is an issue in both cases.

The cases illustrate a general pattern for agriculture and environmental issues. Farmers enjoy existing property rights that give them wide discretion in the use of land and water. Farming practices that have environmental impact provide a basis for both rights-based and utilitarianist arguments urging a restriction or redefinition of these rights. Farmers correctly perceive these restrictions as interference in their use of property, and to the extent that they feel ethically justified in holding these property rights, they will tend to use libertarian arguments to oppose changes in existing policy. However, it is also plausible to interpret environmental impact as an instance of market failure and to propose policies that will redirect resources to their most valued use. Utilitarian arguments are typically employed in making the ethical case for such changes, and the doctrine of allocative efficiency is often advanced as the standard for evaluating policy option for achieving particular environmental goals.

In the Edwards and Kesterson cases, however, there are environmental groups who, while supporting policy change, might be dissatisfied with an analysis that utilizes the efficiency doctrine. Like preservationists who opposed the development of the Hetch-Hetchy reservoir, these groups may have objectives that can only be achieved through fundamental changes in policy structure. Such changes might include the extension of rights to wildlife, to endangered species, or even to forests and ecosystems. They might also be expressed in terms of the way that the experience of natural environments leads to the formation of ethical values, and they might argue that future generations must not be denied the opportunity to learn from the experience of nature.

Public policy can be both an *expression* of our collective beliefs regarding what our society should be like and an attempt to *realize* those beliefs through collective action. Environmental/natural resource policy aims to advance many social goals, only one of which is efficiency in the distribution of scarce natural resources. Such policy must not only provide for the efficient exploitation of natural resources (e.g., water, air, timber, petroleum, metals); it must also provide for the preservation of and public access to the natural environment that is such an important part of our national heritage. It must protect the public against environmental threats to its health and safety. Occasionally, indeed often, these social goals will conflict. For example, we cannot have unrestricted timbering in the hardwood forests of Oregon and at the same time preserve the endangered spotted owl. We cannot maintain unrestricted public access to our national parks and at the same time preserve the very natural environment that the public comes to these parks to enjoy. The plurality of social goals forces hard choices upon us, choices for which our public policies must provide a decision mechanism.

Environmentalists, both conservationists and preservationists, often find themselves at odds with agricultural interests regarding environmental or natural resource policy. The reason should be clear. Agricultural production requires scarce natural resource inputs such as water, energy, soil, and habitat; it often produces, in addition to food and fiber, environmental contamination (caused by pesticides, fertilizers, siltation, salination, animal waste), habitat destruction (draining of wetlands, deforestation), and resource depletion (soil erosion, water depletion).

Environmental/natural resource policy affects agricultural production both by limiting access to needed natural resource inputs and by regulating the production of environmentally undesirable outputs. Thus, for example, federal land management policies control the availability of public lands in the West for cattle grazing; federal environmental protection statutes regulate the disposal of some animal wastes. Such regulation of inputs and outputs typically has an adverse impact on agricultural productivity and profitability. The issue separating agricultural interests and environmentalists is whether these regulatory costs are justifiable.

Environmentalists tend to have a somewhat different policy agenda, depending upon where they fall on the continuum between conservationism and preservationism. Conservationists, as one might expect, tend to focus on the efficient allocation of scarce natural resources that are needed in agricultural production. Thus, not surprisingly, they tend to be in the forefront of disputes (mostly having to do with water and land use) that pit farmers against those who favor different uses of these resources. Preservationists, by contrast, tend to focus on the preservation of wildlife, critical habitats, and scenic or wilderness areas that may be endangered by agricultural practices.

Key Terms

allocative efficiency

conservation

market failure

moral preferences

preservation

References

1. Gilroy, John M., and Robert Y. Shapiro. 1986. "The Polls: Environmental Protection," *Public Opinion Quarterly* 50: 270–279.
2. Gilman, Todd J., "The Texas Water War," *Dallas Morning News*, August 19, 1990, p. 50A.
3. Hays, S. P. 1959. *The Gospel of Efficiency*. Cambridge, Mass.: Harvard University Press.
4. Joint Committee on Water Resources. July 1988. *Regional Water Resources Plan*. Sponsored by the San Antonio City Council and the Edwards Underground Water District Board of Directors.
5. Kneese, Allen, and Blair Bower. 1979. *Environmental Quality and Residuals Management*. Baltimore: Johns Hopkins University Press.
6. Lee, John G., Ronald D. Lacewell, Teofilo Ozuna, Jr., and Lonnie L. Jones. 1987. "Regional Impact of Urban Water Use on Irrigated Agriculture," *Southern Journal of Agricultural Economics* 10: 43–51.
7. Pinchot, Gifford. 1910. *The Fight for Conservation*. Seattle: University of Washington Press.
8. Portney, Paul. 1982. "Introduction," in *Current Issues in Natural Resource Policy*, ed. Paul Fortney. Washington, D.C.: Resources for the Future.
9. Prepared statement, *The Environmental Decade: Hearing Before a Subcommittee of the Committee on Government Operations*, U.S. House of Representatives, 91st Congress, 2nd session, 1970.
10. Steinbeck, John. 1939. *The Grapes of Wrath*. New York: Viking Penguin.
11. Tanji, Kenneth, André Läuchli, and Jewell Meyer. 1986. "Selenium in the San Joaquin Valley," *Environment* 28: 6–10, 34–39.

Suggestions for Further Reading

Our chapter begins with a brief discussion of agrarian myth and the steward-ship of farmers. Readers wishing to followup on this subject should read W. Browne et al., *Sacred Cows and Hot Potatoes: Agrarian Myths in Agricultural Policy* (Boulder, Colo.: Westview Press, 1992). Chapter 5, on productivity, and Chapter 8, on the environment, are particularly relevant. A good discussion of farmers' incentives for stewardship and compliance with environmental regulation can be found in Katherine Reichelderfer's article, "Environmental

Protection and Agricultural Support: Are Tradeoffs Necessary?" in *Agricultural Policies in a New Decade,* ed. Kristin Allen (Washington, D.C.: Resources for the Future, 1990).

There is an enormous literature on the environmental impacts of agriculture. We have selected two cases involving water, but one could easily develop cases involving soil erosion, land use, chemicals, or mechanization. The evolution of pesticides and pesticide policy is the best-documented environmental conflict involving agriculture. The pesticide controversy begins, of course, with Rachel Carson's *Silent Spring* (Boston: Houghton Mifflin, 1962), and those who wish to follow it should consult Frank Graham's *Since Silent Spring* (Boston: Houghton Mifflin, 1970); Robert Van den Bosch's *The Pesticide Conspiracy* (Garden City, N.Y.: Doubleday, 1978); Thomas Dunlap's *D.D.T.* (Princeton, N.J.: Princeton University Press, 1981); John Perkins's *Insects, Experts and the Insecticide Crisis* (New York: Plenum Press, 1982); and Christopher Bosso's *Pesticides and Politics: The Life Cycle of a Public Issue* (Pittsburgh: University of Pittsburgh Press, 1987). David Pimentel's prolific writings on pesticide should also be noted. His chapter in *Ecology, Economics, Ethics: The Broken Circle,* ed. F. Herbert Borman and Stephen R. Kellert (New Haven, Conn.: Yale University Press, 1991), includes citations of his numerous articles.

Three articles on resource use in Charles V. Blatz's *Ethics and Agriculture* (Moscow: University of Idaho Press, 1991) do a fine job of illustrating how libertarian, egalitarian, and utilitarian arguments are applied in this area of agricultural/environmental policy. Donald Scherer ("Towards an Upstream-Downstream Morality of Our Upstream-Downstream World") is the libertarian, and Terry Anderson and Donald Leal ("Going with the Flow: Expanding the Water Markets") are the utilitarians. "Replacing Confusion with Equity: Alternatives for Water Policy in the Colorado River Basin," by Helen Ingram, Lawrence Scaff, and Leslie Silko, provides one of the most intellectually coherent statements of egalitarian reasoning applied to resource policy to be found anywhere.

Sources recommended in Chapter 4 are relevant for those interested in pursuing the question of efficiency as a norm for environmental policy. Mark Sagoff has produced the most important philosophical work on this question as it relates to the environment. His book *The Economy of the Earth* (Cambridge: Cambridge University Press, 1988) is the best place to begin. The philosophical significance of the conflict between Muir and Pinchot is nicely covered in an important book by Bryan Norton, *Toward Unity Among Environmentalists* (Oxford: Oxford University Press, 1991). Those who wish to review a wide variety of philosophical writing on the environment might consult the anthology edited by Donald Van de Veer and Christine Pierce, *People, Penguins and Plastic Trees* (Belmont, Calif.: Wadsworth, 1986). Readings suggested for Chapter 9 on sustainability are also relevant.

CHAPTER 7

Farm Animal Welfare and Animal Rights

In the past decade, animal rights advocates have worked to limit the use of nonhuman animals in laboratory experiments, to curtail hunting of wild animals, to end the use of certain wild animal pelts for clothing, and to improve the treatment of domesticated animals both as pets and in animal agriculture. Some animal rights activists have advocated vegetarianism as an ethically preferable alternative to the use of animals for food. The claims that have been advanced on behalf of animals are based upon the advocates' assessment of moral requirements for human–animal interaction. This chapter will focus upon the use of farm animals in production agriculture.[1]

Animal welfare and animal rights have been discussed widely in the last decade. In popular use, those who advocate *animal welfare* wish to promote moderate reform in animal agriculture, while those who promote *animal rights* advocate revolutionary change, often to the point of vegetarianism. As we will see, use of the terms *welfare* and *rights* does not correspond to the more rigorous use that has been developed in Chapter 3. There we saw that welfare was generally a component of a policy evaluation focused upon performance, though utilitarians can offer arguments for establishing legal rights in virtue of the consequences they produce. Rights arguments are generally a component of structure-focused evaluations, as would be offered by those who advocate libertarian or egalitarian social philosophies.

In the past decade, philosophical and political advocacy of animal welfare and animal rights has not identified many specific policy proposals affecting animal agriculture, though such proposals may soon be placed on the Congressional agenda. One specific proposal was put forward in 1989, when

---

[1]This chapter incorporates materials from P. Thompson and S. Curtis, "The Well Being of Agricultural Animals," a manuscript produced for the Workshop on Ethical Aspects of Food, Agriculture and Natural Resource Policy, available from the Committee for Agricultural Research Policy, 223 Scovell Hall, University of Kentucky, Lexington, KY 40546.

animal welfare activists placed a referendum before the voters of Massachusetts that would have extended regulation of animal agriculture in the United States to unprecedented levels. The elements of this case are analyzed in this chapter. Key actors are identified, and the political process that ultimately led to the defeat of the referendum is described. The Massachusetts initiative provides an example of how abstract philosophical arguments on the status of animals may be integrated with the policy analysis framework developed in Chapter 2.

Situation, Structure, Conduct, and Performance for Animal Agriculture

In modern industrial countries, farm animals are raised primarily for food and fiber products that are harvested and sold as a source of income for the farm or ranch operation. Food uses include meat, but also egg and dairy production, which do not necessarily require slaughter. Nonfood uses include wool, leather, and many animal by-products. In nonindustrialized settings, the sale of animal products is often a minor part of the reason for raising farm animals. In most parts of the world, draft animals are still an important part of the agricultural system. Animals utilize parts of the crop that are not easily consumed by humans and return fertilizer to the soil.

In some societies, cattle and swine have religious significance or represent a level of social status for their owners that is not related to their productive potential. For the most part, these uses will be ignored in the discussion that follows, as will uses of animals in medical experiments, for hunting and recreation, and for pets. We shall assume that the term *animal* refers to nonhuman farm animals of the sort commonly used in the production of food and fiber commodities in modern industrialized agricultural systems.

Human Uses of Agricultural Animals

Even if animals themselves were not entitled to moral consideration, animal agriculture would be ethically significant because of the uses that humans have for farm animals. For more than 99.9 percent of their 14-million-year history, humans and their ancestors were food hunters, gatherers, and scavengers. It was less than 10,000 years ago that they started to domesticate animals and cultivate plants. Agricultural animals—that handful of species that have accompanied humans through thousands of years of existence—have played three important roles in civilization. First and foremost, they provide food for humans. Second, animals used for food provide coproducts, or supplementary uses. Third, animals play an often unnoticed role in the economic organization of the household, the region, and the globe.

Humans and other hominids ate eggs, milk, and meat for millions of years, long before the arrival of animal agriculture. As income increased and the number of dietary options became larger, people selected diets higher in animal protein. Today it is possible to provide adequate nutrition for human beings with no foods of animal origin whatsoever in the diet (the vegan approach). Vegan diets and other, less stringent forms of vegetarianism are practical because modern nutritional science has made it possible to monitor the mix of proteins required for a balanced diet and to supplement needs artificially. Even now, a varied diet (including both animal and plant products) is recommended in the U.S. Department of Agriculture food pyramid as the surest way for humans to fulfill their nutrient requirements.

Animals yield numerous useful coproducts that may benefit people as much as the food these animals produce. Work is still an important animal coproduct around the globe, with around 200 million draft animals in current use (4). Several species, including horses, oxen, and water buffalo, provide traction power. Animal traction has been virtually replaced by engine-powered tractors in the United States, but it remains an important part of agriculture in many other societies. Animals also generate materials that serve as fertilizers, clothing fibers and skins, medicines, and household fuels, among other things. Farm animals are also raised for companionship and to serve as social status symbols.

Animal populations serve as a hedge against fluctuating food supplies and income. Whether used to tide a family over a winter season or an entire year of drought, animals have traditionally served as a reserve of wealth or food that may be tapped in times of scarcity. Animal herds can supplement diets depressed by grain shortages and can supply a boost of high-quality protein at a time when it is most needed (5). This role for agricultural animals perhaps was more important in the past than it is today, although the availability of draft and dairy animals for use as food helped thousands avoid starvation in the African Sahel as recently as 1984. Modern grain storage techniques have reduced our need to store protein on the hoof, and animals now serve as a form of savings that can be converted to cash when needed. Even landless peasants can keep animals in many parts of the world. These animals provide an easy way for transients to store and move wealth, and they can be sold when income needs are greatest.

The Structure of Animal Agriculture

The existing structure of animal agriculture includes a host of laws and regulations concerning acceptable practices for the production and sale of animal products. While many of these laws and regulations deal with consumer protection and food safety, a concern for animal welfare has been an enduring feature of U.S. law as well. The existing regulatory policy on the well-being of animals affects animal agriculture in three different ways:

1. Animals are chattel property under existing legal codes. This means that they may be owned, bought, and sold and that the use or disposal of them is left to the discretion of the owner at any given time. Thus,

while it would be illegal for one person to kill or confine another's animal, chattel property rights give the owners a right to do either of these things to their animals. Few property rights give owners absolute control over the use of their property, however, and this is true for chattel property rights. The owners of animals must not allow them to create a nuisance, for example. Restrictions that require humane treatment of are taken up later.

2. When the interests of farm animals are taken as the basis for regulatory policy, production practices that harm animals are prohibited entirely. So-called downer cattle, for example, that do not survive the process of transport to slaughter with the ability to walk must be destroyed humanely, even though doing so imposes costs upon truckers and packing plants. In such instances, animal well-being is deemed more important than any human desire to economize on prices paid for animal products. Farm animals have been protected against cruel treatment since 1641 in some parts of the United States. Humane laws have always enforced the principle that animal well-being is more important than the human freedom to engage in or benefit from indolent or sadistic treatment of farm animals.

3. In addition, existing legal codes for animal agriculture regulate a wide variety of animal species and production environments, with multiple ends in mind. Rules for transport and slaughter, for marketability of certain products, and for human and animal health affect animal well-being. Existing policy does not set standards for weighing human and animal interests unilaterally, but it gives discretion to agencies. The Food Safety Inspection Service and the Food and Drug Administration, for example, have the authority to regulate based upon the wholesomeness and identity of foods. Whether the use of a particular production practice changes the wholesomeness or identity of a food is a decision that is left to the regulating agency.

Chattel property rights assume great importance in animal agriculture because they establish a bargained-exchange system over which there is relatively little direct government control. Animal producers invest in the purchase and production of animals because they expect to sell them at a profit. Their expectation is based upon the market demand for animal foods and coproducts. Although humane laws and other regulations constrain use and exchange, government protects property rights in live animals, animal carcasses, and animal products exactly as it protects property rights in grains, automobiles, houses, or bicycles. The police power of government is used to protect against theft; administrative offices validate and certify the terms of possession, ownership, and exchange; and the courts adjudicate other disputes. These are the background policies that are needed to initiate a market and to allow consumer demand to determine the incentives and opportunities for animal agriculture.

Animal Production in the United States

Although animal agriculture continues to fulfill the three traditional purposes of food, coproduct, and economic stabilizer, the way animals are raised in the United States has changed dramatically since World War II. Given the regulatory structure for animal agriculture and the fact that producers respond to price incentives, the conduct and performance for animal production have changed largely as a function of changing technology. While animals used to roam outdoors and in relatively open spaces, new methods reduce the amount of land and labor needed for animal production by placing them indoors in confined spaces. These new production methods have improved the animals' lives in some respects and harmed them in others.

Confinement systems are so called because they introduce new controls into the production process by confining animals in ways that are novel compared to traditional animal husbandry. The degree and character of confinement vary tremendously. Often confinement involves keeping animals indoors, where producers can control heat and humidity. In egg production, confinement involves keeping birds in wire mesh cages where feed rations can be controlled, eggs retrieved, medicines administered, and production levels monitored. In the egg industry, the design of these cages and the stocking rate (number of birds per cage) vary. The mere existence of the confinement system introduces opportunities for improving living conditions (through protection from weather) and for worsening them (through crowding and physical constraint).

Some confinement systems, such as for feeder cattle, do not typically place animals indoors. Some, such as broiler productions where birds are free to roam through a large building, do not significantly restrict their movement. It is difficult to generalize about the nature and effects of confinement systems. The list of positive and negative effects upon animals varies from species to species, but some effects are fairly widespread. Access to water is easier in confinement, and animals are therefore more likely to receive it. Intensive animal facilities help prevent farm animals from becoming victims of predators. Perforated floors separate the animals from their own excreta. (Infections can cause disease and death; thus perforated floors greatly improve animals' living conditions.) Caretakers can observe individual animals more thoroughly when they are close at hand, living singly or in small groups; they can therefore respond more effectively to deficiencies or illness on a case-by-case basis.

Large operations also obtain economies from purchasing and marketing in large lots, with more or less continuous flow. This enhances the profitability of the enterprise by reducing costs. It is the consumers of animal products who are the ultimate beneficiaries of the lower prices that increased efficiency brings. The price of meat and poultry products purchased in the grocery store has declined as a share of personal income. The benefits from confinement are thus shared by producers and consumers alike.

Managers of large, intensive animal production units still consider sound animal care and management the basis of high productivity and profitability, so they have an incentive to secure the well-being of their animals. Large units make it profitable to spend more time and effort on herd or flock management. However, the efficiency of animal production depends upon the average productivity of all animals in the same management unit. If the cost of securing the well-being of a few individuals in a large unit exceeds the return on average productivity for the entire unit, producers have no financial incentive to alter a production system.

Cost savings from confinement therefore may be obtained at a cost to the welfare of animals raised in a confinement setting. Animals raised in confinement are, as the word suggests, confined. They do not have freedom and room to move about and associate with one another, as they would in traditional livestock systems. Although there is considerable variation in confinement systems, some crowd animals into small spaces and require additional practices that may harm individual animals. Under some conditions, it may be unprofitable to tailor production practices to a particular animal's needs. The individuals that have grown too big or that are housed with aggressive mates may suffer. Confinement appears to increase behaviors such as biting, fighting, and cannibalism. Other husbandry practices, such as culling male chicks by suffocation or grinding, are associated with the large scale of some farms rather than with confinement systems as such. Animal welfare issues, however, extend to transport and slaughter as well as confinement systems of production.

Critics of confinement systems describe the effects on animals in quite different terms. Jim Mason, for example, writes that the principles of confinement "insure that factory animals are crowded, restricted, stressed, frustrated, held in barren environments, and maintained on additive-laced, unnatural diet" (2, p. 92). Mason and Peter Singer (3) published a critical review of animal agriculture that was extensively illustrated with photographs of confinement systems. It is worth quoting Mason at length to get the flavor of his criticisms:

> If the hatchery is turning out birds for egg factories, the first order of business is the destruction of half the "crop" of chicks. Males don't lay eggs, and the flesh of these specialized layer breeds is of poor quality—"not fit to feed," as one hatchery worker put it. At some hatcheries "egg-type" males are thrown into plastic bags and allowed to suffocate. Females of the strain are debeaked, vaccinated and sent to "grow-out" houses until, at about twenty weeks of age, they are ready to start laying eggs. At this point they are installed in the automated cage layer house. After a year or two in the cages their egg productivity wanes and it becomes unprofitable to feed and house them. The factory farmer may decide to use "force moulting," a procedure which shocks the birds into renewed egg productivity for another few months by leaving them in the dark for several days without food or water. After a force moult or two the hens are spent, and they are delivered to the processors to be turned into soup stock, frozen pies and other convenience foods. (2, pp. 92–93)

Ethical Issues in Animal Agriculture

The ethical issues in the use of farm animals are as varied as the ways animals are used. First are a number of personal decisions that each individual must make. Most people think of the animal rights question in regard to their own conduct well before coming to any opinion about farm production or public policy. Western culture has historically made use of animals for a variety of purposes, while Eastern culture, particularly Hindu culture, has rejected some of these uses on religious and moral grounds. Each individual comes to the question of animal welfare and animal rights with a background that implies acceptability for some uses of animals while rejecting others. Westerners eat beef, pork, and poultry, for example, but shun the eating of dogs, horses, and cats. Examining the ethical issues involved in our treatment of farm animals often leads individuals to think more reflectively about dietary habits that they have maintained since their earliest years.

Second, a host of decisions must be made by individual producers who raise livestock and poultry. Most (but not all) producers believe that they have an ethical duty to ensure humane treatment for the animals under their care. Because of this commitment, many farmers and ranchers have been resentful of critics who appear to assume that farmers have an uncaring attitude toward their animals. At the same time, individuals have assessed the requirements of humane treatment in different ways. They have also evaluated the trade-offs between humane treatment of animals and the overall profitability of their operations differently. A calm and objective assessment of the ethical basis for humane treatment may lead producers to reflect upon the decisions that they have made in organizing their livestock and poultry operations. While this assessment may not lead to changes in the methods of production, it inevitably leads to a deeper and more thoughtful rationale for private decisions that a producer makes about the treatment of agricultural animals.

Finally, there are public policy issues. The United States was one of the first countries to adopt laws requiring humane treatment of animals. Although European countries have now surpassed U.S. codes in the strictness of their standards for agricultural animals, proposals for tighter or more specific standards for treatment of farm animals in the United States are constantly being put forward by animal welfare advocates. Such laws would require minimum standards for movement, access to food and water, and even socialization for farm animals or would ban certain methods of animal production entirely. In fact, the long-term goal of some animal rights activists is the total ban of animal agriculture. Actual legal proposals, however, are far more specific and politically realistic. The U.S. Congress and many state legislatures have some form of animal welfare legislation on their calendars almost all the time.

One key issue underlies all others in evaluating animal agriculture: why extend direct moral consideration to farm animal interests and well-being? Put even more bluntly, why suppose that we have any obligation to farm animals? The answer is important because it secures the motivation for ethical concern about farm animals. It also determines whether policy on animal welfare will focus primarily on ensuring that livestock practices improve animals' quality of life or on structuring human action in such a way as to guarantee entitlements or noninterference rights for the animals. This is a policy difference that returns to some of the basic tensions between rights-based and utilitarian approaches to policy. Before considering a concrete case that illustrates these tensions, it will be useful to review philosophical thought on this fundamental moral issue.

Animal Welfare and Animal Rights

When people have tried to specify exactly why animals are worthy of moral consideration, they typically choose between two conceptual paths or philosophical strategies. The first bases concern upon the painful or distressing experiences to which farm animals might be subjected. Moral consideration for animals might attempt to eliminate, or at least minimize, the suffering of animals wherever possible. The focus of concern is on suffering, on the experience of pain. In this context, pain might be understood to include all forms of physical and mental deprivation. The first strategy answers the question "Why should we care about farm animals?" by noting that farm animals, like human beings, are capable of feeling pain. Moral consideration for animals is a simple extension of our general moral duty to minimize the existence of suffering, insofar as it comes within our power to do so.

The alternative way to think about extending moral consideration to animals is to understand each individual animal as a being worthy of respect. Perhaps the best way to approach the second alternative is to see how the first strategy, focusing on pain and suffering, does not seem to place much value on the animals themselves. It does not, for example, appear to provide reasons for regarding the death of an animal as a form of harm, at least not when death is achieved with no suffering. Furthermore, it invites us to add up the benefits and costs, the pleasure and pain, experienced by many individuals and to evaluate our actions in terms of their aggregate effects. This procedure might justify great harms to a few individuals in light of small benefits to the many. Advocates of ethical vegetarianism are particularly sensitive to these points since together they provide a way to justify human consumption of meat. If animals are slaughtered humanely, then the pleasure and nutritional benefits of a meat diet for humans may outweigh the sacrifice of animal lives.

The alternative strategy is to argue that individual animals are entitled to the same kind of respect that we extend to individual human beings. This alternative is an extension of the general moral duty to treat others with respect; it demands that we balance the interests of individual nonhuman animals with those of ourselves and other humans to whom we owe respect. Duties of respect for others are expressed in the concept of moral rights. It is obvious that farm animals would not be entitled to all of the rights of human beings, but it is plausible to think that they, like humans, also act in pursuit of their own chosen interests. If so, perhaps animals are worthy of moral respect, too.

Chapter 3 introduced libertarianism, egalitarianism, and utilitarianism and the corresponding ideas of noninterference rights, opportunity rights, and welfare. The two paths for thinking through the basis of expressing moral concern link up with the social contract tradition in the contrast between rights and welfare. These concepts have been extremely important in the evolution of the animal welfare/animal rights movement and in the ethical judgments that have served as its foundation. Philosophers pondered the differences and similarities between animals and humans long before rights-based philosophies (such as libertarianism or egalitarianism) and welfare-based philosophies (such as utilitarianism) were formulated, but they seldom did so with the aim of extending moral consideration to animals. Greek and medieval thinkers often attempted to establish a natural hierarchy based upon the respective capacities of nonliving things, plants, nonhuman animals, humans, and perhaps God. These hierarchies also included finer-grained distinctions that postulated a "natural superiority" of races, of economic classes, and of gender. The hierarchy specified rights and privileges. Humans had certain privileges and responsibilities with respect to the use of animals, just as a king had privileges and responsibilities with respect to common folk.

Libertarian, egalitarian, and utilitarian philosophies emerged during an historical period in which these allegedly natural hierarchies were being subjected to a period of intense criticism and rejection. Animals often were discussed in criticisms of the old world view, although such discussion took different forms. The French philosopher René Descartes rejected the idea of a natural hierarchy, a great chain of being, in his more scientific approach to nature, but he accepted the notion of a sharp and insurmountable philosophical distinction between human beings and other animals. Humans, he thought, were rational; they possessed a thinking subjectivity, a mind. Animals, in Descartes's assessment, did not. The German philosopher Immanuel Kant developed one of the most penetrating analyses of ethical duty, one that rejected the intrinsic importance of socioeconomic class. Like Descartes, Kant did not think that animals could be members of the moral community. Animals, he claimed, lacked the requisite moral concepts. The English philosopher Jeremy Bentham, however, concluded that an animal's capacity to feel pleasure or pain was enough justification to include all sentient creatures in the calculation of benefits and harms.

The long history of philosophizing about animals has provided the contemporary political debate over the status of animals with a rich and often contradictory record of attitudes toward human duties to animals. Until quite recently, however, few of those who took the trouble to express judgments on the status of animals were primarily interested in the question of how animals should in fact be treated by humans. The reflections of Descartes, Kant, and Bentham, as well as of many others, arose in the context of an attempt to specify what it is about human beings that entitles them to consideration by their fellow humans. These writings appeared in a political context in which the idea that God had bestowed a special status on kings, noblemen, priests, or Europeans was losing its force. The search for an alternative, more defensible statement of the scope and potency of moral claims led them to consider whether and why nonhuman animals could be part of the social contract.

Utilitarian Philosophy and the Measurement of Welfare

Few people today would think, as Descartes did, that animals have no feelings, that they are machines, but no one doubts that animals experience their world very differently from humans. This fact creates a measurement problem for those interested in applying the first strategy to assessment of animal welfare. Bentham's solution to the measurement problem was to rely on hedonism, that is, to equate benefit with the experience of pleasure (or satisfaction) and harm with the experience of pain (or want). Bentham had reason to think that pleasure and pain had a physiological basis; they were mental experiences with material origin. Bentham was confident that animals felt pain, and given his views on suffering, this fact entitled them to moral consideration. John Stuart Mill modified Bentham's hedonism to account for the more refined and long-term sorts of satisfaction that can be experienced by human beings. The recognition of higher forms of satisfaction allowed Mill to count some aspects of personal fulfillment and respect for rights as moral goods. But they were counted as moral goods not because it was "natural" for people (perhaps only people of the upper classes) to obtain them, but simply because, like a full belly and the absence of pain, they represented forms of satisfaction. Although Mill's views allowed him to weigh the well-being of humans more highly than that of animals, they still left him with an obligation to balance whatever benefit an action may have for humans against the harm it may cause other sentient creatures.

In our own time, Peter Singer (10) and Michael W. Fox (1) have applied utilitarian reasoning to the assessment of animal agriculture. The argument they present consists of the assertions that (i) certain contemporary farming methods cause suffering and (ii) this suffering ought to be taken into consideration at all levels of decision: when a producer chooses an animal production technique, when a consumer purchases an animal product, and when a regulatory policy for farm animals is formulated. In each case, any suffering experienced by the animals is to be weighed against any benefits of the production system in question, including any dietary and sensory benefits that humans derive from using the animal products generated.

Utilitarian philosophers have often thought that their approach was appropriate both for public policy and for personal choice. Utilitarians define their view using three assumptions: (i) they assume universality: the experiences of all parties who are affected by the act count; (ii) the decision rule calls for maximizing utility (act to produce the best consequences for the greatest number of people); and (iii) the axiology is determined by whether an affected party is made more or less satisfied with its situation (pain or deprivation is bad, pleasure or absence of pain is good).

The evaluation of a farming practice would be somewhat as follows. First, assess the benefits of the farming practice, including the food produced for consumers and income for farmers. Next, assess the harm, including animals' suffering. Compare this assessment with similarly constructed assessments for alternative possibilities. Choose the option that is expected to produce the greatest total benefit. In this approach, the benefits to food consumers must be weighed against any harms to the animals. If there are alternatives that produce somewhat comparable benefits while producing lesser harms, they are clearly preferable from an ethical point of view.

In Singer's calculation, these benefits are far outweighed by the suffering that farm animals experience while residing in intensive agricultural systems. He thus concludes that consumers are obliged to become vegetarians. In his view, this is not because it is wrong to eat meat, but because our system of animal production makes it impossible to bring meat to the table without first subjecting the animals to unacceptable distress and pain. Of course, a less drastic estimate of the effect of the production systems in question on the well-being of the animals might lead one to seek reforms or to boycott certain products, but not necessarily to become a vegetarian. If, for example, one felt that veal or egg production was unnecessarily cruel, but that beef or milk production was not, one would act only against those practices that involve an excess of negative consequences.

The common sense contained in this approach loses some of its appeal when one actually attempts to assess the consequences of a farming practice for the animals that are being raised under it. Do animals experience pain and deprivation in exactly the same way humans do? Do they, for example, experience friendship or the loss of affection? Do they anticipate death? Do animals have intentions that can be fulfilled or frustrated? Any attempt to answer these question takes one immediately into questions of animal awareness and raises philosophical issues beyond our present scope. Some of the complexities of utilitarian reasoning can be seen in Singer's argument for vegetarianism, however.

First, note that a change in the circumstances of animal production could lead to a change in the moral justification for vegetarianism. If he became convinced that production practices had been modified and were no longer cruel, Singer would have no reason to abstain from eating meat. To the extent that a meat diet contributes to human health and happiness, one would have good reason to reject vegetarianism. As such, Singer's vegetarianism is a means to the end of reducing animal suffering rather than an end in itself. If animals can be raised humanely and slaughtered painlessly (as some animal scientists claim), there can be no utilitarian objection to using them for food. Eating flesh is not itself wrong, but refusing to eat flesh is, on Singer's view, a morally required form of protest against cruelty.

Second, if we are to be thorough utilitarians, we should ask whether or not our act of protest can be expected to achieve its intended consequences (e.g., reducing animal suffering). Singer admits that personal vegetarianism is ethically required only to the extent that it can be expected to reduce the suffering of farm animals (10). Tom Regan (6), an animal rights advocate, thinks it doubtful that Singer's individual choice to boycott meat will have much effect on animal producers and hence on the well-being of farm animals. Vegetarianism will become an effective means of change only if a large number of people join the protest; but then it would not matter if one person decided to sneak a steak now and then. One individual's decision to eat meat or not is ineffective in improving the well-being of farm animals, whatever choice is made. As such, animal welfare advocates face the **assurance problem**, a version of the prisoner's dilemma in which the consequence they hope to bring about cannot occur unless they can be assured that others will act in the same way. Even those who want to end animal suffering will be tempted to take a free ride on the compliance of others since sneaking an occasional steak does not cause harm.

Animal Interests and Animal Rights

As already noted, one of the main motivations for developing an animal rights philosophy has been a philosophical dissatisfaction with utilitarianism among those who advocate vegetarianism and reform of animal agriculture. Most people who have become vegetarians for ethical reasons think that it is always wrong to eat animal flesh and that the immorality of meat eating does not depend upon linking it to a reduction of suffering among farm animals. They do not think that the moral basis for vegetarianism hangs upon social cooperation. They think that killing an animal and eating it is wrong, period. The wrongness of the act is expressed in saying that it violates animals' fundamental rights. No amount of human benefit can compensate the violation of rights.

But why would we say that animals have rights? The working concept of rights that has been developed throughout this book does not provide a good answer to this question. Social contract theory suggests that rights are based upon hypothetical promises that people make to one another, in a state of nature or the original position, but the hypothetical character of these promises means that they may be interpreted in different ways. One way is to think that social contract theory is a way of more rigorously and objectively specifying rules of conduct on the basis of empathy for others or a way of systematically trying to understand what it is like to be in someone else's shoes. Those who believe that farm animals too have rights also may be basing their judgment on empathy. Their thinking may be somewhat like Rawls's original position (discussed in Chapter 3): What if I had been born into this world as a cow or a pig instead of a human being? How would I like to be treated? But social contract theory attains its rigor by asking us to imagine ourselves as real human beings about to become citizens in a state and by taking a tough-minded view of the considerations that would motivate someone to accept social constraints. In order to reason effectively about justice in this position, we must use what we know about human nature. Contract theory assumes that people are more reliably motivated by self-interest than by empathy.

Self-interest bears upon the social contract because accepting the contract is shown to be in everyone's self-interest. People who did not pledge to share the laws and respect the rights of others might be free to pursue their interests in brutal and vicious ways, but they also would be vulnerable to the vicious and brutal acts of others. One way to express this fact is to say that human beings have relatively few natural advantages over one another. The ability to exploit advantages owing to cleverness, industry, wisdom, beauty, or even physical strength depends upon social cooperation. Even the strongest person must sleep and while sleeping would be vulnerable (in a truly lawless society) to attack by the weak. People would be motivated to accept a social contract because the relatively equal distribution of natural abilities among human beings means that everyone is at risk in a state of nature. This is a purely self-interested motivation; it does not depend upon empathy or altruism.

The self-interest argument breaks down, however, when one attempts to apply it to animals. Someone who was not already inclined to extend rights to farm animals would not be motivated to do so by the self-interest considerations of social contract theory. While a selfish person would truly be at risk from attack by weaker humans in a state of nature, it is not plausible to argue that only law and the social order can protect us from attacks by sheep, pigs, and goats. Contract theory seems ill suited to the kind of imaginative thought experiment that would allow us to attribute contractual rights to nonhuman animals.

An answer to the question of why anyone would think that animals have rights requires philosophical concepts that have not figured prominently in other chapters of this book. We must think of rights in nonpolitical terms, and we must determine whether nonhuman animals also possess the characteristics that entitle humans to moral rights. The attempt to specify the basis of rights in metaphysical rather than contractual terms often turns to the capacity for rational thought. Why should we respect the rights of other people? The metaphysical answer (as distinct from the contractual answer) is that to deny their rights is to repress their capacity to make rational choices based upon their own ends and goals. Since rationality is thought to be a crucial component of what it means to be human, to deny someone the capacity to make rational choices is to deny that person's humanity. To deny others the opportunity to choose their own goals is to repress their capacity for realization and actualization of their most essential being.

The capacity for rational thought, in turn, is often linked to the capacity for language. How do people adopt goals and interests? How do they intentionally seek ends that serve their interests? Perhaps their ability to do this depends upon the ability to represent the world abstractly or to make claims that are meaningful to other people. Perhaps the very idea of seeking an end requires the capacity to have an image of some situation in mind. Can this image be formed without concepts? Can there be concepts without language? Perhaps the very idea of natural interests requires a capacity to make a public claim that will be understood (even when it is not respected) by others. Perhaps, in other words, rationality implies the ability to use language. What does this entail for animal rights?

Some would argue that animals have language, and this argument, like the analysis of animal suffering, brings us quickly to questions about animal awareness and intentions. Others, such as Tom Regan (7) have argued that the emphasis upon language is misleading. Not all humans are rational, nor do all humans use language. Regan concludes from this that the rationality condition cannot be the basis for thinking that human beings have rights. Regan thinks it is better to understand human rights in terms of the fact that all humans are the **subject of a life**. Essentially, a man is individuated by the fact of what happens to him; a woman has the life that she has because the experiences that make it up are hers. The internal experience of personal identity is called *subjectivity*. The word *subject* denotes the unity in mental life that has also been referred to as the *psyche* or the *soul*. Subjectivity is shared by all persons, while rationality and language are not. The basis for claiming rights, then, on Regan's view, must consist in being the subject of a life.

However, once subjectivity has been identified as the criterion for possession of rights, Regan thinks that the rationale for extending moral consideration to animals is simple, just as it is for utilitarian philosophy. As the utilitarian finds it reasonable to think that nonhuman animals suffer pain and satisfaction (just as humans do), Regan finds it reasonable to think that animals are subjects of a life, just as humans are. The extension is conceptually simple, but this time it entails a large package of obligations to respect each individual animal rather than the utilitarian's narrow duty to include animal suffering in the calculation of utility. Furthermore, these are obligations owed by one individual to another, so cooperative schemes have no impact upon the relation of rights and duties. Regan's view requires vegetarianism; it would put an immediate end to any form of animal agriculture that required interference with an animal's self-determination. Some animals, such as laying hens and dairy cattle, might be willing to cooperate with humans in a way that would permit us to use their unfertilized eggs and milk, but for the most part, humans' encounter with farm animals would come to an end.

The philosophical basis for the claim that animals have rights thus differs from that of noninterference or opportunity rights. Claims for animal rights use arguments appealing to philosophical assumptions about subjectivity and rationality, while political rights are defended using social contract arguments that do not require us to define what it means to be the subject of a life. Like all rights theorists, however, advocates of animal rights will be far more concerned with the structure of public policy than with the balance of costs and benefits. As such, there is a basis for disagreement about the relative importance of structure and performance even within groups active on behalf of animals. Utilitarians such as Peter Singer are most concerned with overall welfare, including that of animals, while activists such as Tom Regan want policies that protect animal rights and are not willing to allow the consequences to humans to override the claims of animals unless those consequences are severe enough to violate human rights.

CASE

The Humane Farming Initiative

The Humane Farming Initiative was a Massachusetts state referendum that went before voters in 1988. The referendum proposal was written by an activist group called the Coalition to End Animal Suffering and Exploitation (CEASE). The initiative included provisions prohibiting the suffocation or grinding of baby chicks and requiring veal producers to provide calves with larger space requirements, more bedding, and more food, as well as more general requirements to minimize the pain from castration and dehorning of livestock. The initiative also directed the Massachusetts Commissioner of Agriculture to study further regulations in six areas, including humane transport, healthful diets, and scientific advisory reviews and comments on new farm housing costing more than $10,000 (9). CEASE collected signatures and got the initiative placed on the ballot for the 1988 general election after members of the group became frustrated with the Massachusetts Society for the Prevention of Cruelty to Animals' (MSPCA) attempts to move animal welfare legislation through normal channels.

Key Actors and Affected Parties

CEASE, the group proposing the initiative, is obviously a key actor in the issue. The main group opposing the initiative was the Massachusetts Farm Bureau, a state organization affiliated with the American Farm Bureau Federation (AFBF). The AFBF is a conservative organization that represents the divergent interests of producers engaged in all forms of agriculture. The AFBF also provides a number of services to its members, including farm and home insurance. Farm Bureau opposition to the initiative was based on the view that existing legislation adequately protected farm animals and that new regulations and studies would impose needless costs on farmers.

CEASE is most actively associated with an animal rights view; the MSPCA is associated with an animal welfare view; and the AFBF is associated with a traditional utilitarian view that does not include impacts upon animals in its axiology. In this case and others like it, the most radical reform groups are typically affiliated with an animal rights view, while both producer groups and moderate groups are affiliated with a utilitarian view. The agreement of philosophies has made compromise between moderate and producer groups an attractive option since both their philosophy and their political objectives are reasonably close. Producer groups have not always availed themselves of such compromise, however. Though they understand that animal welfare groups support more moderate reform, producers have generally failed to understand the ethical arguments behind their views and have been unable to engage in dialogue with moderate groups.

Other actors who might have played roles in Massachusetts were apparently on the sidelines. Representatives of the animal science community throughout the state and from the U.S. Department of Agriculture expressed doubt about the scientific basis for intervention on behalf of animals. The MSPCA expressed concern that the referendum process was an inappropriate vehicle for advancing the interests of animals. No one in these groups took a strong stand either for or against the initiative. Perhaps because these groups failed to speak decisively, the press argued for the status quo, taking a dim view of the initiative.

Three important affected parties can be identified. First, of course, there were the animals whose interests were represented by CEASE and MSPCA. Second, there were the farmers whose interests were represented by the Farm Bureau. Finally, there were consumers, whose interests were represented by themselves. Consumers, who are also voters, controlled the referendum process and were in a position to make their own interests decisive. Consumers are also actors, but in a somewhat indirect sense. As consumers, the general public could expect to pay more for food if the referendum passed, particularly if the six additional areas of consideration had resulted in additional regulations. As taxpayers, the general public could expect to pay enforcement and research costs of the initiative, but there is no evidence that these costs figured prominently when the voting public defeated the initiative. According to Shurland (9), altruistic concerns were more prominent in voters' minds. Consumers appeared to vote according to how they weighed the impact of the initiative on the other two affected parties. It is the consequences for animals and producers that are emphasized in performance assessment.

Assessing Performance

The Farm Bureau was quite successful in convincing the public that the initiative's effects upon farmers would be devastating. Referring to the initiative as the Anti-Family Farm Bill, the Farm Bureau created broad-based opposition to the initiative among producers. The press also picked up the "Save the Family Farm" theme, and urban voters joined farmers' opposition. Early polls had shown 55 percent of Massachusetts voters in favor of the initiative, but the final result was 71 percent against. Urban voters apparently concluded that small-scale producers (of whom Massachusetts has many) would be harmed by the initiative. This conclusion, coupled with a broad faith in the morality of family farmers, supported a vote in favor of the status quo.

CEASE countered this utilitarian argument somewhat unsuccessfully by noting that the initiative exempted small-scale producers from its more costly provisions. Although it is difficult to assess how animal welfare regulations would affect farmers, it is useful to gain some grasp of the size and structure of the animal agriculture industry. Here we will discuss national data rather than focusing upon the somewhat uncharacteristic Massachusetts industry. First, it is important to recognize that animal welfare regulations affect all components of the animal products industry, at least up to the point of slaughter. Animal products represent about 5 percent of the total value of manufactured goods in the United States, based on 1987 data. This figure includes value added by farms and ranches, as well as processors, transporters, and packing plants, but does not include wholesale and retail markups made at grocery stores and butcher shops. Figure 7–1 compares animal products industries to four other industries in the United States. The point here is simply to note both that animal products industries are comparable to other politically powerful interests in size and that large amounts of money are at stake. The comparison to tobacco is important because tobacco producers and merchandisers have been very successful at promoting their interests through public policy. The animal products industry is four times larger.

It is also important to understand how animal producers' interests are structured. Here it is useful to contrast the beef and poultry industries. Beef production in the United States is broadly diversified, with approximately 85 percent of cattle produced in cow-calf operations. The cow-calf method involves keeping a herd on range or pasture throughout the year and selling

Figure 7–1   Value of Shipments, 1987

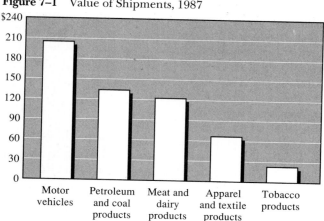

Source: *Statistical Abstract of the United States*

portions of the herd at intervals. Cow-calf farms and ranches vary tremendously in size. On some farms, the cow-calf operation works more like a savings account than a production operation, so that cattle are sold when the farm needs cash. Other farms and ranches are more closely managed to ensure maximum profit. Most cattle from cow-calf operations are "finished" for a few days or weeks in feedlots before being brought to slaughter. A much smaller amount of U.S. cattle production uses the feeder system throughout the animal's life cycle. Cattle producers thus include relatively wealthy and well-capitalized operations, as well as many small family farms. Small-scale cow-calf operations also are operated by many part-time and hobby farmers, some of whom produce not for profit but for pleasure. All of these producers sell into a national market. Their operations and interests are so diverse that they exert little power over prices, and many cattle producers operate close to the margin of economic viability.

Poultry production, by contrast, is controlled by a relatively small number of vertically integrated firms that hatch, raise, slaughter, and market the birds. Companies such as Tyson, Perdue, and Holly Farms either own or contract the entire process that brings the brand name product to grocery meat cases. They keep close watch over supplies, and the relatively short time needed to raise a bird (four to six weeks, compared to an average of eighteen months for cattle) allows them to adjust production to maintain price levels. This is not to say that the poultry industry is uncompetitive: competition among the large poultry firms is so intense that poultry producers are under more pressure to maximize production efficiency than are many cattle producers. In the poultry industry, the farmers who actually raise the birds are either employees of the large firms or, more likely, operating under contract to a large firm that both guarantees the price and specifies the production process down to the last detail. Many of these contract farms consist of a few poultry houses built on farms that had been too small to be profitable for crop production. Families have borrowed the capital to build the confinement systems used in poultry production and are quite dependent upon the contracts that they hold with major poultry firms.

Massachusetts is a state with both an unusually large number of small-scale producers and an unusually large number of nonfarm people living in rural areas. Massachusetts voters may have been more willing to reject the CEASE initiative than would voters in states where people see little of agriculture or where they associate farming with large-scale enterprises. Massachusetts voters concluded that small farms would bear many of the costs of complying with the initiative. Compliance costs would most likely be borne by producers in diversified industries (like that of cattle, although beef cattle production was not targeted by CEASE) where a large variety of production methods exist. Some producers would undoubtedly find it easier to comply with new regulations than others, meaning that only a fraction of the increased costs are likely to be passed on to consumers. Highly organized and integrated industries (like poultry) are probably more likely to respond to regulations with an industrywide pattern of compliance, and the big companies' control over prices would allow them to pass on the costs either to consumers or to the contract farmers who supply them. Costs will not be transferred to consumers in any case where producers across state or national boundaries are free to market noncomplying products along with those of regulated producers. It thus appears that utilitarian arguments were foremost in the minds of voters.

Arguments For and Against the Initiative

While it is important to think through the human impact of policies such as the CEASE initiative, the point of such policy proposals is to extend protection to the interests of farm animals themselves. In its current form, public law gives humans the right to choose from among a broad range of potential production conditions for farm animals, though the need to earn a profit narrows the range considerably in industries such as poultry. Laws that would extend legal protection to farm animals might be justified because there are important nonhuman interests to be protected (a rights argument) or because the benefits to nonhuman animals would in some sense outweigh the costs to human producers and consumers (a utilitarian argument). Either argument might be used to defend the legal rights—constraints upon the acts of others—of nonhuman animals. The ethical components of animal welfare policies depend upon whether ethical rights (human or nonhuman) are violated by existing and proposed structures of legal rights and upon whether the performance of a policy is consistent with utilitarian decision rules. Determining the ethical components of animal welfare depends upon many other philosophically contentious issues, however.

CEASE members may have supported the initiative because they felt that farms animals have moral rights that should be legally protected, without regard to the impact on humans. Conversely, they may have felt (like Bentham) that the notion of moral or natural rights was far less important than suffering, and they may have supported the initiative because they felt that animal suffering outweighed human benefits. Those who opposed the initiative may have done so out of a philosophical rejection of animal rights, or they may have done so because they felt that CEASE had overstated the amount of suffering endured by farm animals, particularly in comparison to the human suffering that would be endured as farmers and food purchasers tried to adjust to new regulatory requirements. Most philosophers who have written on the issue of animal welfare/animal rights have offered arguments that would be used to support one of these judgments. The animal welfare/animal rights debate gets its name from the philosophical difference between the two types of reasoning that can be brought to bear on determining the moral status of animals; but note that either form of reasoning might support arguments for legal rights for animals, as in the Massachusetts initiative. Similarly, either form of reasoning might deny legal rights to animals.

While the philosophical debate between animal rights activists such as Tom Regan and animal welfare proponents such as Peter Singer may have given the issue its name, it now seems that the terms are used differently. Animal rights activists are often thought of as advocates of radical change. They, like CEASE, see the current situation as lacking morality and in dire need of sweeping reform. Animal welfare activists, by contrast, are thought of as advocates of evolutionary reform. They are, like the Massachusetts Society for the Protection of Animals, anxious to work within the system to improve conditions for animals while at the same time respecting the legitimacy of existing interests. Used in this way, the distinction between animal welfare and animal rights has less to do with the philosophies of welfare and rights than it does with the strategies and goals of the respective groups. Any fit between the philosophical welfare/rights distinction and the political welfare/rights distinction is therefore loose.

Holding the rights view does not necessitate advocacy of radical reform. One might, for example, think that animals have a right to live under conditions that allow them to fulfill their biological functions, and these functions might require exercise, sunlight, or socialization (in the case of herd animals). Such a right need not presuppose a right protecting the animals from slaughter. Holding an animal rights view need not entail ethical vegetarianism. Similarly, a utilitarian who thought that animals were harmed by practices commonly considered humane might make an assessment of the consequences that produced an argument for radical reform. Welfare and rights views cannot be identified simply by whether they promote moderate or radical reform.

Learning from the Humane Farming Initiative

The Massachusetts initiative was resoundingly defeated at the polls, but it continues to provide a focal point for discussing the issues of animal welfare and animal rights. Public referenda often allow a full airing of the philosophical reasons for choosing one policy rather than another, but they also provoke confusing and contradictory claims about the likely consequences of an initiative. It is sometimes the group that can proclaim its particular view of the facts most loudly that wins. This raises the secondary ethical question of whether voter referenda are the best way to make policy with respect to farm animals. The MSPCA clearly thought CEASE's action inappropriate.

The Massachusetts initiative also gives us an opportunity to reflect on the importance of facts. To what extent are questions of animal suffering under confinement conditions matters of fact? Are there true and false claims to be made about animal suffering, and if so, will science or common sense provide the test of truth? Perhaps questions of animal suffering are only answered by value judgments, but if so, what philosophical arguments bear on these judgments? Rights theory is capable of deciding policy on purely hypothetical or a priori grounds. Does this give the rights approach an advantage in evaluating policies that govern our use and treatment of farm animals? This list of difficult questions concludes the chapter but points the way toward continuing discussion and debate.

Summary

Throughout history, humans have used animals for food; for coproducts such as work, companionship, fiber, and leather goods; and for moderating the effects of ecological or economic fluctuations in protein and business cycles. The existing structure defines animals as property that can be bought and sold. Markets for animals and animal products therefore determine the incentives for engaging in animal production. Proposals to change public policy for animal agriculture focus on constraints on human use that are designed to extend consideration to the animals themselves. Two strategies for extending such consideration are widely discussed, one that emphasizes performance in the form of animal suffering or welfare and another that emphasizes structure by establishing the claim that animals should enjoy certain rights.

The two strategies for supporting policy change are reflected at a philosophical level in terms of utilitarian arguments that stress welfare and rights arguments that stress respect for animals' vital interests. Utilitarians such as Peter Singer argue that animals experience satisfaction, suffering, or pain in ways that also are experienced by humans. Since utilitarians would include the satisfaction, suffering, and pain of humans in their analysis of an issue, they should also include such consequences as experienced by nonhuman animals. Rights theorists such as Tom Regan find utilitarian analysis inadequate because in their view it does not adequately protect the interests of individual animals, particularly when aggregate gains outweigh the costs to specific individuals. Instead, they rely on a tradition of moral rights, which protects the vital interests of all beings that can be understood as the subjects of a life. This notion of rights differs from contractual rights. It is difficult to extend contractual notions of right to animals.

The attempt to get Massachusetts voters to pass an initiative that would have restricted farmer's use of animals is a case study of changes that animal activists would like to make in animal agriculture. Groups advocating radical reform were labeled as animal rights activists, while those advocating moderate reform were labeled as pressing for animal welfare. There is, however, little correspondence between these labels and the philosophical views indicated by the terms *welfare* and *rights*. Farm groups demonstrated little ability to communicate or negotiate with either group. The likely performance of the law was a key component in the political debate prior to the referendum. In that debate, impacts upon humans (small farmers) were pitted against impacts upon farm animals. Advocates of the initiative were not successful in framing the issue as one of animal rights that must be respected, whatever

the Reagan administration's original view of the Ethiopian government was not unfounded. The media attention to the famine probably influenced the regime in Addis Ababa to be more cooperative with the international relief effort than it might have been. To the extent that world attention did moderate policies in Ethiopia, the change in U.S. policy may have been as much a response to an improvement in the prospects for effective humanitarian assistance as to the growing public outcry. In any case, once the issue became sharply defined in terms of saving lives and relieving misery, any support that might have existed for withholding aid from Ethiopia evaporated.

While few people object to giving emergency assistance, particularly in the face of dramatic photographs of the victims of hunger, longer-term solutions to the problem of hunger are more difficult. Despite the common sense behind the idea of teaching others to fish, the U.S. government has always found it difficult to make long-term commitments to development assistance. While many people see development assistance as a responsibility of justice, many others see it as a purely voluntary or discretionary activity. Some individuals view development assistance as a luxury—something to do when times are good, but see it as a policy that must be curtailed when budgets are tight and the needs at home are too great. For this reason, development assistance generates ethical controversy over when and why government should promote this policy. Both emergency and development assistance must be ethically evaluated in terms of their impact upon affected parties. How are policies that are intended to influence another country's policies to be evaluated ethically? Are U.S. policy makers justified in trying to help those who are not U.S. citizens or residents? How do alternative views of justice affect our evaluation of aid? The sections that follow present two cases where these questions can be raised and the interests of various parties to the policy decision examined.

CASE 1

The African Desert Locust

The African desert locust (*Schistocera gregaria*) has been a menace to agriculture since biblical times. The situation that underlies attempts to counter this pest include facts about the locust's biology. Locusts differ from ordinary grasshoppers in that they can form swarms that number in the billions and have a density of between 20 and 150 million individuals per square kilometer. The natural causes that contribute to swarming are not fully understood. Desert locusts exist as individual insects or in low-density swarms across North Africa and into the Middle East. The swarms that attracted the attention of biblical authors are sporadic and can extend far beyond the desert locust's normal territory. In 1988, a swarm apparently made it across the Atlantic Ocean and was sighted in the Caribbean. When swarms reach this huge size, they are referred to as an *outbreak*, or a *plague*. One source describes a plague of locusts that descended upon Somalia in 1958 containing 40 billion insects and capable of eating 80,000 tons of food in one day—enough to feed 400,000 people for a year (5).

Although the consequences of a desert locust outbreak can be catastrophic for farmers who are unlucky enough to have the swarm attack their fields, desert locust outbreaks have been infrequent in recent decades. Until 1986, the desert locust had been in recession throughout most of its range since 1963. Africans were not prepared to control an outbreak of locusts following this long period of recession. When locust and grasshopper populations began to build in 1985–86, regional pest control organizations required massive donations of pesticide, application technology, emergency assistance, and technical expertise. In 1986 these organizations received an estimated $39 million for locust control, including $9 million from the United States. An additional $15 million of U.S. funds was pledged for control in 1987 and 1988. This money was spent almost exclusively on pesticides to kill the locusts in areas where population densities were building and machines and personnel were available to apply these pesticides (5).

Once it was established that locusts were building to plague levels in 1986, the problem identification stage of the policy process was effectively over and key actors launched into policy formulation. A series of decisions were made about what to do. Generally, these decisions presumed that action was needed to avert or at least mitigate the effects of a plague on crop production and hence food availability for the people of Africa. Similar decisions to request and then apply pesticides were made by many regional organizations in Africa. These decisions were not made by individual producers but by official agencies whose goal was to destroy high-intensity locust populations before they had an opportunity to move from one field to another. Decision making by regional organizations was coordinated by the Food and Agriculture Organization (FAO) of the United Nations. FAO has a staff that monitors pest populations in Africa, coordinates the contributions of other donors, and provides technical assistance for those in regional and national organizations that actually conduct pest control operations. FAO's management responsibility is not, however, highly formalized. For the most part, regional organizations for locust control are based upon a series of bilateral and multilateral agreements among the governments of specific African nations. FAO interacts with these organizations by sharing information and supplying resources but does not have administrative authority over their actions. Despite the lack of statutory or administrative formalization of decision making, coordination by FAO is generally quite effective. Even if they were inclined to take a different path, regional organizations would have little ability to finance operations that varied substantially from the wishes of FAO and the donor community.

Just as the relation between FAO and the regional organizations is not highly formalized, relations between donor organizations and the FAO are based more on informal rules and contacts than upon explicit policies and statutes. Officials at each organization have expectations of how the others will and should behave. They bring an inclination to cooperate with one another in pursuit of shared goals but maintain control over their share of the funds in order to retain their influence on policies.

Additional decisions are made by officers of donor organizations such as the United States Agency for International Development (USAID). USAID is an agency of the U. S. government that supervises a number of development and emergency assistance operations around the world. It has a limited annual budget for this work. When USAID officials decided to allocate funds for chemicals and technology to control desert locusts, they were in effect also deciding not to fund other worthwhile assistance efforts. From the perspective of USAID officials, then, the decision to help pay for the control of the desert locust outbreak must be justified by the judgment that this activity is not only worthwhile, but that it is the most important use of limited aid funds.

Ultimately, the decisions made by USAID officials can be traced back to decisions made by the U.S. Congress and even the President of the United States. Congress makes three kinds of decision. First, it passes authorizing legislation that creates an agency such as USAID and specifies its broad goals and purposes. Second, it makes appropriation decisions as to how much money USAID can spend in any given year. Third, it makes decisions regarding oversight of USAID's activities by requesting information and conducting hearings to ensure that the agency is acting in a manner consistent with the intent of Congress and the national interest. The President is involved in that the top leadership of USAID consists of presidential appointees. These leaders act in the name of the President and generally try to make case-by-case decisions that are consistent with the President's general political views. In extreme cases, the President may even become personally involved in a decision.

In addition to the decision makers themselves, many people are affected by the sequence of decisions that results in an operation to suppress a locust outbreak. The people most obviously affected by the use of pesticides to subdue the locust plague are the small farmers of rural Africa. About 70 percent of Africans live on small farms, often less than an acre. Although patterns differ widely, it is common for women to oversee most of the farming, while men are employed (or otherwise involved) away from the home. Most of the staple food that African families eat is produced on these small plots, though their basic diet of wheat or maize may be complemented by meats, vegetables, and other condiments (including insects) that are purchased or foraged from the countryside. This pattern of life is the basis for two broad categories of impact upon the people of the African countryside.

First, it is these people who are most vulnerable to the locust plague itself. A swarm descending upon the fields of poor subsistence farmers could wipe out a year's harvest. Experts on African agriculture compare the damage done by a swarm of desert locusts to that of a tornado or flood. Selected individuals can be wiped out entirely, and if they do not receive help from friends, neighbors, or government, they will die of starvation and disease.

Preventing the famine brought on by the locust plague is one of the main justifications for a decision to use pesticides. If plagues can be stopped, then the small African farmers are among the primary beneficiaries of doing so.

There are secondary impacts upon small farmers that are not positive, however. People of the African countryside may be exposed to the chemicals used for pest control. Even when applied in recommended doses, pesticide residues can contaminate food webs and create health problems for humans. Some of the pesticides that are reportedly used for locust control in Africa are not approved for similar uses in the United States. Reports from the field in 1987 and 1988 indicated that persistent organochlorine compounds such as BHC, dieldrin, and lindane were being used against the desert locust. These chemicals retain their toxic properties for many years and pose health risks to humans and other animals that come in contact with them. Though banned for use in the United States, these chemicals can be used legally in most African countries. A recent study revealed only five African countries that have any pesticide regulations at all. Dieldrin is an attractive choice for locust control because it is inexpensive to purchase, because large stocks of dieldrin have existed in some parts of Africa since the 1960s, and because its persistence in the environment means that it remains effective long after its initial application. USAID enforces EPA regulations for pest control programs paid for with U.S. funds. This policy has resulted in a substitution of less toxic (but more expensive) pesticides such as fenitrothion and malathion.

Some of the effects of chemical pesticides are subtle and long-lasting. In addition to killing locusts, pesticides being used in Africa kill a broad spectrum of beneficial insects that help pollinate crops and feed upon a wide array of pests. When beneficial insects are killed, yields are adversely affected. What is more, widespread use of chemical control (such as that conducted in Africa from 1986 to 1989) can help pest insects such as locusts develop resistance to the control agent. When beneficial insects are lost and pests develop resistance, farmers are far more vulnerable to future catastrophic crop losses than if no chemical intervention had occurred. What is more, use of chemical pesticides has a broad range of effects upon wildlife populations that are used for food and that contribute to the basic ecology of Africa. Not surprisingly, some scientists express considerable uncertainty about the long-range impact of desert locust control on African ecology (5).

Health and environmental effects are normal costs associated with the proper and recommended use of chemical pesticides. Risks from normal use can be multiplied several times over when chemicals are mismanaged and misapplied. The extent of misapplication in Africa is not known with certainty, but experts estimate that the problem is serious. Pesticides may be used by technicians lacking adequate training in their use and unable to read the protocol or warnings supplied with them. The general lack of regulatory apparatus for pesticides in Africa allows mistakes to occur undetected and intentional violations to go unpunished. Furthermore, the density of the rural population in Africa means that humans may be more readily exposed to aerial sprays, and the human consumption of insects may mean that pesticide residues are introduced into human diets at levels that far exceed those of the developed world.

Others besides small farmers are affected by locust control. People in African cities need food, too, and the preservation of African crops helps ensure a constant and inexpensive food supply. People in cities, too, are affected by pesticide residues and ecological impact, though less directly and perhaps less seriously. More subtle effects of locust control include economic spinoffs of the control program itself. Large-scale pest control efforts provide temporary employment for many people, not the least of whom are the chronically underfunded scientific elites of African universities, research institutes, and ministries of agriculture. The purchase of pesticides is, of course, beneficial to the Western multinational corporations that produce them. In addition, large farmers in Africa—producers of export crops such as coffee, tea, or peanuts—may be able to divert substantial amounts of the pesticides intended for use against locusts to spray on their own crops for a wide array of pests. When this happens, consumers of these products back in the developed world where the pesticides originate become the victims of pesticide contamination too. Clearly, a wide variety of people are affected, both positively and negatively, by a decision to use chemical pesticides to suppress an outbreak of desert locusts in Africa.

Structure and Performance in North Africa

If we assume that USAID will be involved in decisions about desert locust control in Africa, what should the goals of U.S. policy be? The situation includes many factors that will affect the possibility of achieving the goals, of course. The fact that northern Africa is embroiled in civil wars makes the airplanes and trucks used for locust control vulnerable to attack or capture. The fact that many African governments have their power base in the cities may make their leaders less concerned about what takes place in the countryside as long as urban food supplies are not disrupted. Recent U.S. conflicts with Libya and with the government of Ethiopia introduce further diplomatic and military considerations into the situation. These factors will become very important as decision makers select a specific policy, but they do not address the larger question: What is the U.S. government trying to accomplish by offering development assistance to North Africa?

The answer most likely to be offered by officials of USAID stresses performance objectives. Americans would like to see an end to famine and malnutrition in the region. Americans would like to help ensure that low-resource farmers and herders will be able to produce enough food and fiber to feed and clothe themselves in the future. Americans would like to see general economic growth in the nations of North Africa so that their people will not be forced to live in conditions of poverty. These goals can be defined in terms of improvements in the health and wealth of the people of North Africa. A policy that achieved these goals would produce an end state in which many people would be better off. While measurement of the benefits and costs of such a policy might prove difficult, the policy is designed and implemented from the utilitarian perspective that Peter Singer has described in his writings on hunger. Since these people are desperately poor and since American citizens are far from being asked to make comparable sacrifices, there can be little doubt that such a policy serves utilitarian goals by producing more benefit than cost.

The alternative is for development goals to be defined in terms of structure rather than performance. If we think of how libertarians and egalitarians evaluate policy in Western democracies, for example, we find that they are less concerned with whether governments bring about health and wealth for their citizens than with whether the laws and policies imposed by government guarantee civil rights. Most rights theorists believe that respect for rights also encourages better health and economic growth, but they also believe structures are not *justified* by these performance outcomes. For the rights theorist, an efficient policy would be ruled unacceptable if it entailed the violation of individual rights. Given a rights-based philosophy of government, the question in Africa should be whether the structure that is presumed by any given policy is acceptable. The question is complicated by the fact that the legal rights in place in African countries are not components of U.S. development policy.

These two definitions of development goals do not necessarily come into conflict, for a given policy may be justified by both utilitarian and rights-based criteria. They can come into conflict one way when performance evaluation looks only at aggregate outcomes or when individual rights are examined at a very localized level. In the desert locust case, decisions must be made for a region that includes several countries. Although losses from a locust swarm may be relatively localized, decision makers cannot prevent the losses once it is known which individuals will be affected. They must apply pesticides to locusts at locations that may be many miles from the site at which the most serious damage would occur. The basis for the decision cannot be the protection of individual rights; it must be promotion of the general good.

A second tension between utilitarian and rights criteria arises because the use of potent chemicals in Africa may violate rights of the people exposed to chemical sprays or residues. Decision makers who favor chemical control must not ignore the fact that their efforts expose people to risks. They must be sure that the benefits to people whose crops will be saved outweigh the risks to people exposed to pesticides. The aggregated performance outcomes must be positive; they must satisfy the Kaldor-Hicks criterion. A strict application of noninterference rights would imply that these risk exposures are unjustified under any circumstances.

Even those who take rights very seriously in evaluating public policy admit that there are emergency situations in which decisions that expose individuals to risks and harms must be made in order to avoid disaster. There are, in short, cases where rights cannot be respected. They would, however, want to be assured that the rights and interests of all affected parties are considered when policies are formulated. But do the rights and interests of farmers and herders in Africa receive adequate consideration? Are they considered when USAID officials in Washington make decisions about the conditions for using U.S. technical assistance to control locusts? Even if the rights and interests of farmers and herders are represented by African scientists who participated in the decision (which is questionable), it is hard to see how they are represented in the USAID decision to support locust control. But if they are not represented, they are probably not adequately considered. If the U.S. government is to take the rights of foreign citizens seriously, it may have to confine its assistance efforts to projects that work directly with the farmers and herders who are affected. For only then can USAID officials be sure that their aid efforts respect the rights and interests of affected parties.

Although this philosophical tension underlies many foreign assistance policies, the situation itself may be more important in determining policy in the desert locust case. If it is clear that a locust plague is imminent and that timely application of chemicals can control it, objecting to chemical control out of concern for the autonomy of the affected parties is an objection that pays lip service to their interests while allowing events to overwhelm them. On the other hand, if it is clear that natural causes will make the locust swarm subside or that chemical applications will not have much impact anyway, the chemical control effort appears to sacrifice the rights of affected parties needlessly. In either case, facts about the situation dominate philosophical differences about goals.

CASE 2

The Bumpers Amendment

In November 1985, Senator Dale Bumpers offered an amendment intended to prohibit foreign aid activities that would encourage the export of agricultural commodities from developing countries. The bill stressed the competition for world markets between potential exporters from the developing world and U.S. farmers. The amendment (No. 1129) reads in part:

> None of the funds to be appropriated to carry out chapter 1 of the Foreign Assistance Act of 1981 may be available for any testing or breeding feasibility study, variety improvement or introduction, consultancy, publication, conference, or training in connection with the growth or production in a foreign country for export if such export would compete in world markets with a similar commodity grown or produced in the United States. (9)

A similar version, which we will refer to as the Bumpers Amendment, was reintroduced in May 1986 and has become law.

The Bumpers Amendment requires USAID to suspend projects that could enable poor foreign farmers to increase commercial production of commodities (such as meat, maize, or wheat) that are exported from the United States and also of commodities (such as palm oil) that are substitutes for U.S. commodities (such as soybean oil). These restrictions also apply to U.S. contributions to the World Bank and the International Agricultural Research Centers (IARCs), famous for the "green revolution" success in strengthening the developing world's production of wheat and rice.

The Bumpers Amendment was justified by the ethical principle that provides a powerful challenge to foreign development assistance. In Bumpers's words, the act is to "prevent American tax dollars from being used to help foreign countries who are trying to take our export markets" (8). This argument for limiting foreign aid appeals to the idea of a social contract. Foreigners are not part of the contract, so it is wrong to use our resources to provide services to them. The principle states that the poor of other nations have no standing in the social contract. They are not entitled to the protection of rights and the provision of benefits that contract theories promote. As discussed in Chapter 3, social contract theories establish a government's goals and obligations by describing a hypothetical bargaining situation in which the principles of government can be negotiated; but only those in the bargaining position (the state of nature), or the original position, are in a position to negotiate. The borders of the bargaining position correspond to the borders of the society that emerges from it. Noncitizens cannot be entitled to foreign aid as a matter of justice, since their interests have been excluded from the social contract. The justification of the Bumpers Amendment depends upon a defense of this principle, but the importance of principle in public policy can be appreciated only by reviewing the situation in which the Bumpers Amendment was formulated.

The Situation and History of the Bumpers Amendment

The Bumpers Amendment in 1986 followed a series of attacks against foreign aid. In 1982, farm state newspapers criticized USAID's Collaborative Research Support Project on peanuts. Three years later, national newspapers ran items linking trade problems to the success of international agricultural development projects. An erroneous report said that USAID had spent $341,137,588 helping foreign farmers. The general thrust of this criticism was that USAID programs harmed U.S. foreign trade in agricultural commodities and hence reduced the incomes of U.S. agricultural producers. As such, it was felt that these programs represented a misuse of public funds.

After a decade of unprecedented growth and dominance of world markets, the U.S. agricultural economy had fallen into a slide that reached crisis proportions by 1983. Farm bankruptcies dominated the national news, and farmers complained bitterly about federal policies. The Reagan administration had worked hard to limit inflation and restore the value of the dollar.

Increases in the foreign exchange value of the dollar put U.S. producers at a disadvantage in world markets, however, lowering farm profits at just the time that interest costs seemed to be increasing without limit.

The increasing competitiveness of foreign growers was a big problem for American farmers. There was, nevertheless, a gap between the problems of U.S. producers and foreign aid. The new competitors for U.S. growers were, for the most part, other industrialized growers in Europe and Australia who were responding to subsidized production incentives of the sort that U.S. producers had enjoyed for years. Among developing countries, only the most wealthy (such as Brazil, Taiwan, or Argentina) were emerging as competitors to the United States in world markets, and even then not as a result of USAID funding. So why did American farmers attack foreign aid?

U.S. farmers receive government support through specific commodity programs for major crops such as wheat, corn, cotton, rice, or soybeans. Farmers have organized to concentrate on these commodity programs. Commodity organizations are supported by growers of the particular commodity, and the professional staff of commodity organizations must justify this support by offering services to the members. These services include lobbying in Washington for policies that favor members' interests. It is in the interests of the staffs of these organizations to present their members with a never ending string of battles in which lobbying, letter-writing campaigns, or media attention succeeds in affecting public policy. The monetary policies affecting farm interests in the 1980s did not present many opportunities for commodity representatives to display their influence. The need to be perceived as active in influencing international trade created an incentive for commodity organizations to seek out weak targets, even if the victories obtained were merely symbolic.

The American Soybean Association (ASA), a producer organization for soybean growers located mostly in the central and southern United States, devoted a June 1985 newsletter to the topic "ASA Leaders Draft Resolution Aimed at Government Export Policies." This mailing to the ASA membership said, "Citing the U.S. government's lack of commitment to an aggressive export policy as the root cause of the current farm crisis, ASA farmer leaders recently proposed a resolution calling for an end to administration policies that adversely affect exports." Among the nine initiatives listed, three addressed development assistance:

- Eliminate the grants and technical assistance that directly or indirectly assist foreign nations to expand the production of competing commodities.
- Vote against loans by the World Bank and other multinational financial institutions that expand the production or export of competing commodities by foreign countries.
- Redirect research funding from federal monies currently aimed at assisting foreign competitors to research aimed at boosting U.S. agricultural

productivity, lowering costs of production, and boosting overall U.S. agricultural competitiveness. (1)

A subsequent newsletter to members criticized U.S. approval of a World Bank loan to Brazil for the purpose of improving its railroads. It was feared that improved railroads would help Brazilian producers "get their farm products to export markets faster!"

Newsletters requested soybean producers to write their congressmen in support of the ASA initiatives, and many did. Dale Bumpers, Democratic Senator from Arkansas, represents a region where soybean production is important and where soybean growers were among the most vocal and active of respondents to ASA mailings and news articles. Bumpers's primary arguments in support of the amendment were more carefully worded versions of the case presented in ASA mailings. Bumpers cited the decline in the dollar value of U.S. agricultural exports from 1981 to 1986, noting that 40 percent of U.S. farm production is harvested for export. He then stated:

> Yet, the Agency for International Development has awarded grants for research and development of export crops from foreign countries with whom we directly compete for agricultural products. Certainly, the U.S. needs to provide strong support to less developed nations for food security and subsistence agriculture. But the U.S. should not provide assistance for countries to better their export capability and undercut the ability of U.S. farmers to compete effectively. (3, p. 17)

Given the barrage of letters sent by angry farmers, this argument was sufficient to ensure passage of the amendment. The only reluctance (expressed by Bumpers himself) came from those who feared that the law might affect development assistance aimed at helping the genuinely poor peasant classes in the developing world. The senators assured themselves that this would not be the case in light of the fact that such recipients tended not to be in countries that exported the major grain commodities grown by U.S. farmers; in any case, poor subsistence farmers contribute virtually nothing to the store of commodities traded on world markets.

Justifying the Bumpers Amendment

Although the Bumpers Amendment regulates the projects that USAID may support, it provides for an exception when these projects benefit low-resource farmers. Since USAID concentrates on poor farmers anyway, the amendment may have had little impact on development assistance activities. In addition, the people who carry out development assistance projects in the field are far from the policy makers who sit in Washington, D.C. One can question whether any attempt to fine-tune development aid in the way specified by the Bumpers Amendment can really affect the daily activity of development specialists in the field. Despite the limited direct consequences of the Bumpers Amendment, the law does entail enforcement costs in monitoring aid programs. Administrators must review proposals for compliance with the law, a process that adds an additional layer of bureaucracy. Since the law applies to U.S. contributions to the World Bank and to international centers, these enforcement costs are not insignificant.

A utilitarian might object to the Bumpers Amendment on the grounds that it creates enforcement costs while securing few if any benefits. Aside from its limited effectiveness, both utilitarians and egalitarians might object to the philosophical spirit of the law. Utilitarians and egalitarians alike might prefer a principle something like this:

> *The Good Samaritan thesis*: Public policy should aim to maximize the benefits accruing from public expenditures or should use funds to benefit the most needy.

Either maximizing benefits or helping the worst off would constitute support for aid. In contrast, libertarians would oppose aid because it aims to secure an opportunity for recipients rather than protecting noninterference rights. However, all three considerations may miss the point. Anyone who believes in a social contract might support the Bumpers Amendment on the basis of the following principle:

> *The social contract thesis*: Government is a contract among citizens. Public policy should not compromise vital interests of citizens in order to provide benefits to noncitizens.

The tension between the Good Samaritan thesis and the social contract thesis is an enduring philosophical controversy. The problem is related to the issue of charity discussed at the beginning of this chapter. Most people think that charitable acts are acts of good will rather than acts that fulfill obligations. Charitable public policies, including foreign development assistance, are no different. But when foreign aid harms some of our own people, any duty to be charitable seems to be overridden by social contract obligations to fellow citizens. The philosophical tension between the Good Samaritan thesis and the social contract thesis is more serious than in the problem of charity, though, since the Good Samaritan thesis explicitly recognizes a duty to promote development assistance. The social contract thesis, by contrast, implies that the policies required by the Good Samaritan thesis may sometimes be acts of social *in*justice.

In its present form, the Good Samaritan thesis combines utilitarian and egalitarian principles. What is crucial in this context, however, is that either approach to policy requires impartiality regarding the interests of U.S. farmers and farmers of the developing world. Given the disparity of wealth between the United States and developing countries, transfer programs would be justified either by a standard utilitarian injunction to do the greatest good for the greatest number or by John Rawls's more pointedly egalitarian *difference principle*, which requires just policy to benefit the worst-off group. Many economists and moral philosophers who might disagree on fundamental philosophies would share an assumption that in weighing the benefits and harms, the full range of consequences to all parties must be taken into account, without bias toward any particular group. In the case at hand, the utilitarian maxim and the difference principle would almost certainly coincide in favoring a humanitarian policy toward the poor of other lands.

Yet the primary arguments in support of the Bumpers Amendment reject the impartiality condition of the Good Samaritan thesis. Indeed, the entire point of the ASA campaign and of Senator Bumpers's legislative response was to establish the priority of U.S. agricultural trade interests against actions that might return larger or more needed benefits to producers in other lands. The Bumpers Amendment constrains the Good Samaritan thesis and establishes a right of U.S. producers to be protected against harm by development assistance policies without regard to the weight of benefits received by noncitizens. The argument for the Bumpers Amendment must therefore rest upon the social contract thesis. In fact, farmers' letters to Congress persistently complained about the use of public funds for projects that help noncitizens at the expense of citizens. It therefore seems likely that something like the social contract thesis is being advanced as the principle that justifies the Bumpers Amendment.

The Good Samaritan thesis is not, however, abandoned entirely, for remarks in the *Congressional Record* that form the basis for interpreting the law are clear in limiting its intent. It is not to be construed as an attack upon the legitimacy of aid to the poor of the developing world. A harsh reading of the social contract thesis might be thought to invalidate noncitizens' claims as beneficiaries of U.S. policy entirely. In fact, the Bumpers Amendment places the Good Samaritan thesis and the social contract thesis in tension without giving clear priority to either. In the actual language of the law, the clause giving USAID authority to promote food security constrains the primary clause establishing the priority of U.S. trade interests. Since the humanitarian clause constrains the assertion of contractual rights, one might think that the corresponding humanitarian principle is more fundamental. The political history of the Bumpers Amendment, however, indicates the opposite. The trade opportunities of U.S. producers must be acknowledged as a constraint on both utilitarian and Rawlsian principles. The entire point of the ASA campaign was, of course, to establish this point, and the Bumpers Amendment would appear to serve as a congressional endorsement.

The Good Samaritan thesis is not the only way to argue for foreign aid, however. If the social contract thesis is correct, it means that national objectives may override the interests of individual citizens. If foreign assistance helps achieve justified national policy goals, then it may be justified as a means to secure those goals. There are, in fact, several authors who feel that foreign agricultural assistance is vital to the future growth of world markets. They feel that growth in world markets is in U.S. interests. They argue that U.S. aid to foreign farmers and herders is justified as a means of improving future prospects for foreign trade. They argue that world agricultural markets will be among the first to grow. Hence, ironically, U.S. agricultural producers will be among the first to benefit from aid that appears to help their competitors.

If this argument is interpreted as an appeal to U.S. national interests, then it might be an adequate reply to the way that the Bumpers Amendment was justified by the social contract thesis. Notice that this new argument does not depend upon the Good Samaritan thesis. Indeed, it redefines the purpose of development assistance in a way that accepts the social contract thesis. Aid is given not as a duty to the poor but as a means of achieving U.S. national objectives. By changing the intention of foreign assistance actions, the new argument makes them consistent with the social contract thesis. These actions no longer intend to benefit the foreign poor (at the expense of U.S. producers); they now intend to enhance world markets. This new goal will benefit U.S. producers (though not necessarily the same producers who are harmed by aid in the first place). The foreign poor are no longer the intended beneficiaries of the policy; they benefit as if by accident.

U.S. foreign aid programs continue to be swept by the political currents represented by these philosophical conflicts. A majority of Americans favor humanitarian assistance but do not approve of foreign aid programs intended to achieve more self-interested objectives. However, when aid programs become specific enough to compromise the interests of an identifiable group, the balance of opinion shifts and foreign aid projects become perceived as illegitimate "give away" programs that harm Americans. The politics of the Bumpers Amendment makes this point clear. These philosophical issues are not confined to agricultural policies, but they have had an impact on agricultural assistance as well as on U.S. agriculture. They can be expected to continue to influence aid debates and, in turn, aid policies.

Summary

It is obvious that famine and hunger will be among the most important topics for any study of agricultural ethics. This chapter has concentrated on policies that render assistance across international borders. U.S. foreign assistance policy is divided between emergency relief from the threat of starvation that results from disasters and development assistance that attempts to lift poor farmers out of the desperate poverty that pervades agriculture throughout much of the developing world. Both forms of foreign aid raise ethical questions about how the interests of affected parties should be taken into consideration.

The desert locust case illustrates this problem. Currently, foreign agricultural assistance is almost always evaluated in utilitarian terms. Assistance programs are considered successful if they reach end-state targets that are defined in terms such as total food production, increased societal income, and reduced infant mortality. The emphasis upon the consequences of development assistance projects may lead project managers and policy makers to overlook the rights of affected parties. The poor may indeed benefit from a project that exposes them to risk, forecloses the opportunity to make their own choices, or gives them no representation or voice in the decision-making process. Rights theorists might argue that such projects are unjustifiable even when benefits outweigh costs.

The Bumpers Amendment case illustrates ethical issues that are associated almost exclusively with development assistance. One way to understand foreign aid is by analogy to personal charity. Charity is voluntary, and the recipients of charity are thought to have no enforceable claim upon the donors. If foreign aid is a form of public charity, however, the national interests that influence foreign policy taint the voluntariness and altruism that are characteristic of charitable acts. What is more, libertarians will have little sympathy with any notion of public charity. One alternative is to understand foreign aid as a duty of justice owed by relatively well-off countries to relatively poor ones. This interpretation would be favored by egalitarians and by at least some utilititarians.

The Bumpers Amendment shows why it is difficult to make the case for foreign aid as a duty of justice. If aid is a duty of justice based upon the idea of a social contract, the interests of foreigners ought not to count equally with those of our fellow citizens, with whom the social contract has been made. It is on this basis that American farmers object to policies that create new competitors for them even when those competitors are currently quite poor.

Key Terms

development assistance
emergency assistance

References

1. "ASA Leaders Draft Resolution Aimed at Government Export Policies," *ASA Newsletter*, August 1, 1985.
2. Hardin, Garrett. 1976. "Carrying Capacity as an Ethical Concept," in *Moral Dilemmas of World Hunger*, ed. George R. Lucas and Thomas Ogletree. New York: Harper and Row.
3. Johnson, Glenn L. 1987. *Objectivity in Public Decision Making.* Lexington: Committee for Agricultural Research Policy, University of Kentucky.
4. Nagel, Thomas. 1977. "Poverty and Food," in *Food Policy*, ed. P. Brown and H. Shue. New York: Free Press.
5. Office of Technology Assessment, U.S. Congress. 1990. *Plague of Locusts: A Special Report, OTA-F-450.* Washington, D.C.: U.S. Government Printing Office.
6. Sen, Amartya Kumar. 1982. *Poverty and Famines.* 2nd ed. New York: Oxford University Press.
7. Singer, Peter. 1972. "Famine, Affluence and Morality," in *Philosophy and Public Affairs* 1:329–337.
8. U.S. Congress. 1986. *Congressional Record—Senate, June 6, 1986, S7028.* Washington, D.C.: U.S. Government Printing Office.

9. ———. 1985. *Congressional Record—Senate, Nov. 22, 1985, S16269.* Washington, D.C.: U.S. Government Printing Office.

Suggestions for Further Reading

The literature on ethics, development, and world hunger is large. Three anthologies from the 1970s define the field. *World Hunger and Moral Obligation,* ed. William Aiken and Hugh LaFollette (Englewood Cliffs, N.J.: Prentice-Hall, 1977), collects seminal papers by Garrett Hardin and Peter Singer, along with other important papers by philosophers. A companion is *Lifeboat Ethics: The Moral Dilemmas of World Hunger,* ed. George R. Lucas and Thomas Ogletree (New York: Harper and Row, 1976). This book follows Hardin in defining the issue in terms of *triage,* a concept borrowed from medical ethics that stresses the importance of using scarce lifesaving resources efficiently, even when doing so requires the conscious sacrifice of human lives. The best book for a public policy approach is *Food Policy: The Responsibility of the United States in Life and Death Choices,* ed. Peter Brown and Henry Shue (New York: Free Press, 1977). Virtually all the papers in this collection continue to be important and deserve a wider audience than they have had.

Henry Shue's *Basic Rights* (Princeton, N.J.: Princeton University Press, 1980) presents a detailed argument for an egalitarian/opportunity rights approach to the responsibility to give aid. Onora O'Neill's *Faces of Hunger: An Essay on Poverty, Justice and Development* (Boston: Allen and Unwin, 1986) presents a philosophically sophisticated argument for duties to the poor of developing countries that is based upon Kantian moral theory. Paul Thompson's *The Ethics of Aid and Trade: U.S. Food Policy, Foreign Competition and the Social Contract* (New York: Cambridge University Press, 1992) examines the themes raised by the Bumpers Amendment in detail.

Works on development theory and development ethics are far too extensive to be summarized here. There is perhaps no better starting point for those interested in food and agriculture than the anthology edited by Carl Eicher and John Staatz, *Agricultural Development in the Third World* (2nd ed.; Baltimore: Johns Hopkins University Press, 1990). A fine overview of the philosophical considerations bearing on development theory can be found in David Crocker's article "Toward Development Ethics," *World Development* 19:457–483, 1990. Roger Riddell's *Foreign Aid Reconsidered* (Baltimore: Johns Hopkins University Press, 1987) is also a philosophically sophisticated treatment. We would be remiss to neglect at least a mention of the two giants at integrating ethics and development. They are Denis Goulet, whose 1977 work *The Uncertain Promise: Value Conflicts in Technology Transfer* (New York: IDOC/North America) deserves careful study, and Amartya Sen, whose writings are so prolific that they overwhelm. Readers who are totally unfamiliar with Sen's work might begin with the elegantly written 1990 essay entitled "Individual Freedom as a Social Commitment," *New York Review of Books* 37(10):49–53.

CHAPTER 9

Sustainability

Conventional agricultural production practices were subjected to a variety of criticisms in the 1980s. Some of the more specific points of criticism focused on certain aspects of food safety, environmental quality, and the well-being of farm animals. In each of these areas, specific regulatory policies or property rights were proposed to reform agriculture. These issues and proposals have been discussed in other chapters. In some cases, however, criticisms were expressed in the form of a broad philosophical critique of conventional agriculture. A **philosophical critique** is a three-stage argument that first describes in broad terms the values and assumptions that provide reasons for a given pattern of decision making or a particular course of conduct. The second stage produces evidence or reasoning intended to show the error in these values, assumptions, and patterns of choice. The third stage produces an alternative set of values and assumptions intended to correct the errors of the original view. Critics want to substitute their alternative vision for an existing set of values, assumptions, and choices. Philosophical critique relates to public policy because policies are influenced by the broad set of values, assumptions, and choices shared by the parties who are active in policy formulation.

Sometimes a philosophical critique follows the divisions of ethical criteria introduced in Chapter 3. An egalitarian, for example, might offer a critique of utilitarian thinking as it relates to food safety or natural resource policy and might argue that the emphasis upon predicting consequences has led people to formulate unacceptable policies. The egalitarian might then substitute an alternative vision in which the structure of opportunity rights is advanced as the key criterion for assessing policy. Some, but not all, conflicts over policy follow this pattern. However, it is also possible to develop a philosophical critique of contemporary agriculture that does not follow the lines of division sketched in Chapter 3. Many critics writing in the last two decades have felt that decisions in American agriculture—decisions of producers, consumers, and agribusiness firms, as well as those of policy makers—have been based upon an erroneous set of values and assumptions.

In broad terms, the critique states that American agriculture has been evaluated as an industry just like the steel or automobile industry. Critics feel that agriculture is different from other industries. One theme of the criticism is that agriculture differs because it is an ecologically and economically foundational form of production, one that must be maintained or sustained if society is to prosper. A related theme is that agriculture differs because it is the source of important moral values and lessons. This chapter examines the first theme: that an alternative agriculture should be sustainable. Chapter 10 examines the second theme: that agriculture should be organized to promote the values and existence of the family farm.

The Impetus for "Sustainable" Agriculture

American agriculture and rural life underwent massive change in the decades following World War II. The typical farm in the late 1940s closely resembled the diversified family farm of popular imagination. It was relatively small (about 200 acres), was farmed by a single family that was large by today's standards, and supported several different farm enterprises (wheat, corn, vegetables, beef, pork, poultry, dairy crops, cotton, etc.). Three decades later, Old McDonald's farm had all but disappeared. Far fewer people were farming more acreage in fewer enterprises; mixed livestock-grain operations were largely a thing of the past. There were other changes as well. In 1950, there were some 5.6 million farms; by 1981, there were only 2.4 million. The surviving farms were on average almost twice as large, growing from 213 acres in 1950 to 425 acres in 1981. (Total acreage under cultivation remained nearly unchanged at about 340 million acres.) During this same period, farm population fell sharply from 23 million to 5.9 million. Farm population as a percentage of rural population also fell, from 36.8 percent in 1950 to 9.8 percent in 1981. Farm productivity, on the other hand, increased dramatically. For example, during the period 1950 to 1981, wheat yields (bushels per acre) doubled and corn and sorghum yields tripled. During this same period, farm labor input fell from fifty-five hours per acre planted in 1950 to eighteen hours per acre planted in 1981. Far fewer farmers were farming larger farms and producing much higher yields (5).

The primary cause of these changes is simple: American agriculture became a capital-intensive industry dependent upon chemicals, heavy farm equipment, and irrigation. American farmers had long used various arsenic-based insecticides, beginning with Paris green (a copper acetoarsenite) in 1867 and then lead arsenate in the 1910s and 1920s. But only after World War II did agricultural use of chemicals really take off. During the period 1950 to 1981, chemical use jumped over 700 percent. Herbicides are a case in point. In 1945, 2,4-D, 2,4,5-T, and other phenoxyacetic herbicides first came on the market. By 1949, farmers were using twenty-five different herbicides on 23 million acres of corn, wheat, and turf. By 1959, one year after the introduction of atrazine, the number of acres treated with herbicides had more than doubled. But this 52 million acres still represented only 15 percent of total cropland in the United States. The real explosion took place in the 1960s, when herbicides such as alachlor were introduced. By 1974, more than one-half of all cropland in the United States was being treated with herbicides, a total of more than 160 million acres. By 1987, more than 95 percent of the acres devoted to corn and soybeans and 60 percent of the acres devoted to wheat were being treated with herbicides, typically atrazine and alachlor.

As Comstock points out:

> The rapid expansion in the use of herbicides after World War II has gone hand in hand with the use of industrially produced pesticides to control insects, synthetic anhydrous ammonia—and now ureas—to supply nitrogen, manufactured superphosphates to provide phosphate, large amounts of capital to purchase the inputs, and large tracts of land over which to spread the costs. (4, p. 276)

Comstock notes that the use of one chemical often entails the use of another. If, for example, a corn farmer uses 2,4-D to control weeds, he or she will need fungicides to control smut and Southern corn-leaf blight, which seem to accompany the use of this herbicide; sooner or later, the farmer will also need insecticides to control the corn-leaf aphids that seem to follow the use of the herbicide.

By 1981, U.S. farmers were using annually a total of 23 million tons of synthetic nutrients (e.g., some 130 pounds of nitrogen per acre of corn), 225,000 tons of herbicides, 60,000 tons of insecticides, and 20,000 tons of fungicides. During this same period, tractor horsepower per acre planted tripled and total land under irrigation doubled. The turn to synthetic nutrients, notably nitrogen, was especially significant because this meant that nitrogen-producing leguminous forage crops no longer had to be grown in order to replenish soil nutrients. Traditional crop rotation practices could be largely abandoned. Without these forage crops to support livestock, mixed livestock-grain operations were soon replaced by monocultural cash grain operations. Livestock operations became concentrated in large off-farm factories, which like the emerging monocultural grain operations depended heavily on purchased off-farm chemical inputs. Thus, for example, the use of antibiotics in animal feeds to enhance weight gain rose from essentially zero in 1950 to close to 9 million pounds in 1980. Old McDonald's multi-enterprise farm had been replaced by a single-enterprise farm that grew only one or two crops. The barnyard animals of which young children sing had been moved to large single-product confinement systems. Old McDonald himself had probably sold his farm and moved to the city. The modern farm family no longer grew their own food; they shopped at the local supermarket like everyone else.

These dramatic increases in productivity and production were accompanied by a corresponding increase in the income of individual farm workers, from $7,400 in 1950 to $19,600 in 1981 (measured in 1982 dollars). But these increases were achieved only because many had been forced out of farming. Commodity prices, measured in constant dollars, actually fell during the period. Total net farm income was constant or even fell slightly during the 1950s and early 1960s before rising sharply in the 1970s in response to a growing export market.

Farmers who survived this period were not only better paid than their 1950 counterparts; they were also more indebted. The farm debt-equity ratio, which measures farm indebtedness as a percentage of farm equity, jumped from 8.7 percent in 1950 to 18.9 percent in 1981. This is hardly surprising. Chemicals, heavy farm machinery, and irrigation are very expensive. Farmers had to purchase these inputs if they were to remain competitive. If they didn't have the money, then they had to borrow it. Farming had become a capital-intensive industry in which, like most other industries, a substantial portion of gross revenues went for the purchase of the inputs necessary for producing a product.

The late 1970s were the halcyon days of postwar American agriculture. Agricultural exports were soaring to new heights; individual farm income was at an all-time high; agricultural productivity had surpassed nonfarm business sector productivity; cropland under cultivation had reached an all-time high. Farmers were prospering. They were no longer poor country cousins to America's suburban middle class. They, too, were able to afford the latest modern conveniences, take winter vacations, and send their children to better colleges and universities. By some standards they were even wealthy. Land values had skyrocketed from an average of $53 per acre in 1950 to $713 per acre in 1981; better farmland was selling for prices in excess of $2,000 per acre.

But ominous clouds were already gathering on the economic horizon. Interest rates were soaring to unprecedented levels. By 1981, the prime rate of interest (the rate that big banks charge their best customers) was 18.9 percent. At the same time, changes in federal monetary policy curbed inflation dramatically. The real cost of servicing farm debt was now very high. In addition, commodity prices had begun to drop, while the price of purchased off-farm inputs continued to increase. Demand for American agricultural commodities in international markets also declined as a result of the increased value of the dollar, increased foreign competition, and loan rates in federal commodity programs (i.e., the prices that the government guarantees farmers) that were set well above international market prices. The prosperity of the 1970s quickly turned into the global recession of the early 1980s. Farmers who had assumed heavy debt in order to expand their farm operations were severely strained. The debt-to-asset ratio suddenly became the crucial barometer of a farm's viability. Unable to service their debts, many farmers were forced into bankruptcy. Especially vulnerable were the owner/operators of moderate-sized farms who, unlike the owner/operators of large farms, were not well capitalized and, unlike the owner/operators of small part-time farms, could not depend on off-farm income to carry them through these hard times. The changes in farm structure were dramatic. By 1982, 72 percent of American farms were small, typically part-time operations accounting for only 11 percent of total farm sales; 14 percent were large, often very large, and accounted for some 63 percent of total sales. (At present, in California, 20 percent of the state's farmers account for 90 percent of the state's total agricultural production.) By 1988, 38 percent of all American farmers held full-time, off-farm jobs; farm income as a percentage of total income had fallen to 27 percent. For most farmers, farming no longer paid the bills. Nor were most farmers contributing significantly to the nation's total agricultural production.

Although many farmers experienced financial hardship during the 1980s, many prospered. Net farm income rose sharply during the mid-1980s, but only at a significant cost to American taxpayers as a result of record levels of government support ($25.8 billion in 1986). Such support accounted for almost 50 percent of net farm income in 1986 and 1987. The financial plight of farmers also affected farm lending institutions and suppliers of farm inputs. One-fourth of all farm loans—$33.7 billion—were nonperforming or delinquent in 1984 and 1985. Agricultural bank failures accounted for more than one-half of 1985 bank failures, although they represented only one-quarter of all banks. Suppliers were also hurt by bad debt, as well as by reduced sales; many rural communities saw their local farm implement dealers, car dealers, and chemical suppliers go out of business. Rural communities that had survived the precipitous decline in farm population during the 1950s found themselves further ravaged by the events of the 1980s. Many communities emerged from the 1980s little more than ghosts of their 1940s selves (8).

All of these developments might have provided little impetus for the philosophical critique that has come to be associated with sustainable agriculture. These events created dissatisfaction with the status quo, but the growing concern in the 1970s and 1980s about the apparently harmful effects of post-World War II agricultural practices on environmental quality and human health provided a link between these events and the popular understanding of ecology. A number of critics beginning with Rachel Carson, in her influential book *Silent Spring* (3), argued that a capital-intensive American agriculture dependent upon chemicals, heavy machinery, and irrigation is not simply financially and spiritually disastrous for many farmers and their families, destructive of many rural communities, and expensive for most American taxpayers, but is also a clear threat to both the environment and human health. (See Chapter 6 for a brief description of the environmental hazards posed by modern agricultural practices.) It seemed to these critics that whatever the benefits to some farmers, to the industries that fueled the new agricultural technology, and perhaps to the publicly financed universities that provided much of the basic research in support of this technology, American society simply could not, and indeed should not, support or sustain the financial, social, spiritual, environmental, and health costs of this new agriculture. What was needed, these critics argued, was an **alternative agriculture**, one that is a **sustainable agriculture**.

What Is Sustainable Agriculture?

Critics of postwar American agriculture have raised concerns about the long-run consequences of current agricultural production practices for (i) human health and safety, (ii) the environment, and (iii) the future availability of the natural resources required for food production. They have also criticized current farm policy and agricultural technology on the grounds that (iv) they favor capital-intensive farming practices and/or (v) they decrease the profitability of medium-sized, owner-operator (i.e., family) farms. These criticisms focus on various unwanted and generally unintended consequences of current practices and policy, notably polluted water supplies, depletion of potentially renewable soil and energy resources, harmful effects on wildlife, chemical residues on food, depopulation of rural areas, and an unprecedented concentration of capital within the agricultural sector. What these critics have in common is the conviction that an agriculture that has these consequences cannot be sustained indefinitely. In place of conventional agriculture, they promote the alternative vision of sustainable agriculture, which, they assume, would not have these undesirable consequences.

But why, we should ask, do they assume this? Is it obvious that an agriculture could not have some or all of these undesirable consequences and nonetheless be sustainable? It certainly does not seem to be true as a general principle that undesirable consequences are always, or even typically, unsustainable. Poverty and sickness, for example, are undesirable but seemingly sustainable features of virtually all societies. The issue here is important because proponents of sustainable agriculture believe that recognizing sustainability to be one of the major social goals of agricultural policy would serve to eliminate these undesirable consequences. In order to be clear on this issue, we must first look more closely at three alternative accounts of sustainability to which proponents appeal. Wes Jackson and Miguel Altieri are two maverick agricultural scientists who have developed philosophical critiques of conventional agriculture as a basis for promoting their alternative visions. Generally, agricultural scientists and extension personnel have tended to define sustainability in less ideological terms, settling on a standard view of sustainability that stands in contrast to the critiques of Jackson and Altieri.

Critique 1: Wes Jackson's New Roots for Agriculture

Wes Jackson is a geneticist who established his own experimental center, the Land Institute, for research on sustainable agriculture in 1976. His 1980 book *New Roots for Agriculture* (revised and republished in 1985; see Ref. 6) provided a rationale for his alternative vision. Jackson begins by noting a series of failures associated with conventional agriculture in the postwar period. He notes the financial problems facing farmers who have relied on irrigation, chemical inputs, and large monocultures, and he links these problems to a variety of environmental impacts, especially soil fertility. Public policy is discussed in a chapter that notes the inability of organizations such as the Soil Conservation Service to affect farming practices in a manner that would mitigate their environmental impact. Jackson places these failures within the context of a broader spiritual failure. This spiritual failure is seen in the way that the pursuit of wealth and the ethic of self-interest become dominant values in the modern world. Jackson feels that humanity has ceased to understand its fundamental aims and goals in terms of establishing the proper relationship with the land.

Jackson presents his alternative vision for agriculture as a contrast between the farm as a food factory—the conventional view—and the farm as hearth. As a hearth, the farm is understood as a homestead for family activity. This theme links Jackson's alternative vision to that of poet and essayist Wendell Berry, discussed in Chapter 10. Though Jackson and Berry clearly see each other as collaborators on a common vision for an alternative agriculture, Jackson's alternative vision differs from Berry's by providing more explicit discussion of what it would mean for the farm as hearth to produce sustainable agriculture. The key to this vision is Jackson's emphasis upon declining soil fertility as the dominant spiritual and practical failure of conventional agriculture. Jackson writes:

> A profound truth has escaped us. Soil is a placenta or matrix, a living organism which is larger than the life it supports, a tough elastic membrane which has given rise to many life forms and has watched the thousands of species from their first experiments at survival, many of them through millennia-long roaring success and even dominion before their decline and demise. But it is itself now dying. It is a death that is utterly senseless, and portends our own. In nature the wounded placenta heals through plant succession; enterprising species cover wounds quickly. (6, p. 10)

Jackson's vision of soil as "living organism . . . larger than the life it supports" is the basis for his vision of sustainable agriculture. A pattern of life that interrupts the healing process of plant succession is unsustainable because it destroys the "placenta" on which all life forms depend.

Jackson sees this as a solvable problem through the development of alternative agriculture organized around perennial polyculture. Here agriculture would mimic the natural prairie, where many plants grow simultaneously. Humans would harvest from a variety of plants blooming and fruiting at various times of the year. Since soil would not be disturbed, soil building processes could continue as in a natural prairie. Agricultural research should be dedicated to producing food crops that can thrive in such a setting, replacing the cultivation, irrigation, and chemical inputs of conventional agriculture. Jackson writes:

All of our research [at the Land Institute] centers around four biological questions:

- Can perennialism and high yield go together year after year?
- Can a polyculture of perennials outyield a monoculture of perennials? We know it is possible for annuals and forage perennials.
- Can an agricultural ecosystem sponsor its own fertility, especially the nitrogen and carbon?
- Can high yielding "domestic prairies" be put in place so that the problems of insects, pathogens, and weeds are sufficiently minimized? (6, p. 136)

These four questions stipulate the technical content for the vision of the farm as the hearth. Although Jackson clearly thinks that the criteria implied by these questions depend upon spiritual commitment to the vision of the hearth rather than the food factory, he does not provide detailed discussion of why this is so.

Critique 2: Miguel Altieri's Agroecology

Trained as an entomologist, Miguel Altieri has done extensive work on biological control, the use of plant and insect enemies rather than toxic chemicals to control pest outbreaks. As his research focused increasingly on peasant agriculture in developing countries, Altieri noticed that peasant farmers were already using a sophisticated mix of crops and production practices to limit the risks from pest outbreaks, drought, and other natural forces. These peasant practices had been refined through trial and error over centuries. Differing widely from one region to another, these farming practices were an adaptive response to the variation in local environmental conditions that peasants were likely to experience in a given locale. As adaptations to local conditions, peasant practices were shaped by the ecosystem in which their farms were located. Altieri's observations led to a theory of agriculture that he calls *agroecology.*

Altieri sees peasant agriculture as offering a sharp contrast to the industrialized agriculture of the United States. U.S. farming practice is based upon agricultural research conducted in universities. This research has been guided by reductionist research norms borrowed from seventeenth-century scientist/philosophers such as René Descartes and Robert Boyle. Altieri (1) argues that scientific emphasis upon universal laws and the replicability of experiments has inadvertently substituted a set of values that are inappropriate for agriculture generally, not only in developing countries but also in the United States. It is his criticism of scientific values that makes Altieri's agroecology stand as a critique of conventional agriculture, and the lessons he has learned from peasants provide the alternative vision.

With a series of coauthors, Altieri writes that university scientists have responded more to their personal incentives for tenure, promotion, and recognition by peers than to the real problems of farmers. Working within universities, agricultural scientists have increasingly emulated the norms and laboratory practices of pure biology, physics, and chemistry. This practice has meant that a successful research project should identify natural laws, or statistical correlations that have a high degree of generality. Scientists have been interested in very general understandings of how plants and animals respond to nutrients, for example, or how genetic traits are passed from one individual to another. What is more, scientific findings must be replicable. That is, a scientist in one university must be able to reproduce the same result in another university or lab, given the same experimental conditions. This norm has led scientists to place great emphasis upon eliminating the sources of variability from one lab to another. Farmers, however, are interested in specific crops growing in a specific location (their farm), and there will always be a wide variety of factors that differentiate one farm from another. Philosopher of science Frederick Suppe (9) has documented this problem in some detail.

Altieri criticizes industrial agriculture on the grounds that it attempts to reproduce the conditions of controlled variability that are necessary for good science within the farmer's fields. It does this by altering the environment through massive inputs of chemicals and capital-intensive equipment for irrigation and standardized cultivation. Although these practices have been profitable over the short run for U.S. farmers, they also make them completely dependent upon new science (as well as upon the agribusiness firms that develop and distribute new technology).

An example of this dependence can be seen in the resistance to pesticides that insects quickly develop under field conditions. Spraying kills many insects, but those that survive are likely to have genetic traits that give them the ability to resist the effects of the chemical. Within a few generations, these traits are dominant throughout the insect population, and new chemicals must be introduced. At the same time, the natural enemies of the pest are killed by sprays, but the enemies do not bounce back as fast. Since they eat the pest insect, their numbers do not start to grow until there is already a large population of the pest species to provide food for them. The farmer cannot wait, however, for the crop is at risk from a resistant pest, now uncontrolled by natural enemies and hence present in larger numbers than ever before. The farmer must depend upon scientists and chemical companies to come up with new, more powerful chemicals or face a devastating loss of production.

Altieri notes that while this cycle suits the interests of scientists (who have a steady flow of research funds) and chemical companies (which can introduce a steady flow of products), it is far from clear that it truly serves the interests of farmers. In his view, a more rational approach would use the knowledge and techniques of science to do what peasant farmers have been doing all along. Rather than altering the environment, the ecological forces affecting the farms, scientists should find a mix of plants and animals that is uniquely suited to each farm's environmental niche. Though such research may produce relatively few important scientific breakthroughs, it is far better suited to the farmer's need to develop a production system that is well adapted to the ecological forces likely to affect a given farm over time.

Like Jackson, Altieri (2) links his vision of sustainable agriculture to criticisms that emphasize the protection of family farms. Altieri's basis for doing so is less spiritual than political, however. He sees chemical companies and other agribusiness input firms making inroads in the Latin American countries where he has worked with peasant farmers. Land and credit policies can make it difficult for farmers who do not adopt these industrialized farming techniques to compete with those who do. As such, sustainable agriculture depends upon policies that do not distort the costs of agricultural production, either by making purchased inputs artificially cheap (through government subsidies of fertilizer, irrigation, or chemicals) or by failing to internalize environmental costs (see Chapter 6). Altieri interprets such agricultural development policies as part of a conspiracy to make farmers dependent on technologies that cannot be abandoned once subsidies are removed. Since such policies are widely advocated by those who emphasize the need to increase farm income, Altieri's critique, like Jackson's, takes issue with the goal of producing wealth. Unlike Jackson's critique, Altieri's has Marxist overtones, for he rejects the need to introduce capital (in the form of machinery and purchased inputs) into the agricultural production process.

The Standard View of Sustainability

Jackson and Altieri produce alternative visions of sustainable agriculture that fulfill the criteria for a philosophical critique. They note the assumptions of conventional agriculture and present reasons for finding them in error. They then present alternative visions that are based upon alternative assumptions and values. Jackson's critique stresses the greed of the conventional view and offers the hearth as a spiritual and technical alternative. Altieri's critique focuses on the way that industrialized agriculture serves the interests of scientists and agribusiness rather than those of farmers. His vision of an agriculture researched and adapted to meet the local conditions of a specific farm is another alternative. Neither Jackson nor Altieri makes specific recommendations about the policy requirements of his alternative vision.

Most participants in the development of sustainable agriculture have not undertaken the systematic philosophical critique developed by Jackson and Altieri. Most are either ill equipped to do so, lacking the vocabulary and vision, or have little incentive to engage in the reflection and argument that a critique requires. Farmers find themselves in such a position, being faced with practical problems of day-to-day management that tend to make them pragmatists, advocates of "what works." In general, groups such as those led by William Leibhardt at the University of California have attempted to develop sustainable agriculture that uses traditional agronomic research methods to find solutions to farmers' problems. These groups have evolved toward a vision of sustainable agriculture that is less sweeping than those of Jackson or Altieri. Because such researchers and farmers represent the majority of those advocating sustainable agriculture, we call their concept the **standard view**.

In the standard view, the concept of sustainability is drawn from theories of natural resource management according to which a level of exploitation of a renewable resource is said to be sustainable if that level can be maintained indefinitely without impairment of the resource base. Thus, for example, an annual harvest rate of some species of fish or game is said to be sustainable if that rate can be maintained indefinitely without impairing or endangering that species. More generally, there are many different sorts of things that we speak of as being sustainable or unsustainable: yields, soil fertility, human activities, public policies, social institutions, and even life itself. To say of one of these things that it is sustainable is to say that it can be kept going, that it can be kept in existence, that it can be supported, maintained, or carried on indefinitely.

Judgments of sustainability, especially as applied to various human practices, activities, and institutions, will often be contentious. Involving as they must a judgment as to the system's ability to sustain, support, or maintain something over an indefinite period of time, there will often be considerable room for dispute, not simply about the period of time over which the ability is to be exercised, but also about what is to be counted as a successful exercise of the ability to sustain. To the extent that there is no agreement on these matters, there can be no agreement on judgments of sustainability. Such disputes, it should be noted, are conceptual rather than factual. Agreement on empirical facts does not entail agreement on our judgments about sustainability. Empirical facts do not dictate how we are to understand and use the concept of sustainability.

The potential for conceptual disagreement over sustainability as a goal of American agriculture creates a need to clarify the meaning of sustainability in any given context. Lowance et al. suggest that sustainability is to be understood as a multidimensional, hierarchical concept that includes agronomic, microeconomic, ecological, and macroeconomic aspects:

> Agronomic sustainability refers to the ability of a tract of land to maintain productivity over a long period of time. Microeconomic sustainability is dependent on the ability of the farm, as the basic economic unit, to stay in business. Ecological sustainability depends on the maintenance of life-support systems provided by non-agricultural and non-industrial segments of a region. Macroeconomic sustainability is controlled by factors such as fiscal policies and interest rates which determine the viability of national agriculture systems. In our view, there are critical constraints to sustainability at different scales of the agricultural hierarchy. (7, pp. 169–173)

On the standard view, too, sustainability is a multidimensional concept. It does not describe the ability of a single person, institution, or thing to sustain or maintain certain farming practices or systems. It variously describes the ability of *land, farms, farm families, rural communities, banks, farm credit associations, governmental units,* and *natural ecosystems* to sustain certain farming practices or systems without increasing their vulnerability to the particular sort of disintegration or collapse that each of these entities faces—loss of productivity in the case of land, bankruptcy in the case of farms, depopulation in the case of rural communities, and so on.

Is Sustainability the Right Criterion?

At first, sustainability seems to be an appropriate criterion for evaluating farming practices and systems. History provides many examples of ways of life, communities, governments, and even entire societies and civilizations that have failed because their agricultural practices and systems were unsustainable. The demise of the Babylonian empire is sometimes attributed to the unsustainability of the irrigation practices upon which agricultural production depended. Postwar American agriculture, some critics believe, promises to provide history with yet another example. On more careful consideration, however, sustainability appears *not* to be the right criterion. It appears to be at once too strong and too weak to support the moral evaluation of American agricultural practices and systems that proponents of sustainable agriculture intend.

Sustainability seem to be *too strong* a criterion inasmuch as it appears questionable whether any agriculture could count as sustainable, at least on these proponents' understanding of that notion. Farming practices and systems may be sustainable relative to one criterion but not relative to another. Thus, for example, conservation tillage may prevent soil erosion and thus may contribute to the agronomic sustainability of this tillage system; but if this system relies on the regular use of herbicides that pollute water supplies and harm the health of wildlife, farm workers, and consumers, then it might be unsustainable environmentally. An alternative tillage system may be agronomically and environmentally sustainable but may earn such low profits as to be unsustainable for the farm that employs such a system. Proponents of sustainable agriculture promote sustainability as an appropriate goal of agricultural policy; however, such a goal may be impossible to achieve. There may simply be no farming practices or systems that are simultaneously sustainable with respect to all the criteria that proponents of sustainable agriculture have in mind (e.g., land, farms, farm families, rural communities, ecosystem, nation). Sustainability of the sort that proponents envision may thus be an unattainable ideal. It is unsatisfactory as an evaluative criterion because it fails to provide us with any guidance for evaluating farming practices and systems that invariably fall short of this ideal. It provides no guidance for deciding the relative importance of preserving land productivity, of saving the family farm, and of providing low cost food to consumers.

Sustainability would also seem to be *too weak*, that is, too impoverished an evaluative criterion, inasmuch as certain farming practices and systems might be sustainable according to one set of criteria but unacceptable on other ethical grounds. Farming practices and systems that, for example, impoverish farm families and rural communities, cause sickness among farm workers or consumers, or harm wildlife do not have to be unsustainable in order to be unacceptable, any more than do agricultural systems that depend on slaveholding or sharecropping. Farming practices and systems may have any number of undesirable consequences, and they may depend upon rights structures that violate liberties or foreclose opportunities. The criteria by which we evaluate farming practices and systems should state these norms explicitly rather than attempting to sneak them in under the rubric of sustainability.

A careful examination of the rhetoric of sustainable agriculture reveals that sustainability is rarely understood as it is in resource economics or ecology. Rather, it is most often used as a proxy (i.e., replacement) for one or another term of positive normative evaluation, such as *good, desirable, acceptable, justifiable*, and so on. The term *unsustainable*, by contrast, is most often used as a proxy for one or another term of negative normative evaluation, such as *bad, undesirable*, or *unjustifiable*. In many instances, the notion of sustainability would seem to be a normative concept masquerading as a descriptive one.

It is understandable that proponents of sustainable agriculture would attempt to clothe their normative evaluation of current farming practices and systems in the garb of a scientific description. The rhetoric of sustainability seeks to invest such evaluation with the authority of indisputable scientific fact. But such rhetoric is not simply misleading; it is also counterproductive in two important respects. First, it focuses the dispute over current farming practices and systems in the wrong place. If the issue were really sustainability, then many of the criticisms leveled by proponents of sustainable agriculture against current farming practices and systems would simply be beside the point since they do not actually address that issue. Many of their proposals for changing these practices and systems would also be undercut since these proponents fail to provide any arguments that would show that the proposed alternative practices and systems are themselves any more sustainable. Second, such rhetoric forgoes the resources of a more subtle and nuanced normative vocabulary in terms of which current farming practices and systems might be more effectively evaluated. Proponents of sustainable agriculture, it will be recalled, criticize current farming practices and systems on a number of different grounds. For example, they deplete potentially renewable soil and energy resources; imperil human health and safety; endanger wildlife; decrease the profitability of the moderate-sized family farm; put farm families under significant financial and hence emotional strain; and lead to the depopulation of rural communities. These consequences may indeed render current farming practices and systems unsustainable; however, whether they do or do not, these consequences are undesirable in themselves. They should, if possible, be avoided for that reason alone. The point here is that proponents of sustainable agriculture are offering what is in fact an ethical criticism of current practices and systems and would do well to formulate their criticism in those terms. They are arguing that (i) the consequences of these practices and systems are ethically unacceptable and that (ii) an ethically acceptable alternative agriculture that lacks those consequences can and should be developed.

Evaluating Alternative Agricultures

If we abandon the notion of sustainability and think of sustainable agriculture as simply alternative agriculture, then it becomes clear how we should both understand the criticisms that proponents of sustainable agriculture levy against conventional agriculture and how to go about evaluating their positive proposals. These proponents are attempting to initiate a change in agricultural policy that would shift American agriculture away from what they perceive to be its harmful dependence on chemical inputs. In its place, they propose to install a system of food and fiber production that systematically pursues the following goals:

1. More thorough incorporation of natural processes such as nutrient cycles, nitrogen fixation, and pest-predator relationships into the agricultural production process;

2. Reduction in the use of off-farm inputs with the greatest potential to harm the environment or the health of farmers and consumers;

3. Greater productive use of the biological and genetic potential of plant and animal species;

4. Improvement of the match between cropping patterns and the productive potential and physical limitations of agricultural lands to ensure long-term sustainability of current production levels; and

5. Profitable and efficient production with emphasis on improved farm management and conservation of soil, water, energy, and biological resources. (8, p. 4)

So defined, this alternative agriculture attempts to reduce, to the extent possible, the use of purchased synthetic chemical inputs. It is generally thought to include such farm practices as (i) crop rotations designed to reduce pest damage, increase available soil nitrogen, and reduce soil erosion; (ii) integrated pest management (IPM), which reduces the need for pesticides by a careful combination of crop rotations, scouting, weather monitoring, use of pest-resistant cultivars, timing of planting, and biological pest controls; (iii) low-intensity animal production systems that emphasize nonpharmaceutical methods of health maintenance; and (iv) tillage and planting practices that conserve soil and water resources and help control weeds. This alternative agriculture promotes diversified, multi-enterprise farming operations, which tend to be more resilient in the face of drought, pest infestation, and unexpected market fluctuations. It also promotes the agricultural research necessary to develop effective alternative farming practices.

The criticisms of conventional farming practices are intended to initiate a policy process by providing what in Chapter 2 we described as "problem identification." The proposed alternative farming practices and diversified farming system are offered as a solution to the problems identified by these criticisms. These practices and system are the *conduct* that proponents would like to secure from American farmers. What remains to be specified is the particular agricultural policy or policies that would produce such conduct. Such policies will be necessary because current policies have served to entrench, if not promote, the farming practices that an alternative agriculture would replace. To provide a specification of these policies, we would need to develop a specification of the *situation* and then determine the sort of *structure* that would have to be imposed on that situation in order to secure the desired conduct. Once determined, this structure would constitute a concrete policy proposal that could receive consideration during the policy formulation phase of the policy process.

A concrete illustration would be helpful here. Agriculture, we noted in Chapter 6, is the major nonpoint source of surface- and groundwater contamination in the United States. Preventing, or at least reducing, such pollution will require changing current farming practices. Among other things, farmers will have to be weaned away from their heavy dependence on synthetic nutrients and pesticides. No single policy is likely to achieve this goal; rather, it will probably take a set of different policies, each of which focuses on one aspect of the problem. Put in terms of our analytical framework, these policies will have to change farmers' conduct in such a way that it no longer results in the undesirable performance characteristic of current conduct. These policies will probably include ones that both more closely regulate the farmers' use of these chemicals and provide farmers with significant economic disincentives for their use. Federal statutes already give the EPA significant regulatory powers in this area. The Clean Water Act of 1972 is the major federal statute regulating both point and nonpoint source pollution of surface- and groundwater. It empowers the EPA to develop industrywide discharge standards for conventional and toxic pollutants. The Federal Insecticide, Fungicide, and Rodenticide Act (FIFRA) provides for the registration of all pesticides and the uses to which they may be put, the certification of individuals who apply certain restricted pesticides, and premarket testing of all new pesticides. The EPA has used FIFRA to ban all crop uses of some pesticides, including DDT, aldrin, and dieldrin; most crop uses of others, such as heptachlor and aldicarb; and some crop uses of still others, as noted in Chapter 5.

FIFRA requires the EPA to reregister pesticides as new data on their health effects become available. There is good reason to believe that the reregistration process will result in further restrictions in the permitted agricultural uses of many pesticides, especially fungicides. The EPA has only recently begun to move under the Clean Water Act to control nonpoint source water pollutants, including fertilizers and pesticides. It has ordered all states to develop plans for monitoring and regulating nonpoint source pollution of surface- and groundwater. It is unclear what form these state regulations will take; however, it seems likely that they will both restrict the use of fertilizers and pesticides and increase their cost to the farmer. It is quite probable not only that certification procedures for applicators will be tightened but also that there will be effective regulation of application rates. Such regulations will inevitably increase the cost of using these chemicals, either because chemicals currently in use will be forced out of the market in favor of safer, more expensive chemicals or because the regulations will add significantly to the cost of their application.

Proponents of alternative agricultures predict that the shift away from heavily chemical-dependent farming practices would have a number of consequences. Broadly speaking, this shift would reduce the environmental and health risks posed by the current use of these chemicals. But it would also reduce crop yields, thus requiring that additional land be brought under cultivation. Because this increased acreage would have to include more slope lands, soil erosion would increase. Increased reliance on leguminous crops for nitrogen would reduce the productivity of cash grain and vegetable farms. Farmers would probably reintroduce livestock in an effort to make more efficient use of leguminous crops, thereby possibly creating a new source of nonpoint source water pollution. The reduction of chemical inputs, especially herbicides, would increase the demand for farm labor and hence could be expected to revitalize rural communities. Net farm income would increase (every 1 percent decrease in production is predicted to bring about a 2–4 percent increase in the farm-gate price and an increase in retail price to consumers of about one-third that amount). Increased net farm income, coupled with the increased acreage under cultivation, would lead to higher land values throughout the United States. There would be a reduction in the energy required to produce and use agricultural chemicals, although this energy saving would be at least partly offset by the energy inputs for increased tillage. Finally, decreased production, coupled with a shift to leguminous crops, would lead directly to a decrease in the grains available for export markets; however, this loss in exports might be offset by a diminished need for price support and stabilization programs, since farm surpluses, especially in commodities such as corn and soybeans, would be significantly reduced.

There is considerable disagreement among both proponents and critics regarding the accuracy of these qualitative predictions, as well as about the magnitude and significance of the predicted consequences of adopting alternative farming practices. Such disagreement is understandable given the difficulty of predicting accurately the impact of adopting these practices on dynamic systems as complex as American agriculture, the farm economy, and the environment. But fortunately for our discussion, it is enough simply that we know the sorts of consequences that might be entailed by the adoption of alternative farming practices. The crucial lesson to be drawn here is that the adoption of these practices would have consequences far beyond the fields that would be farmed using alternative, minimally chemical-dependent practices. Not only would surface- and groundwater quality be affected, but also wildlife, rural communities, consumers, chemical producers, export markets, and taxpayers. These effects would not be uniformly beneficial to everyone involved. There would be winners and losers. In some regions of the country, for example, where farm production is less dependent on pesticides, farmers would benefit considerably, whereas farmers in other regions would suffer. The use of fungicides is a case in point. In some regions it is virtually impossible to produce apples of marketable quality and appearance without fungicides; in other regions, it is quite easy. A ban on fungicides would give apple growers in the latter regions a significant competitive advantage.

Once we realize that there will be winners and losers in any large-scale shift to alternative agricultural practices, then it becomes clear that the policies that would be necessary to bring about this shift pose ethical issues that would have to be addressed at some point in the policy process. The question, we realize, is not simply whether we want an alternative agriculture free of current practices' chemical dependence; it is also whether the policies necessary to bring about such an agriculture would be ethically acceptable. For those of us who adopt a rights-based perspective on this issue, the question will be whether the structures imposed by these policies are consistent with what we take to be the relevant moral rights of those affected by these policies, namely, farmers, rural communities, taxpayers, consumers, and so on. For those of us who adopt a consequentialist perspective, the question will be whether the consequences of these policies maximize (or satisfy) our chosen decision rule (or criterion). From either perspective, the ethical acceptability of proposed policies will turn on the details of those policies— details of policy *structure* in the first case, details of policy *performance* in the second. And as undesirable as certain aspects of modern agriculture may be, it does not follow that any alternative lacking those undesirable aspects is, ethically speaking, any better. Alternative agricultures, like any agricultural system, have their strengths and weaknesses. It remains an open question whether they would be better overall than what we already have.

Some Anticipated Ethical Issues

In the absence of concrete policy proposals, as well as detailed analyses of the conduct and hence performance that these proposed policies could be expected to entail, it is difficult to foresee all the ethical issues that would be likely to arise; however, some of the issues can be anticipated.

There are the costs, both direct and indirect, to consumers. The shift away from chemical-dependent farming practices may lessen the health risk posed by contamination of foods and water supplies, but if achieving this decreased risk entails higher food prices for consumers, then we must look at how these benefits and costs are distributed across society. Malnutrition and hunger are no less a health risk than is pesticide contamination. In the absence of public policies that effectively combat malnutrition and hunger, the existing health risk posed by agricultural chemicals may be more equitable in its distribution than the risk that would be imposed by increased food prices since the latter would have a disproportionate impact on the poor.

Proponents and critics alike anticipate a significant decrease in grain production and hence grain surpluses. The loss of export revenues might, as some argue, be at least partly offset by decreased federal price support payments, but we must also look at the issue of food security. Commodity surpluses are costly to maintain; however, they do provide a cushion against crop failure and resulting famine. In the absence of the cushion provided by surpluses, not only might consumers be unacceptably vulnerable to interruptions in the food supply, but also food prices to consumers might fluctuate widely, again with a predictable effect on the poor.

Perhaps these costs to consumers might be more than offset by the effect that these policies would have in preserving and encouraging what some see as a morally exemplary or virtuous agrarian lifestyle (see Chapter 10). But we need to look closely at the impact that these policies would have on rural communities and farm structure. Proponents anticipate that the significantly larger labor force required by an alternative agriculture would revitalize rural life and communities. They further anticipate that an alternative agriculture would both render moderate-sized family farms more competitive and arrest the ever-increasing concentration of capital in the hands of large corporate farm owners. But would this happen? The predicted increase in land values and in acreage under cultivation might well accelerate rather than reverse the current trends in farm structure change. Instead of the rebirth in family farming that proponents envision, these policies might conceivably lead to a more thoroughly industrialized agricultural system, worked almost entirely by largely unskilled wage laborers who did not live on the farms on which they worked. Even if these laborers lived in rural communities (rather than commuting from nearby cities), they would hardly have the wealth to contribute significantly to the reconstruction and revitalization of rural communities and infrastructures. The point here is not that this is what would happen, only that we must look closely at the impact that these policies could be expected to have. Our cities are full of people whose parents came to escape the grinding poverty of rural life. Policies that would return significant numbers of people to those conditions would be ethically unacceptable. They would, of course, also be a failure; people wouldn't go.

There is also the issue of the impact of these proposed policies on wildlife and livestock. Proponents anticipate that the shift to alternative farming practices would promote the reintroduction of livestock in order to make more efficient use of nitrogen-fixing leguminous crops. They assume that this shift, perhaps accompanied by policies restricting the nontherapeutic use of antibiotics, would move American animal agriculture away from its dependence on confinement systems. It seems doubtful that these policies would be sufficient to return animals to the barnyards of an earlier era; however, they might lead to production systems that would be less confining than current systems. The impact of these policies on wildlife is equally unclear. The decreased reliance on agricultural chemicals, especially synthetic nutrients, might well result in dramatic improvements in surfacewater quality, to the great benefit of wildlife, especially aquatic life, if these improvements were not offset by the anticipated increase in soil erosion. The anticipated increase in total acreage under cultivation would result in the destruction of some wildlife habitat; this loss in habitat might be offset by the anticipated return to pasture rotation practices, coupled with greater production of leguminous crops.

There would, no doubt, be still other ethical issues. The main point to be made here is that we have the appropriate analytical framework and conceptual tools for evaluating the ethical acceptability of the proposed policies that would implement an alternative agriculture. Furnished with detailed analyses of the structure and performance of the proposed policies, we know how to go about making the necessary evaluation. There is, then, an important distinction between piecemeal criticism of problems related to food safety, environmental quality, animal welfare, and the financial viability of farming and the systematic philosophical critique of agriculture that is implied by the call for sustainable agriculture. Critics who advocate sustainable agriculture may be using the term as a convenient way to note the need for change in policies affecting these diverse issues. If so, there is no particular ethical significance to sustainable agriculture as such. What is argued is the need to understand a broader set of values in evaluating each of these distinct areas of public policy. Narrow, technical notions of sustainability drawn from agronomy, population genetics, or ecology might be incorporated into conventional utilitarian criteria for evaluating policy performance.

If sustainable agriculture is to be interpreted as a genuine philosophical critique of conventional agriculture, the alternative vision must be specified as a general world view, a coherent and comprehensive set of assumptions and values that could guide production, consumption, and policy decisions along an alternative path. Wes Jackson and Miguel Altieri have attempted to offer such a vision. Jackson, Altieri, and others, writing on sustainable agriculture, often merge their arguments with those of the agrarians discussed in Chapter 10. More frequently, the alternative is simply a list of agronomic practices, the standard view, that reduce chemical and other purchased inputs and advocate crop rotation, reduced tillage, and IPM. Although these practices might be components of an alternative agriculture, they are also consistent with the economic and political goals of conventional agriculture as it has been conceptualized over the past decade.

As philosophical critiques of conventional agriculture, visions of sustainability criticize conventional practices. They have substituted alternative visions that do seem to be more consistent with principles of ecology, but they have not yet succeeded in translating these visions into policy prescriptions.

At the time of this writing, conventional utilitarian, egalitarian, and proce-dural norms appear to be more effective vehicles for assessing policy and for making adjustments in existing policy. Jackson, at least, would not be satis-fied with this assessment since he views the norm of enlightened self-interest (the basis of contract arguments) as a fundamental part of the problem. He would see the need for an environmental ethic, one that makes dramatic change in the norms and concepts that have been the basis for this book. The theme of alternative approaches to ethics, critical of the approach taken here, is considered again in Chapter 10.

Summary

The recent popularity of sustainable agriculture is due to the convergence of several political forces affecting agriculture. The management challenges fac-ing farmers have become more complex as farm policy, monetary policy, and foreign trade interact to affect the prices of farm commodities and the costs of farm credit. Farmers have become more aware that changes in farm tech-nology can have unpredictable effects on farm structure. Rural communities have undergone dramatic change in the past two decades, becoming less de-pendent upon farming as their economic base. These three forces have led farm groups and rural communities to seek policies and technologies that would produce a steady state farm economy, one in which farms and agribusiness could operate in a predictable fashion for the foreseeable fu-ture. These forces are joined by growing public concern for the environmen-tal consequences of agriculture and by popular understanding of nature or ecology as a closed system of checks and balances. In the public's mind, agri-culture has become unsustainable because it has violated the limits of the ecosystem, threatening to throw it out of balance.

A closer examination of these problems shows that multiple goals are be-ing collapsed under the umbrella of sustainability. Farm groups are con-cerned about rural quality of life, especially as it is related to farm income and the continued economic viability of existing farm communities. Urban groups are interested in environmental impacts, food safety, and water qual-ity, as well as the more abstract value of ecosystem integrity. In combining these concerns under a call for sustainable agriculture, farm and urban groups attain some political effectiveness because of their larger numbers, but they sacrifice the ability to make specific or even accurate statements about the values that are truly being sought. It is quite possible that social and farming systems that sacrifice one or more of these values are sustainable in the sense that they can be continued indefinitely.

The National Research Council proposes an alternative agriculture that consists largely of reducing chemical inputs to the agricultural production process. No single policy is likely to achieve this goal. Instead a package of policies will be needed to change incentives so that farmers reduce their use of chemicals in a variety of areas. Regulatory policy provides a means to do this, but it will also impose costs upon farmers, as well as upon agribusiness firms themselves. Once this is realized, the ethical questions associated with sustainability can be seen in more familiar terms. When should individual rights to make decisions or use property be compromised to achieve public goals? How and when should losers be compensated as public policy alters incentives to use chemical inputs? Should food consumers share in the cost burdens through increased food prices, particularly given that the greatest burden from increased food prices falls upon the urban poor? These are familiar ethical issues raised independently in other chapters of the book. Framing them in terms of sustainability does not change their content.

Key Terms

alternative agriculture   standard view

philosophical critique   sustainable agriculture

References

1. Altieri, Miguel A. 1987. *Agroecology: The Scientific Basis of Alternative Agriculture.* Boulder, Colo.: Westview Press.
2. ——. 1991. "An Agroecological Analysis of the Environmental Degradation Resulting from the Structure of Agriculture," in *Beyond the Large Farm: Ethics and Research goals for Agriculture,* ed. Paul B. Thompson and Bill A. Stout. Boulder, Colo.: Westview Press, pp. 125–135.
3. Carson, Rachel. 1962. *Silent Spring.* Boston: Houghton Mifflin.
4. Comstock, Gary. 1989. "Genetically Engineered Herbicide Resistance, Part One," *Journal of Agricultural Ethics* 2:263–306.
5. Hallberg, M. C. 1988. "The U.S. Agricultural and Food System: A Postwar Historical Perspective." Pub. No. 55. University Park: Northeast Regional Center for Rural Development, Pennsylvania State University.
6. Jackson, Wes. 1985. *New Roots for Agriculture.* Lincoln: University of Nebraska Press.
7. Lowance, Richard, Paul F. Hendrix, and Eugene P. Odom. 1987. "A Hierarchical Approach to Sustainable Agriculture," *American Journal of Alternative Agriculture* 1(4):169–173.
8. National Research Council. 1989. *Alternative Agriculture.* Washington, D.C.: National Academy Press.
9. Suppe, Frederick. 1987. "The Limited Applicability of Agricultural Research," *Agriculture and Human Values* 4(Fall):4–13.

Suggestions for Further Reading

The cited paper by Lowance et al. (1987) and the National Research Council report on *Alternative Agriculture* (Washington, D.C.: National Academy Press, 1989) provide a good starting point for a discussion of sustainable agriculture. There are dozens of recent books that argue for sustainable agriculture (or sustainable development), many written for an audience of educated nonspecialists. The publications of Lester Brown's Worldwatch Institute have consistently taken sustainability as their organizing theme, and many articles on different aspects of sustainability can be found in each year's edition of *The State of the World* (New York: Norton). Sympathetic treatments of sustainability as a concept can be found in Herman E. Daly and John B. Cobb, Jr., *For the Common Good* (Boston: Beacon Press, 1989) and in John Young, *Sustaining the Earth* (Cambridge, Mass.: Harvard University Press, 1990). A perceptive and critical treatment of sustainability in international development is found in Michael Redclift, *Sustainable Development* (London: Methuen, 1987). Few philosophical discussions of sustainability are in print. Readers may consult Patrick Madden and Paul B. Thompson, "Ethical Aspects of Changing Agricultural Technology in the United States," *Notre Dame Journal of Law, Ethics and Public Policy* 3(1):85–116, 1987, or Mark Sagoff, *The Economy of the Earth* (New York: Cambridge University Press, 1988), but neither provides detailed analysis of sustainability as a concept. The German philosopher/sociologist Niklas Luhmann has raised some of the most difficult issues in his concise but technically complex book *Ecological Communication* (Chicago: University of Chicago Press, 1989). In addition, many of the suggested works listed in Chapter 6 are also relevant to the issue of sustainability.

Readers are, of course, invited to consult the works of Wes Jackson and Miguel Altieri cited in the references to this chapter. Jackson is also coeditor with Wendell Berry and Bruce Coleman of *Meeting the Expectations of Land: Essays in Sustainable Agriculture and Stewardship* (San Francisco: North Point Press, 1984). A book entitled *Our Sustainable Table*, ed. Robert Clark (San Francisco: North Point Press, 1990), includes popular essays by Jackson and Wendell Berry (as well as a list of additional sources), but these essays are less helpful philosophically than for the way they illustrate how sustainability is interpreted simply as reduced pesticide use in the public mind. In addition to his book, Altieri has published extensively in agricultural journals. He has contributed a chapter to *Beyond the Large Farm: Ethics and Research Goals for Agriculture*, ed. Paul B. Thompson and Bill A. Stout (Boulder, Colo.: Westview Press, 1991). That collection also includes a bibliographic essay on environmental criticism of conventional agriculture that examines the links between agriculture and environmental ethics.

CHAPTER 10

Saving the Family Farm

Since the passage of the original "Triple A," the Agricultural Adjustment Act of 1933, U.S. federal policy has attempted to relieve the financial stress of American farmers. The public rationale for doing so has several stated objectives, including maintaining food security for American consumers and conserving soil and water resources for future generations. Often, however, the broad package of payments to farmers that is known simply as **farm policy** has been defended on the grounds that preserving family farms is itself a valid goal for public policy. In the last decade, farm failures throughout the American South and Midwest were so numerous that the period between 1983 and 1987 became known as a crisis. An alternative proposal to the 1985 Food Security Act was titled the Save the Family Farm Act. The goal of saving family farms surfaced again in the late 1980s as part of an argument against new technologies that were expected to influence agricultural production as a result of advances in molecular biology. This chapter will examine the goal of saving the family farm. Unlike other case study chapters that emphasize the elements of a particular policy decision, the analysis of the family farm issue will stress general philosophical themes that might be applied to many policies. Farm policy is in fact a complex web of many policies, some of which have economic implications that cancel each other out. As such, understanding the economic consequences of any given policy requires sophisticated knowledge of economic concepts, and there is often debate among economists as to what the economic implications of a given policy actually are.

The chapter begins with a broad overview of farm policy and then presents three different ways to think about what is happening to small or family farms. Indeed, the characteristics that define a small or family farm are themselves hotly debated by those who take alternative perspectives on the importance of saving farms. The first philosophy to be discussed begins with a utilitarian analysis of changes in American agriculture that defines the ethical significance of farm policy in terms of its financial and emotional impact upon affected parties. The second philosophy combines elements of libertarian and egalitarian philosophy in a view that we call **agrarian populism**. The third view stresses the impact of farming on personal moral character and presents an important challenge to some of the broad approaches to ethics and policy that have been developed in this book. We call this view **agrarian traditionalism**.

Farm Policy

The wealth and financial viability of a farm is, in the final analysis, a simple matter of the farmer's ability to bring in more income from the sale of commodities than is spent to produce them. Farms that persistently lose money or that make profits that are insufficient to meet family needs eventually fail. In this respect, farms are no different from any family owned business. There are many things that can affect a particular farm's capacity to earn income, however. Soil fertility, water availability, and climate make profitable production far more difficult in some locations than in others. Farm management skill and even luck can also play a role. These imbalances in the productive potential of farms are not usually thought of as appropriate for policy redress. Instead, public policies take aim at problems that affect either all (or most) farms or all farms of a certain type.

The most serious general problem may be that U.S. farmers have exhibited a century-long ability to produce more agricultural commodities than can be sold at a profit, even when world markets are included. If prices for food and fiber were established by supply and demand, farmers would experience persistent shortfalls. Those who could not survive an extended period of losses would be forced out of farming, and this phenomenon would continue at least until the production capacity was reduced, prices rose, and agriculture became profitable. Such a situation would be a textbook picture of how competition is supposed to control prices in a free market economy, but Americans have been unwilling to allow market forces to have these effects in agriculture. One reason is that it may be better to tolerate a chronic oversupply of food than to deal with the hunger, deprivation, and political instability that might accompany even a temporary undersupply. We can tolerate a little inconvenience in the availability of dry cleaning, automobiles, or even energy, but the prospect of food shortages strikes many people as something to avoid at all costs. A second reason is that bankruptcies of even 2 to 5 percent of agricultural firms would affect hundreds of thousands of Americans. The relocation costs, the suffering of affected families, and the political repercussions for farm state politicians might be too great to bear. A third reason is that chronic overproduction in agriculture might continue to be a problem as long as there are enough producers to ensure true competition.

Although farmers go bankrupt, their land usually does not go out of production; rather typically it is purchased or leased by successful farmers who may more than make up for the production that would have been lost by bankruptcy. Furthermore, the seasonal nature of agricultural production makes it easy for farmers to increase expected yields after the crop is in the field by extra plantings or additional fertilizer, but difficult to decrease expected yields without writing off the investment entirely. As such, an expectation of high prices increases the supply of food, but an expectation of low prices does little to reduce it. Any of these reasons for failing to allow market forces to control supply might be questioned, but their cumulative impact has been a reluctance to leave the oversupply problem to the market.

A related general problem is resource depletion. As noted in Chapter 6, farmers face a prisoner's dilemma situation in respect to conservation of soil and water. While it might be good for everyone to reduce their use of these resources, any individual can gain an advantage by failing to do so. This is particularly the case with pumping of aquifers and erosive effects that may harm lands far from the site of abuse. There are incentives for everyone to overutilize these resources, then, and the result is the worst case outcome. Irreplaceable resources are consumed to produce food that is not needed and that cannot be sold at a price that compensates farmers for input costs, let alone the long-term costs of resource depletion.

Although these problems plague all agriculture, some farmers are especially vulnerable to the economic forces set in motion by the imbalance between incentives to produce more rather than less. As already noted, financially secure farmers without debt are far more capable of enduring years of narrow profits than are farmers who have recently started farming, expanded their operations, or made equipment purchases that must be amortized over several years. Diversified farm businesses are also stronger in difficult times, particularly when some of their income is drawn from nonfarm sources. Although large and small farms may be equally efficient in production, large operations may be able to accumulate larger cash reserves in good years, may find it easier to expand into supply or processing components of agribusiness, and may be able to negotiate more favorable terms with both suppliers and buyers. There may also be a tendency for successful farms to grow larger as they buy out failed competitors. Though it is clear that large or corporately owned farm operations have weaknesses as well as strengths, small farms tend to fall into the categories of vulnerability more often than large ones.

The issue of farm size is, for most people, related to the idea of family farms. There has been a historical pattern of family ownership and management of small and **medium-sized farms**. Some key elements of this pattern that are important to the policy debate are discussed later, but it is important to recognize that there is no intrinsic connection between farm size and family ownership. Some small farms are operated as hobbies and may be owned by wealthy individuals who rarely see them. Some large farms are owned and, with the aid of technology, farmed by single families. Some medium-sized farms often thought of as family farms are owned by absentee landlords, and some families farm under contract to food marketing corporations that specify the production process in great detail. Is it farm size or a pattern of ownership and work that is most relevant to public policy? The three philosophies we will discuss take different views on this question, with utilitarians stressing size and the two agrarian views stressing other characteristics better conveyed by the term *family farm*.

Farm policies, then, aim to redress at least three problems at once: imbalance between supply and demand, resource depletion, and the perceived bias against small or family farms. In fact, many other policies, including taxes, money supply, and foreign exchange, may have as strong an effect upon the fortune of farmers as do those intended to fix agricultural problems. It should come as no surprise that some policies have economic implications that tend to cancel the intended effects of others. An adequate account of the way that any given policy affects farms quickly requires sophisticated economic concepts, and economists debate the implications of a given policy. Marty Strange (10) concludes that price support policies and tax policies provide advantages for farmers who make large investments in land and equipment. Since farmers who do this either farm large operations already or expand rapidly, Strange finds the aggregate effect of farm policy to be biased against relatively small-scale family-run operations. Luther Tweeten (13), on the other hand, completes an extensive review of major farm policies by concluding that family farms receive greater benefit per dollar of farm income than do large farms. He notes that although large farms have advantages over small ones, the policies that create or maintain these advantages are not unjust. A greater emphasis on saving family farms would, in Tweeten's view, be achieved only at the expense of higher food prices, which in turn would harm the poor.

Analysis of particular policies and their effects upon farms of any given type becomes technically complex, and experts do not always agree. The sheer complexity of farm policy analysis may permit the goal of helping family farms to dominate the policy debates, without being effectively addressed by any specific policy. The general framework of goals, values, and ideas that surfaces in the political discussion of family farms is quite vague. Many different interest groups can claim to support policies that further these goals, and the policies they support may contradict one another or cancel out each other's effects. Bonnen and Browne (4) have argued that concern for family farms, which they call the *agrarian myth*, dominates and muddies discussion of agricultural policy. In their view, the vagueness and complexity of family farm issues has the effect of making farm policy hard to reform. The values are so vague and the issues so complex that policy makers come to prefer the status quo. Reform would require a clear and convincing statement of how the proposed changes would affect family farms, but since no one is entirely sure what family farms are or how the current package of policies affects them, such clarity is virtually impossible to obtain. If Bonnen and Browne are right, we might do better to forget about family farms altogether and to formulate agricultural policies on the basis of goals that can be more clearly stated. Such a proposal has been made by some followers of a utilitarian analysis, but first it is important to take a closer look at the problems raised by new agricultural technologies.

Technology Policy and Farm Structure

It is important to distinguish between the terms *production* and *productivity* as related to agricultural technology. Agricultural production can increase through expanded use of resources, such as occurred on the land frontier in this nation, or it can result from improved technology or improvement in the quality of managerial ability, labor, and land. Productivity refers to a ratio of output to input. Total productivity of agriculture is the ratio of total output to total input, with both numerator and denominator usually measured in terms of current market value. Total productivity is often used to measure economic efficiency. Partial productivity, on the other hand, measures the output attributable to a selected input or group of inputs. The common example is land productivity, such as yield of wheat per acre harvested. Livestock productivity is often measured in terms such as milk production per cow or number of eggs laid per hen. The concept of productivity is implicit in the following economic definition of technology:

> A specific state of art and science which is used to transform a set of inputs (resources) into a set of outputs (goods or services). . . . The significance of technical change is that it permits the substitution of knowledge for resources, or of inexpensive and abundant resources for scarce and expensive resources, or that it releases constraints on growth imposed by inelastic resource supplies. In the process this change generally provides some economic benefit by a cost-reducing productivity dividend. (11, p. 2).

The initial beneficiaries of the development and utilization of new technology are the businesses or institutions receiving royalties or profits from supplying the technology to users. The employees of these organizations are also direct beneficiaries. Other beneficiaries are the early-adopting firms or innovators who enjoy a lower average cost of production per unit of output while the prices are still keyed to the older (higher-cost) technology. Consequently, early adopters earn increased profits. The secondary impact of most technologies is to increase production of the agricultural commodities. In agriculture, the increase in output is ordinarily accompanied by a more than proportionate decline in prices and, therefore, a lower total income for the producing sector of the industry after the adoption has reached an advanced stage. Conversely, the marketing sector, whose income is keyed to the volume of output, tends to receive higher income as a result of reduced commodity prices at the farm level. Consumers then become the ultimate beneficiaries through lower commodity prices than those they would have to pay if the new technology had not been adopted. The national economy also benefits through real income gained (increased purchasing power) and sometimes through increased exports of the farm commodity.

Clearly, improved technology typically increases the output generated from a given amount of input, defined by economists as an increase in productivity. Early adopters often find their average cost of production declining and profits rising while the total quantity of the commodity produced by the industry has not risen enough to suppress prices. However, as more farmers adopt the new technology, output tends to increase significantly, thereby putting downward pressure on product prices, except in those cases where demand is expanding significantly or government price support programs intervene. Farmers who fail to innovate soon find themselves at a disadvantage; they incur the higher cost associated with the older technology but receive lower prices for the commodities they produce. Feeling this pressure, some of these farmers will adopt the new technology as part of the widespread adoption pattern, but their profits often decline in spite of this late adoption unless they can expand the size of the farm sufficiently to compensate for the loss. Early adopters are more likely to be able to finance expansion out of the temporarily high profits. Farmers who do not adopt the new technology may continue to incur costs above the falling commodity prices; ultimately they either go out of commercial farming entirely, become part-time operators, or shift to production of other agricultural commodities in which they may have a competitive advantage. Meanwhile, the early adopters who had the skill and capital to apply the technology appropriately typically capture a larger share of the market. Some may now operate larger farms, but they do not necessarily have higher profits than they did before the new technology was introduced.

Adoption of new technology can also accelerate changes in the size distribution of farms, with subsequent impact upon rural communities. The effects may include the failure of less efficient farm operators, the demise of agribusiness firms, geographic shifts in production, and a further concentration of production in fewer and larger firms. When local farmers capture an increased share of the production of the commodity affected by that technology, employment and income benefits accrue to firms and employees involved in the processing, transportation, and sale of the commodity and of secondary products manufactured from that commodity. The ultimate beneficiaries of the technology, then, are consumers (through lower commodity prices), early-adopting firms (through an initial surge of profits and an increased share of industry sales), and the firms or institutions providing the technology to users (through royalties and profits).

Typically, adaptive or applied research is necessary to select or modify technology appropriate to local climatic, soil, and market conditions. This adaptive work has been a significant contribution of public universities and the U.S. Department of Agriculture; hence technology research and development is a public policy issue for agriculture. However, commercial development of new agricultural technology is increasingly done in the private sector—primarily by agribusiness firms. Roughly two-thirds of the total research and development expenditures for the farm and food system in the United States are now made by the private sector (11). An even higher percentage of the agricultural technology transfer is provided by agribusiness sales personnel and consulting firms.

This trend is especially significant among the new biotechnology firms that have emerged in recent years. The potential effect of biotechnology on the structure of American agriculture, its employment, income, and competitiveness, is unknown at present. If the nation's technology delivery system—both the public sector (primarily extension) and the private sector (sales and service organizations)—quickly and effectively helps farmers and agribusiness to adopt appropriate biotechnology, the competitive edge of the nation's agricultural industries against foreign competitors can be strengthened. At the same time, biotechnology can have the same disruptive effects upon rural communities that chemical and mechanical technology have had in the past.

CASE

The in vitro *Production of BST*

One example of the effect of biotechnology is the *in vitro* production of bovine somatotropin (BST) by genetically altered bacteria. Cornell University scientists have estimated that this hormone, when correctly administered to lactating dairy cows, can increase their annual milk production by about 25 percent. The Monsanto Company, which is presently awaiting FDA approval of BST, contends that adoption of the enzyme technology will be extremely profitable for the dairy industry, but this assessment is not universally shared. As adoption of the technology becomes widespread, the surplus of dairy products will expand significantly, thereby increasing pressure on federal price support programs and ultimately causing lower prices for dairy products and reducing the number of dairy farmers (9). Fallert and Hallberg (6) review several scenarios for adoption of BST. Under the assumption that BST is adopted throughout the United States, they predict that consumer expenditures on milk and dairy products would decrease by 5.7 percent. Milk prices and producer revenues would decline by 8 percent and 7 percent, respectively. In a worst case scenario, consumers' fears about the health effects of BST might provoke a reduction in the consumption of milk, leading to a 12 percent decline in price and a 10 percent decline in the size of the nation's dairy herd. Fallert and Hallberg note that this would provoke major adjustments on the part of dairy farmers in the United States. After reviewing the comparative impacts of BST on small versus large farms, Loren Tauer concludes:

> Since BST use will increase aggregate milk production and thus require fewer cows in total, more of those reductions may come from smaller farms that

cannot as effectively use BST than from larger farms. Since there will be fewer cows, many small farms may be eliminated before milk demand and supply are balanced.

There are those who argue that since BST increases production per cow, farmers will reduce the number of cows in their herd and produce the same amount of milk. If all farmers reduce their herd size accordingly, there would be no need for a reduction in farm numbers. This line of reasoning is economically illogical, and empirical evidence does not support it. It rarely makes economic sense for farmers to reduce the number of cows they have capacity for on their farms. (12, p. 209)

The structural adjustments would be particularly painful for those farmers forced to leave the industry who do not have profitable alternatives. States where farmers lag behind in adoption of the BST technology could be most severely affected.

The case of BST illustrates how the family farm issue affects the general policy environment for agriculture in indirect and surprising ways. Dairy producers in Wisconsin and New York were alarmed by economists' predictions on the effects of BST on the dairy industry. Many feared that the productivity gains available from BST would be disproportionately captured by large dairy producers, who in turn are disproportionately located in the southern United States. When the issue was described as a regional competition rather than as a technology that would affect inefficient operations, it became much easier to mobilize political support on the grounds that BST would undermine family farming in the North and Northeast. The activism of these small farm advocates attracted allies from unusual sources. Animal welfare activists raised concerns about the effects of BST on cattle. As the issue of BST became more generally known, consumer groups began to raise questions about the health effects on humans who drank milk from cattle treated with BST. A consortium of grocery chains pledged not to stock dairy products that had been produced by dairies using BST, even though BST occurs naturally in milk and scientists see no health hazard associated with the levels of BST that may occur in milk produced with the new technology. This decision had little to do with preserving family farms, but it seems likely that it would not have been raised if family farm activists had not made the introduction of BST into a political issue.

The BST case also illustrates the complexity of policy issues in which concern for family farms plays a pivotal role. Legislatures and government agencies may be pressed to issue regulations on the use of BST in the coming years. These regulations may involve labeling of milk and milk products produced by injecting the hormone into dairy cows. They may involve animal welfare restrictions. They may call for a total ban on BST as a dairy production tool. Any of these regulatory proposals might be expected to draw support from family farm activists, yet the connection between these regulatory proposals and the family farm issue is indirect at best. The agrarian values that lead people to try to help family farms are mingled in this web of policy proposals with concern for human health and safety, for informed consent, and for humane treatment of farm animals. In addition to being economically complex, the issues are philosophically complex. The value alliances among family farm activists, consumer activists, and animal welfare activists create significant pressure for policy action, but they are fragile alliances. They may fracture at any time, and there is little reason to think that they will be maintained when BST fades from the policy agenda.

Technology Conflicts and Public Policy

In one sense, it is easy to see why some dairy producers have opposed the introduction of BST. Those producers who have relatively small, integrated dairy operations may well be hurt by the new technology. Many Northern dairies are operations in which the farmer raises the feed for the ten to forty cows that are milked. These farmers operate profitably because they purchase little, if any, feed and incorporate the value that is added from growing, processing, and transporting feed into their milk price. Many larger dairies make a profit by carefully managing larger numbers of cows, but such management requires time. These producers must either purchase feed or hire additional labor to manage crops. Although economists continue to debate the actual effects of BST, many producers in the first group think that the technology would give an additional advantage to producers in the second group. If this is so, it is in the self-interest of the first group to oppose the new technology.

There is nothing wrong with these integrated dairy farmers acting to advance their self-interests. From the policy perspective, however, the issue emerges as one in which their interests stand in opposition to those of another group of dairy farmers: those who emphasize herd management. That is, the policy issue appears to be one in which two groups of producers are distinguished by their choice of production strategies. They may also be distinguished by region or by whether they are, according to some definition, large or small, but these additional distinctions appear at the outset to be something of an accident. How should public policy address this question of competition between two groups? Two answers can be sketched.

The first answer is libertarian. The conflict between these two producer groups is a market conflict. Government cannot intervene in this conflict without violating noninterference rights. If government bans BST simply because integrated producers want it banned, government interferes with the way herd management producers can use their property. Government is telling them that they cannot spend their money on BST. Government is also telling them what they can and cannot do with their cattle, and it is telling the biotechnology industry that it cannot market a product that it has invested a great deal of its property in developing. The integrated dairy farmers are not entitled to government help on this view, but everyone else is entitled to government noninterference. Acting on behalf of the integrated producers would be an instance of government picking the winners and losers.

The second answer is utilitarian. Contrary to the libertarian view, for the utilitarian this is not purely a market conflict. Government is already intimately involved in the dairy industry. Public universities helped develop BST. U.S. Department of Agriculture price supports already affect milk production. Government has established the rules of the game and has had a big hand in deciding who wins and who loses. As such, the only recourse is to evaluate the regulation of BST in terms of its likely consequences. A ban on BST would be a decision to continue the status quo. The alternative, allowing BST to come on the market, would have the usual pattern of consequences. Producers and distributors of BST would benefit, as would early adopters among dairy producers. Some producers would be harmed. If milk prices are allowed to fall, the big beneficiaries would be consumers. Since it is likely that the aggregate benefits to consumers would outweigh the harms to producers, a utilitarian would probably endorse the introduction of BST, though for very different reasons than would libertarians.

There are several factors that would complicate utilitarian analysis. Calculation of benefits and harms become far more complex when the effects of international markets are included. What if the United States allowed BST but Europe did not? Would the effect be to make U.S. milk cheaper (hence helping U.S. dairy producers), or would other countries refuse to accept U.S. milk (hence harming them)? What about the effect upon the dairy cows themselves? Should the benefits and harms to cattle be counted in the utilitarian calculation? What about the alleged consumer health consequences? Should we count these consequences as harms despite the fact that there is no scientific evidence that they are harmful? These factors might tip the balance against BST, but what is important is to see that none of these considerations have anything to do with favoring integrated producers in virtue of the claim that helping this group serves the policy goal of preserving the family farm. The value of the family farm is out of the picture entirely in both the libertarian and utilitarian analyses of the issue.

Why, then, should saving the family farm be introduced into the issue at all? It is easy to see why integrated producers would use the family farm issue as part of their appeal if they expected that this would help them get political support. It is harder to see why anyone should take the family farm issue seriously, that is, why it should be part of a rational argument intended to sway disinterested parties toward sympathy with the integrated producers' point of view. Many policy analysts have faced this difficulty and have concluded that family farm arguments are irrational, founded on nostalgia and emotion. They acknowledge that they are a political force, but they do not regard the family farm issue as one that has a legitimate basis in any viable interpretation of the public interest. As such, they salute the value of the family farm because it is politically necessary to do so while privately discounting the force of arguments that appeal to the family farm issue. These policy analysts concede that there may be good reason for policies that help retrain dislocated farmers, preserve resources or protect the public health, and lower costs to food consumers. But there is no good reason for policies to save the family farm. The family farm issue is little more than a cloak for interest group politics. Those who support farm groups because of their alleged status as family farms are dupes, taken in by empty rhetoric and emotional appeal. It may be politically suicidal to oppose the family farm publicly, but there is no ethical content to the notion of the family farm, and in an ideal world, this issue would disappear from the policy agenda.

This conclusion is hasty, however, for it ignores the arguments that have been given to support a policy goal of preserving the family farm. The following three sections will examine some of those arguments more carefully, but it should be noted in advance that the connection between the family farm issue as a policy goal and the interests of any given group of agricultural producers will always be tenuous. Some interest groups do use the family farm issue as a cloak. As such, there is good reason to regard family farm arguments with skepticism, even if the response described in the preceding paragraphs is an overreaction.

Utilitarian Policy Analysis and Farm Structure

Most conventional farm policy analysts have training in agricultural economics. They tend to analyze farm policy by attempting to predict the consequences of policy change. They evaluate the expected consequences in terms of their impact upon individuals. This general approach to policy is an example of the philosophy that has been called consequentialist or utilitarian in this book. Agriculture policy analysts do not always use the same decision rule to convert their assessment of expected policy consequences into a policy prescription and have often been reluctant to offer prescriptions at all. Their reluctance is based on the assumption that the application of a particular decision rule would introduce bias into their otherwise objective analysis. The mere fact that farm policy issues are described in terms of their impact upon individuals, however, implies a bias toward utilitarian philosophy. These impacts would not be crucial to someone who wished to argue for certain policy goals or structures on a priori rights-based grounds. For this reason, we will refer to conventional agricultural policy analysis as utilitarian.

Policy analysts have tended to emphasize financial impacts. The reasons for doing so derive from the difficulty of measuring and comparing the emotional stress endured by different individuals. The emphasis upon financial outcomes has led utilitarian policy analysts to think of the key questions in farm policy as problems that relate to **farm structure**. Farm structure refers to general financial characteristics of agriculture analyzed at the aggregate level. For example, the number of farms in which more than 20 percent of the land under cultivation is owned by absentee landlords is a fact about farm structure. The percentage of U.S. farms engaged in both crop and animal production is a fact about farm structure. Facts about farm structure do not refer to particular farms but rather to all agriculture, defined on a regional, national, or even global basis.

Utilitarian agricultural policy analysts have documented a pattern of change in farm structure in the years since World War II. They have interpreted expressions of concern about the decline of small or family farms in terms of the declining number of medium-sized farms. This way of analyzing the family farm issue suggests that the ethical evaluation of farm policy should be made by determining why this fact about farm structure should be of any ethical significance. Two answers to this philosophical question have been suggested. The first answer analyzes the ethical significance of changes in farm structure in terms of the well-being or welfare of the individuals affected. The second answer determines whether there are ethically significant consequences associated with changing farm structure other than those associated with the welfare of individuals who experience financial impact and resulting emotional stress.

The first way of answering the question of why medium-sized farms should be protected is by far the most widely accepted approach among agricultural policy analysts. People living on the farms that fail or that endure periods of financial difficulty in connection with structural change are harmed by these changes. They can be harmed when their incomes and assets decline in value, and they can endure enormous personal loss, sadness, and regret when they are forced to change their lives in response to economic pressures. What is more, people who live in rural communities can be affected in similar ways. When the farm population declines, there will be fewer people using banks, farm implement dealers, drugstores, schools, and hospitals in rural areas. Fewer medium-sized producers means a decline in total rural population, so the unwanted impacts upon human lives are multiplied many times over throughout the small towns of rural America.

Although it is not easy to measure these impacts, estimating the decline in farm income and in the number and volume of businesses operating in rural areas provides some indication of the costs that are borne by individuals as a result of changing farm structure. This assessment is only the first stage in a utilitarian analysis, for others are affected by farm policy as well. As noted earlier, it may well be the case that changes in farm structure are causally linked to policies and technologies that create low prices for food consumers. Food consumers—all of us—benefit from these low prices. A utilitarian will want to weigh the costs or harms that are borne by producers and by residents of small towns against the benefits that are obtained by food consumers. If it turns out that the benefits outweigh the harms, a utilitarian may well conclude, as previously, that changes in farm structure are a good thing for society.

Even if low food prices produce benefits that outweigh the harms to producers (and this conclusion can be debated), a utilitarian policy analyst may be reluctant to end the analysis there. Use of a Pareto principle decision rule might require that the losers be compensated, or it may be that there are ways to produce the benefits of low food prices while minimizing the harms of structural adjustment. It may also be possible to help people in rural communities make economic transitions by offering them training in new occupations or by encouraging development of new industries in rural areas. Some conventional discussions of farm policy take up these options in great detail. These discussions all presuppose agreement on the utilitarian approach to farm policy, however, and we will forgo any further development of them here.

It is important to note that by analyzing structural change in terms of its financial impact, utilitarian analysts have not identified anything that would distinguish change in farm structure from changes in the pattern of financial characteristics for any industry. Buggy whip manufacturers went out of business, and they too experienced financial and emotional hardship. It may be that changes in this industry did not cause similar hardships for the communities in which they were located, but changes in manufacturing industries certainly do. Utilitarian policy analysts tend to see farm structure change as just another form of economic adjustment, much like adjustments in the steel or auto industries, where many people are adversely affected by plant closings. While utilitarians may be more inclined to do something about events that cause such massive disruptions of individual welfare than are strict libertarians, their reasons for policy intervention have nothing to do with the fact that it is agriculture as such that is being affected. Similar dislocations in any industry would stimulate similar arguments for a policy response.

The second utilitarian strategy for analyzing structural change shows more promise for finding a reason to resist structural change in agriculture. It may be that medium-sized farms possess a value beyond that of the goods they produce in the form of income, personal satisfaction, rural economic activity, and, of course, food for human consumption. An argument of this sort has been applied to many areas of social life where dollars and cents seem to be inappropriate units of measure. The existence of art, music, and poetry, for example, may be valuable well beyond the dollar value that paintings, performances, and poems contribute to the gross national product. The existence of wilderness areas may have value well apart from any uses that we expect to make of them. It may be possible to describe medium-sized farms in similar terms.

There are three candidates for this broader kind of value. First, it may be that such farms have **aesthetic value**. Medium-sized farms may break up the rural landscape in ways that are visually attractive. The pattern of barns and farmhouses appearing at intervals of a few miles may be preferable to one in which very large tracts of unbroken land are laid out in uniform patterns of production. Second, it may be that medium-sized farms have **historic value**. Farms run by independent families, plus rural communities spread across the landscape, have played a pivotal role in the American experience. It may be that the reasons for preserving the middle group of farms are similar to the reasons we preserve historic buildings or neighborhoods. Third, medium-sized farms may be of **symbolic value**. Such farms continue to be the subject of films and literature, particularly in books written for children. It may be that these farms are emblematic of a broad category of values that we want to preserve and promote. Just as we value the American flag or the pictures of George Washington as emblems of our values and goals, medium-sized farms may have value in their ability to represent a vague but important class of feelings and political allegiances.

Many critics of utilitarianism have stressed the fact that utilitarians tend to underrate such values, and they have expressed this criticism by claiming that utilitarians ignore noneconomic values. There is a philosophical debate over whether the tendency to ignore such values is a characteristic of utilitarianism or a failure to complete the full comparison of values that utilitarianism demands. There is also a terminological debate over whether the critics make appropriate use of the word *economic*. What is more important than either of these debates is whether these values deserve serious consideration, and if so, how to weigh them in comparison to more familiar forms of suffering and enjoyment associated with financial loss or gain. As we have described utilitarian consequentialism in this book, whatever values are allowed to count in the assessment of policy performance, it is their weighting with respect to the chosen decision rule that will determine the policy evaluation. Utilitarianism differs from other approaches in this respect because rights or procedural approaches find ways to prescribe policy in ways that reduce (and even nullify) the importance of assigning value to a policy's impacts.

Agrarian Populism

American agrarianism is often traced to Thomas Jefferson. Jefferson's writings on American farmers have provided some of the most frequently cited aphorisms in the corpus of American political thought. The most frequently cited passages are from the *Notes on the State of Virginia*, where Jefferson writes that "those who labor in the earth" have (if anyone has) been chosen to receive God's "peculiar deposit for substantial and genuine virtue" (8, p. 290), and the 1785 letter to John Jay, where Jefferson writes:

> Cultivators of the earth are the most valuable citizens. They are the most vigorous, the most independent, the most virtuous, and they are tied to their country and wedded to its liberty and interests by the most lasting bonds. (8, p. 818)

These passages, as well as others, have served time and again to remind the American public of a political duty to preserve and protect its farm population. Jefferson's words are ambiguous, however, in that they hint at a more broadly moral notion of virtue in addition to their political message.

These famous passages were written between the writing of the Declaration of Independence and the constitutional convention that established the United States as a republic in 1789. This was a time of constitutional debate and momentous philosophical deliberation unprecedented in recorded history. American Federalists such as Alexander Hamilton and James Madison were advocating that the United States should invest power in an elite, not unlike the English House of Lords. The rationale for doing so is as old as philosophy itself. Plato identified democracy's flaw in a citizen's tendency to take a free ride, to shirk responsibility for securing public goods, while simultaneously pressing for personal interests. The Federalist solution presumed that an educated class of gentlemen, whose financial interests were tied to large landed estates, would moderate the mob's tendency to vote themselves benefits while defeating the taxes for needed public services. Part of the rationale for the Federalists' solution lay in their view of education and human nature, but part of it lay in the view that estate holders would not be able to separate their interests from those of the state in the way that manufacturers, merchants, and tradesmen could. People in these predominantly urban occupations could always convert wealth into capital and abandon a crumbling state; planters could not.

The cited passages from the *Notes on the State of Virginia* and the letter to Jay are part of Jefferson's reply to the Federalists. Jefferson is pointing to the fact that in America it is not the aristocrat but the common farmer who occupies the land. This argument accepts the view that landowners make a stronger identification between self-interest and common good than do others (hence landowners are more virtuous *as citizens*) and accepts the idea that a landed population is less susceptible to the temptations of short-term, unsustainable government policies. In America, however, the land is owned not by aristocratic landlords who employ landless labor but by the tillers themselves. Jefferson's argument is less a rationale for land to the tiller than for constructing political power in accordance with a previously existing pattern of land holdings. In the American context of the age, the argument favored democracy and undercut key premises of the antidemocratic view of constitutional choice. Small farms were important to Jefferson because they promised temporary protection from the danger of mob rule. The structure of the society would eventually change, but if it could be established on a democratic basis, perhaps new traditions would emerge that would protect the public good from the dilemmas of public choice.

In more recent times, the Jeffersonian argument is most readily recognizable in writings by Harold Breimyer and Jim Hightower. Breimyer, an agricultural economist who served in several Democratic administrations, stresses the role of farming as an entry-level occupation that serves as a safety valve for the American economy. In his view, the American concept of liberty has always included an assurance that no one would be forced to work for wages in order to live. American society would guarantee that everyone has an opportunity to be his or her own boss, though neither success nor great wealth would be secured under this opportunity right. The small family farm has secured this opportunity right throughout American history. Those who did not want to work in the factories could, with little formal training, take up farming. Breimyer fears that the changes that have taken place in agriculture have all but eliminated this important opportunity right, and that as it disappears, the political legitimacy of American capitalism goes along with it. If people cannot farm as a way to escape bosses and factory jobs, then our society is truly guilty of fostering wage slavery, just as Karl Marx predicted (5).

Breimyer's argument interprets liberty in terms of opportunity rights. The argument is populist in that it stresses the interests of the poor and the relatively weak over the interests of property and efficiency. Populist arguments generally stress the needs of the average person. Populist politicians have often championed small and family farmers. Since family farms have historically been populated by relatively poor and powerless Americans, there has been a persistent identification of agrarian interests and populist themes. That argument has become more difficult to make since World War II as farmers have climbed out of poverty and into the middle class. One of the most effective voices in making the argument is Texas politician Jim Hightower.

Hightower has been careful to state the agrarian theme in language that includes most contemporary farm families. Like all agrarians, Hightower celebrates the hard work and independence of the farm family, but like Breimyer, his focus is on the farmer as an entrepreneur who declares independence from big business and wage labor. Hightower identifies farming as one of the few careers open to the entrepreneur in contemporary society, and one that is unique because it is open to people with relatively little formal training and few specialized skills.

According to Hightower, this fact becomes crucial to understanding the political value of the family farm. A democracy in which economic opportunities are open only to the wealthy and well educated is intolerable to Hightower. In this view, it is essential for a democracy to have a place where the average person can make it. A society without such an outlet becomes vulnerable to radicalism, anarchy, and revolution. Capitalist democracy, in short, depends on maintaining access to entrepreneurial opportunities for all citizens. Hightower thinks that, historically, agriculture and the family farm have ensured the legitimacy of American political institutions by providing an opportunity to people who are excluded from other sectors of the economy. It is thus a moral and political imperative not to lose this component of the U.S. economy (7).

Hightower's views are essentially an update of turn-of-the-century populism, a political philosophy that stressed the average citizen's need for protection from powerful business interests. The agrarian populist theme was always strong, and it led to the formation of farm-based political movements such as the Grange and ultimately to many of today's farm cooperatives. To the extent that populism remains a force in American politics, the agrarian values articulated by Hightower and others can be expected to exert influence. Moreover, the populist tradition provides a way of reconciling the rhetoric of agrarian traditionalism advocated by Wendell Berry with the realities of contemporary farm life. Laying stress on entrepreneurship, rather than backbreaking sweat and toil, allows the majority of American farmers to jump on the agrarian bandwagon and provides a point of political focus and action against the corporate middlemen and suppliers who have traditionally been portrayed as enemies of the farmer.

Agrarian Traditionalism

Agrarian traditionalism provides a third approach to farm policy and public perceptions of farm policy issues. It probably comes closest to Bonnen and Browne's agrarian myth in their 1989 article showing why farm policy is so difficult to reform (4). Agrarian traditionalism is not a clearly developed philosophical view, however. Some of its central claims are stated in the nineteenth-century writings of Ralph Waldo Emerson, but its most eloquent contemporary advocate is poet and essayist Wendell Berry. Berry's writings are strongly recommended to people who want to understand agrarian traditionalism, even though he does not attempt a philosophical, as opposed to a literary or evocative, statement of the central ideas. In fact, it is not easy to describe the philosophical viewpoint that we will call *agrarian traditionalism* from the vantage point on ethics and public policy that we have developed in this book. A philosophically deep statement of this view must begin by rejecting many of the ideas about ethics that were advanced in Chapter 3. Only then can we begin to appreciate why traditional agrarians say what they do about family farms and farm policy.

Social contract theory presents the ethics of public policy by constructing a perspective on social life that is admittedly artificial. Whether we talk about the state of nature, the original position, or the prisoner's dilemma, we are describing a hypothetical situation in which individuals are expected to negotiate cooperative agreements (the social contract) on the basis of their perceived self-interests. This approach makes it appear that the ethics of public life consists of nothing more than enlightened self-interest, of showing that respecting rights, procedures, or ensuring cooperation is in everyone's long-term interest. Most people probably think that truly ethical action requires more than self-interest, however. Indeed, many think that when people do good works on the basis of self-interest (by seeing what is in it for themselves), they are not acting ethically at all.

There are many philosophical strategies for understanding ethics in terms that reject self-interested motives. One stresses the notion of loyalty. Many of our clearest examples of non-self-interested action seem to be instances of loyalty. When we visit an ailing friend, for example, we do it not for our own sake but for the sake of the friendship itself. It is our loyalty to our friend that is the basis of our duty and our desire to visit when this person is ill. A person motivated by self-interest also might visit the sick because he or she expects the sick friend to return a favor after recovery, but the self-regarding motive sours the visit. It is no longer an act of friendship. Other loyalties create reasons for acting on behalf of family, neighbors, coworkers, or fellow countrymen. In these cases, to act ethically is to understand that one's relationship to these other people carries with it responsibilities to perform certain kinds of actions on their behalf. The specific acts that may be required depend not only upon the nature of the relationship but also upon the particular situation. We should visit some friends and coworkers when they are sick, but not others, for example. We may know that one friend would prefer solitude, while another would welcome visits. Whether we should visit and how long depends upon many contingent factors that could be discovered in any given situation but that would be difficult to specify in any general rule about visiting the sick.

Another way to describe this common form of morality is to talk about character. A person who calculated whether visiting a sick friend was in his or her own interest might be described as having a defective character. People of good character would make the visit for the sake of the friend. In the same vein, one might describe loyalty to friends as a virtue possessed by people of good moral character and obsession with self-interest as a vice. One does not set out to develop good moral character because of the personal rewards that character brings. Moral character is a trait that one acquires through the conduct of one's affairs with others, through the performance of one's family and social roles, and through virtuous action.

The discussion of loyalty and character may seem to fit in the category of personal morality: those moral codes or rules that we accept as vitally important for ourselves but that do not exert a claim upon public policy. It is quite possible, however, to paint a picture of social ethics in which loyalty and character are crucially important. The very notion of loyalty suggests a web of relationships with others. Our loyalties are formed through our relationships with others, not by personal moral codes that we can choose to accept or reject.

The most common picture of these relationships places family loyalties at the center, closest to the heart. Relationships between husband and wife or between parent and child produce vivid examples of moral obligation fulfilled and realized through loyalty. Similarly, a person's conduct toward a spouse, parent, or child is taken to be an important indicator of character. In traditional societies, family loyalties extend in concentric circles, like the ripples from a pebble dropped in still water. The very ideas of family role—grandparent, uncle, aunt, nephew, cousin—carry with them a pattern of relationships that must be realized and fulfilled through different forms of loyalty. Friendship, neighborhood, and community extend these circles beyond blood relations, ending, in traditional society, with loyalties to one's fellow countrymen.

The vision of personal loyalties embedded in a web of concrete social relationships suggests a vision of society in which social structure and individual role are codetermined. It becomes impossible to say what an individual is and should be apart from a broad specification of social roles, but in specifying these roles, one describes a social order. Social morality thus becomes fixed by the web of relationships as much as personal morality does. Questions of how the community should comport itself can be answered by understanding how the community provides a context in which good moral character can be realized and how the interpersonal loyalties that emerge from the web of social relations can be fulfilled.

This picture of community and public morality can be evoked by describing traditional tribal societies or by an account of the feudal system. The European feudal economy is an important reference point for ethics because social contract theory took shape during the time that European states were making the transition from rural societies organized under the manorial system of peasants bound to a liege lord to diversified societies organized around manufacturing and trade centers in the cities and towns. In the manorial system, peasants worked land owned by aristocrats. In addition to being the owners or bosses of the production process, the aristocrats held political rank, and the peasants owed political as well as economic obligations to them. In the manorial system, participating in primary agricultural production activities was part of one's duty to one's lord.

The key moral concept in this system was personal loyalty, in deed if not in spirit. The ethical code of both peasant and aristocrat could be spelled out almost entirely in terms of the status of specific individuals who were well known to those who had duties to perform. Loyal peasants worked the land to which they were bonded; loyal lords protected their serfs from invasion and from thieves. It is possible to describe the duties and obligations of the peasant and lord as those of particular and concrete loyalties, loyalties owed to a particular person and to be performed in a particular place at a particular time. Even the agricultural price system was grounded in traditional fees and tariffs specified in terms of particular obligations owed between miller and peasant, peasant and lord. Any attempt to exploit an advantage arising from supply and demand was regarded as an attempt to shirk a moral and political obligation to exchange at the traditional rate.

This picture of duty and obligation should be seen in contrast to the modern idea of legal obligation and rights, which stresses the universal, the general principle, specified for all times, places, and peoples, and which sees moral action as an application of universally valid laws to particular cases. Although feudal Europe was not lacking in a concept of universal law, police power and judicial authority ultimately resided in the person of the liege lord, extending hierarchically (again like the ripples in a pond) to regional lords and the head of state and finally to God. As peasants owed duties to their lord, the duke or baron owed duties to his king.

The fact that the manorial system was agricultural is significant. Traditional values for agricultural production are in fact traditional values for society as a whole. Any given plot of land is unique, entirely particular. Tying obligations to a particular place was feasible, even natural, for agriculture since the land itself had a permanent location that provided a measure of security to medieval relationships. As long as the peasants stayed on the land, the lord could not abandon them entirely, for the lord's own interests were in the land, and these interests could not be easily moved. Furthermore, it was land that knitted political and economic relations into a seamless web. Politics of the feudal area was essentially concerned with territory. Political rank was based on domain over a specific parcel of land. People who could move their production from one territory to another could change their political loyalties, but agricultural producers could do so only by abandoning their claim to their key productive asset, the land. The ethic of this status system, however, may have became dysfunctional as societies came to emphasize trade and manufacturing. Both of these activities required entrepreneurs to take risks and to deal with much larger circles of people. They did not require that their practitioners remain in the same place indefinitely, and sometimes they presented great incentives for relocation. Further, the morality of location-bound loyalties did not support the norms required for trade. As trade and manufacturing spanned the globe in search of materials and markets, the serviceability of a moral code based solely on personal loyalties to particular individuals became obsolete. Commerce required rules for upholding covenants with people from many different places.

Trading societies needed an ethic whereby people could be trusted to honor contracts, and it needed a legal system that could enforce them. The ethical content of the business contract was, in contrast to the particular duties of personal loyalty, spelled out by the entirely impersonal rights and privileges specified in the terms of exchange. Contractual agreements did not depend upon the uniqueness of their particular signatories, and indeed, one could agree to the same set of contractual terms with indefinitely many people. Moral duty consisted not in loyalty to a particular person, but in fulfilling the specified obligations without regard to the particular identity of the other signatories. It should not be surprising, therefore, that philosophers should have gotten around to thinking of morality in contractual terms, either literally, as in the case of Hobbes and Locke, or as a similarly faceless and universalized specification of entitlements, rules, expectations, and obligations, as in the case of Bentham and Kant.

To the extent that this very simplified story of the transition between feudal Europe and the modern era is accurate, social contract theory (and indeed almost all forms of modern morality) can be understood as a deep historical challenge to the morality of personal loyalty and character. Furthermore, the peasant's role in feudal agriculture was one of severely restricted opportunity and liberty. In some instances, the relation between the master and the commoner was one of virtual (if not actual) slavery. The language of loyalty and character can be and has been applied to the relationship between master and slave, but this is a form of loyalty that few would endorse today. Social contract theory reflects both economic changes in

European society and a deep philosophical opposition to the repressive relationships that the feudal order enforced.

Nevertheless, describing morality in terms of a web of interpersonal loyalties, rather than as a contract or deal struck among self-interested and autonomous individuals, continues to have an attraction. The difficulty in retaining this view is that one must have some plausible (and attractive) picture of how loyalties, character, and community coalesce into mutually reinforcing social relationships. The web of loyalties and community ties that would establish this picture consists in concrete relationships among people united by a common heritage, geography, blood, marriage, and mutually supporting visions of the future. These relationships would vary in their details from one community to another and from one time to another. The web would consist of particularized points at which real people come into contact with one another, and it would derive its capacity to serve as a framework for the evaluation of moral character from elements that could not be generalized or stated in concepts that apply universally.

It is possible that Wendell Berry's writings on agriculture provide just such a picture, especially in his poems and novels that examine the relationships of a rural world in their particulars. It is impossible to summarize a poem or novel, and if it is the details that are important, a summary would miss the point in any case. As such, the discussion that follows of Berry's vision should be regarded as a pointer toward the larger view. Berry's writings on the ethics of agriculture seem to lack philosophical arguments in the usual sense, but his literary picture of rural communities as places in time where human action attains meaning from the specific web of relations among his characters forms an argument that must be grasped in its entirety in order to become convincing.

Wendell Berry's Agrarianism

Although his novels and poems may be the key sources for Wendell Berry's vision, he has produced a series of essays on farming that express his views in didactic form. These essays stress the importance of work, nature, and community in the traditional agrarian way of life. Berry's essays often criticize the effects of modern technology on that way of life. He shows how modern farming techniques have altered the character of each of these three key elements in the agrarian way of life.

The following passage from *The Gift of Good Land* describes the impact of technology on work.

> But good work and good workmanship cannot be accomplished by "slaps" and "swipes." Such language seems to be derived from the he-man vocabulary of TV westerns, not from any known principles of good agriculture. What does the language of good agricultural workmanship sound like? Here is the voice of an

old-time English farmworker and horseman, Harry Groom, as quoted in George Ewart Evan's *The Horse in the Furrow*: "It's all rush today. You hear a young chap say in the pub: 'I done thirty acres today.' But it ain't messed over, let alone done. You take the rolling, for instance. Two mile an hour is fast enough for a roll or a harrow. With a roll, the slower the better. If you roll fast, the clods are not broken up, they're just pressed in further. Speed is everything now; just jump on the tractor and way across the field as if it's a dirt-track. You see it when a farmer takes over a new farm: he goes in and plants straight-way, right out of the book. But if one of the old farmers took a new farm, and you walked round the land with him and asked him: 'What are you going to plant here and here?' he'd look at you some queer; because he wouldn't plant nothing much at first. He'd wait a bit and see what the land was like: he'd prove the land first. A good practical man would hold on for a few weeks, and get the feel of the land under his feet. He'd walk on it and feel it through his boots and see if it was a good heart, before he planted anything; he'd sow only when he knew what the land was fit for."

Granted that there is always plenty of room to disagree about farming methods, there is still no way to deny that in the first quotation we have a description of careless farming, and in the second a description of a way of farming as careful—as knowing, skillful, and loving—as any other kind of high workmanship. The difference between the two is simply that the second considers where and how the machine is used, whereas the first considers only the machine. The first is the point of view of a man high up in the airconditioned cab of a tractor described as "a beast that eats acres." The second is that of a man who has worked close to the ground in the open air of the field, who has studied the condition of the ground as he drove over it, and who has cared and thought about it. (2, pp. 106–108)

The following passage from *The Unsettling of America* describes the impact of technology on our experience of nature.

I am writing this in the north-central part of Kentucky on a morning near the end of June. We have had rain for two days, hard rain during the last several hours. From where I sit I can see the Kentucky River swiftening and rising, the water already yellow with mud. I know that inside this city-oriented consumer economy there are many people who will never see this muddy rise and many who will see it without knowing what it means. I know also that there are many who see it, and know what it means, and not care. If it lasts until the weekend there will be people who will find it as good as clear water for motorboating and waterskiing.

In the past several days I have seen some of the worst-eroded corn fields that I have seen in this country in my life. This erosion is occurring on the cash-rented farms of farmer's widows and city farmers, absentee owners, the doctors and businessmen who buy a farm for the tax breaks or to have "a quiet place in the country" for the weekends. It is the direct result of economic and agricultural policy; it might be said to *be* an economic and agricultural policy. (1, p. 107)

The following passage from *Home Economics* describes the impact of technology on home.

> According to the industrial formula, the ideal human residence (from the Latin *residere*, "to sit back" or "remain sitting") is one in which the residers do not work. The house is built, equipped, decorated, and provisioned by other people, by strangers. In it, the married couple practice as few as possible of the disciplines of household or homestead. Their domestic labor consists principally of buying things, putting things away, and throwing things away, but it is understood that it is "best" to have even those jobs done by an "inferior" person, and the ultimate industrial ideal is a "home" in which *everything* would be done by pushing buttons. In such a "home," a married couple are mates, sexually, legally, and socially, but they are not helpmates; they do nothing useful either together or for each other. According to the ideal, work should be done *away* from home. When such spouses say to each other, "I will love you forever," the meaning of their words is seriously impaired by their circumstances; they are speaking in the presence of so little that they have done and made. Their history together is essentially placeless; it has no visible or tangible incarnation. They have only themselves in view. (3, p. 119)

The message of these passages is that the modern person is losing the ability to derive meaning from work, nature, and community. The capacity to understand moral character in light of the experiences and relationships that are accumulated in the communal life of people who work in nature is disappearing from the modern landscape. By contrast, a traditional agrarian community of the sort that existed across the United States until shortly after World War II made it easy to acquire and interpret the work experiences that give meaning to life. Berry's novels present this story, but his chapter on Thomas Jefferson from *The Unsettling of America* portrays nineteenth century agriculture in similar terms. In that context, Berry interprets Jefferson as being a visionary advocate of agrarianism.

Berry quotes Jefferson on industrialists to contrast his views on the effects of agriculture. Jefferson wrote:

> "I consider the class of artificers as the panderers of vice, and the instruments by which the liberties of a country are generally overturned." By "artificers" he meant manufacturers, and he made no distinction between labor and management. . . . [The quote] suggests that he held manufacturers in suspicion because their values were already becoming abstract, enabling them to be "socially mobile" and therefore subject preeminently to the motives of self-interest. (1, p. 144)

Berry thus finds the farm to be a superior environment for the cultivation of a moral sense and the occupation of the farmer to be a superior activity for the development of moral virtues. These themes represent the keys to an agrarian statement of social and moral goals for agriculture: the anchoring of self-interest in a community and the necessity of self-reliance.

Jefferson himself was very much influenced by social contract theory and was mindful of the importance of self-interest in individual decisions. He and the other founding fathers saw their task as one that would marry self-interest to social unity (and thereby to a broader concept of the good) rather than to dissolution, avarice, unrestrained competition, and social chaos. However, the presupposition that underlies Jefferson's reasoning on the agrarian vision is that an economy based upon agriculture would be superior to one in which self-interest could be attached to movable and consumable assets. Jefferson's reasoning echoes themes from the status system of the feudal past. The farmer was tied to his land; the good of the land was identical to the farmer's self-interest. Since a farmer must stay in one spot, he must learn to get along with his neighbors and take an interest in long-term stability. The virtues of honesty, integrity, and charity promote a stable society and are also the virtues that promote the farmer's own interest. A manufacturer, however, is not so firmly tied to a community. The *artificer*, to use Jefferson's term, can spoil the air, exploit the local work force, poison the wells, and then pick up his assets and move on down the road when the business environment becomes hostile (or demands that these externalities be internalized). Jefferson himself was no enemy of industry, but Berry uses his argument to portray the encouragement of farming as a key to a unified and stable economy.

The second virtue, self-reliance, can also be tied to a distrust of manufacture. The farmer must be adept at a variety of skills. This fact requires the farmer to appreciate the complexity of nature and the need for flexibility and multiple approaches in coping with challenges. The farmer thus incorporates one aspect of the civil society—strength through diversity—in his personal character. The manufacturer, on the other hand, succeeds by learning how to do one thing better than anyone else. Wendell Berry lays heavy stress upon specialization in his critique of modern agriculture:

> What happens under the rule of specialization is that, though society becomes more and more intricate, it has less and less structure. . . . The community disintegrates because it loses the necessary understanding, forms, and enactments of the relations among materials and processes, principles and actions, ideals and realities, past and present, present and future, men and women, body and spirit, city and country, civilization and wilderness, growth and decay, life and death—just as the individual character loses the sense of responsible involvement in these relations. (1, p. 21)

Berry describes a tragic irony in the increasing reliance upon social systems rather than upon diverse skills incorporated in a single self. As human beings become less reliant upon their individual abilities to make flexible and ingenious responses to adversity, they lose the capacity to appreciate the importance of community, becoming destructive of the natural and social systems that have replaced the yeoman farmer's need for self-reliance.

By placing Jefferson's praise of farming in a historical context, Berry shows how one can identify self-reliance and community as the essential virtues of agriculture. Community and self-reliance are sought not only as individual goals or character traits that members of the farm household must acquire, but also as social goals, as traits that all citizens of the new republic must acquire, in part through the experience and example of agriculture, if democratic liberties are to be secure.

The reason small farms are good is that they cultivate virtue in the character of the farm family. The reasons this is alleged to be so do not easily survive condensation and summarization. They have to do with the way farm families experience the unity and diversity of life. Each family member performs diverse roles that are specialized by age and sex, which are in turn precisely the factors that define their place in the social order of the family. The family unifies these roles into an order that makes each person's duty in ensuring farm survival easy to grasp. The diversity of tasks is also reflected in the changing of the seasons and in the breadth of cultural practices, but these too are unified by the farm itself. The farm family is at one with nature, and each person both values and is valued by the role relationships that the production practices of the small farm demands. Similar roles bind all members of the rural community.

What we have in Berry's thought, then, is a revision of the old traditionalism of the feudal system. Moral obligations issue forth from roles that unify economic and political status. Duties are grounded in loyalties to particular individuals who are bound to one another in time and place. Virtue is found in living up to the role requirements one inherits by being situated in a community or a family. The particularity of being so situated means that men have roles that differ from those of women; that adults have roles that differ from those of children; that farmers have roles that differ from those of cobblers, blacksmiths, and carpenters; and that all persons must fulfill the requirements of their roles. Those who do so are virtuous; those who are overcome by jealousy, competitiveness, greed, and other vices fall short in the moral quest. Even the failures know what is expected of them, however, while those of us who live in trading and manufacturing societies have no clear-cut goals to live up to. Berry's most poignant portrayal of the morality of roles is his understated novel *A Place on Earth*, in which a World War II Kentucky farming community perches at the precipice of industrialized agriculture, of sons and daughters who will not take up their parents' roles, and with a community whose inner structure is on the verge of destruction, not by the war, but by the war technologies like DDT that are its aftermath. Berry's celebration of agrarian virtue is a revision, rather than a revival, of traditionalist morality because each farmer is lord of the manor. It is a democratization, or at least a leveling, of the feudal class structure but one that preserves its categories for deriving moral significance.

Wendell Berry's agrarian attack upon the individualistic self-interestedness and universalism of social contract theory has also been taken up in other quarters. Alisdair MacIntyre's *After Virtue* and Robert Bellah's coauthored *Habits of the Heart* attempt to show why Enlightenment morality fails to account for the historical and geographical rootedness of moral relationships. The philosophical themes that emerge from the confrontation between traditional agrarianism and social contract theory go far beyond the scope of a book on ethics, agriculture, and public policy. They may be among the themes that future historians will note as most characteristic of our time.

Summary

The theme of saving the family farm is influential across a broad spectrum of farm policy and American farm politics. The number of farms has decreased dramatically in the twentieth century, and the declining number of farms is often cited as a reason for commodity policies that help farmers. Another prominent theme is that new agricultural technologies may benefit consumers, large farmers, and agribusiness, but they tend to harm small or family farms. This view becomes part of an argument for regulating technologies such as BST. It is also relevant for decisions about how to spend public funds for agricultural research. In general, these themes are consistent with the utilitarian analysis of agricultural policy that has been the backbone of economics-based policy analysis. In that analysis, benefits are weighed against harms to those whose incomes are adversely affected, often to the point where they must leave farming. A more sophisticated application of utilitarian theory would broaden the range of consequences to be considered, including impacts for animals and future generations, as well as for the aesthetic, historic, and symbolic values associated with family farms.

In contrast to the utilitarian approach, agrarian populists have argued that big business and big government have stacked the deck against the small farmer. They think that the "right to farm" is an important component of liberty. Agrarian populists are offering egalitarian arguments to the extent that they see the right to farm as an opportunity right, one that should be protected along with other primary goods. The key to this view is the claim that economic liberty for poor individuals depends upon preserving a structure of rights such that people are never forced to accept low-wage jobs as an economic necessity. Historically, the widespread existence of small farms gave people a subsistence level of food security and a chance at greater success. In so doing, small farms protected economic liberty without extending welfare to the poor. If the opportunity to farm is denied to the poorest people in our society, they will be forced to accept low-wage jobs. Agrarian populists view this form of economic coercion as indefensible and as an affront to justice.

A third viewpoint is provided by the agrarian traditionalist, typified by Wendell Berry. On this view, small, low-technology farms are important because they preserve the work habits that build strong moral character and because they bind farm families into a close-knit community where loyalty and status will determine a set of moral obligations. This view of ethics stands in contrast to the social contract views that have been the main focus throughout this book. As such, the movement to save the family farm can be understood as an alternative ethic for agriculture, one that does not accept enlightened self-interest and the social contract as an acceptable basis for agricultural ethics.

Key Terms

aesthetic value

agarian populism

agrarian traditionalism

farm policy

farm structure

historic value

medium-sized farms

symbolic value

References

1. Berry, Wendell. 1977. *The Unsettling of America*. San Francisco: Sierra Club Books.
2. _____. 1983. *The Gift of Good Land*. San Francisco: North Point Press.
3. _____. 1987. *Home Economics*. San Francisco: North Point Press.
4. Bonnen, James T., and William P. Browne. 1989. "Why Is Agricultural Policy So Difficult to Reform?", in *The Political Economy of U.S. Agriculture*, ed. Carol S. Kramer. Washington, D.C.: Resources for the Future.
5. Breimyer, Harold F. 1965. *Individual Freedom and the Economic Organization of Agriculture*. Urbana: University of Illinois Press.
6. Fallert, R. C., and M. C. Hallberg. 1992. "BST and the Price of Milk and Dairy Products," in *Bovine Somatotropin and Emerging Issues*, ed. M. C. Hallberg. Boulder, Colo.: Westview Press.
7. Hightower, Jim. 1976. *Eat Your Heart Out*. New York: Crown Books.
8. Jefferson, Thomas. 1984. *Writings*, ed. Merrill D. Peterson. New York: Literary Classics of the United States.
9. Kalter, Robert J. 1985. "The New Biotech Agriculture: Unforeseen Economic Consequences," *Issues in Science and Technology* 2:122–133.
10. Strange, Marty. 1988. *Family Farming: A New Economic Vision*. Lincoln: University of Nebraska Press.
11. Sundquist, W. Burt. 1983. "Technology and Productivity Policies for the Future," *The Farm and Food System in Transition*, FS4. East Lansing, Mich.: Cooperative Extension Service, Michigan State University.
12. Tauer, Loren W. 1992. "Impact of BST on Small versus Large Dairy Farms," in *Bovine Somatotropin and Emerging Issues*, ed. M. C. Hallberg. Boulder, Colo.: Westview Press.
13. Tweeten, Luther. 1987. "Has the Family Farm Been Treated Unjustly?" in *Is There a Moral Obligation to Save the Family Farm?*, ed. G. Comstock. Ames: Iowa State University Press.

Suggestions for Further Reading

The literature on saving the family farm is quite extensive. The cited works by Marty Strange and Luther Tweeten provide a good starting point. A wide range of views have been anthologized in Gary Comstock's *Is There a Moral Obligation to Save the Family Farm?* (Ames: Iowa State University Press, 1987). Agricultural research policy is evaluated in Paul B. Thompson and Bill A. Stout, eds., *Beyond the Large Farm: Ethics and Research Goals for Agriculture* (Boulder, Colo: Westview Press, 1991), which includes a bibliographic essay on agrarianism by Nancy Shankle. The themes in this chapter have been systematically linked to various aspects of agricultural policy in W. Browne, J. Skees, L. Swanson, P. Thompson, and L. Unnevehr, *Sacred Cows and Hot Potatoes: Agrarian Myths in Agricultural Policy* (Boulder, Colo.: Westview Press, 1992). The ethics of the BST case is the subject of a chapter by Paul Thompson in M. C. Hallberg's *Bovine Somatotropin and Emerging Issues* (Boulder, Colo.: Westview Press, 1992), and of articles by Jeffrey Burkhardt (in *Technology in Society* 14:221–243, 1992) and Gary Comstock (in *Agriculture and Human Values* 5:36–52, 1988). Other aspects of biotechnology are taken up in L. Busch, W. Lacy, J. Burkhardt, and L. Lacy, *Plants, Power and Profits* (New York: Basil Blackwell, 1991).

Agrarianism as a theme has been studied by James Montmarquet, *The Idea of Agrarianism* (Moscow: University of Idaho Press, 1989). The cited works of Harold Breimyer, Jim Hightower, and Wendell Berry are most important, especially *The Unsettling of America* and *Home Economics* by Berry. Berry's work has been linked to sustainability in a perceptive 1990 review by Bill McKibben entitled "Prophet in Kentucky" (*New York Review of Books* 37:30–34). Readers should also consult Suggestions for Further Reading for Chapter 9 to follow this line of thought.

Index

Index

A

Act consequentialism, 52
Administrative Procedures Act, 18
Administrative systems, 23
Agency for International Development, 197–199, 201–204, 206
Agrarian
  myth, 131, 235, 248
  populism, 233, 247, 257
  traditionalist (-ism), 233, 248, 252, 254, 257
Agricultural Adjustment Act, 232
Agroecology, 217
Alar (daminozide), 108, 122–125
Allocative efficiency, 70, 95, 97–100, 104, 153–159, 162
Alternative agriculture, 215, 216, 223–229
Altieri, Miguel, 215, 217–220, 228
American Farm Bureau Federation, 180
American Soybean Association, 80, 203, 204, 206
Animal
  drugs, 110, 120, 121, 123, 125, 126
  rights, 166, 172, 177–180, 184–187

Animal well-being/animal welfare, 4, 5, 166, 168, 169, 171–177, 180–182, 184–187, 210, 228, 239
Associations, 9, 10, 12, 29
Assurance problem, 61, 177
Axiology, 52–55, 57, 78, 79, 86–88, 95, 143, 176, 180

B

Bargained exchange (structure), 24, 116, 117
Basic rights, 50
Benson, Ezra Taft, 1, 2, 5
Bentham, Jeremy, 50, 51, 55, 59, 87, 174, 175, 184, 251
Berry, Wendell, 80, 216, 248, 252–257
bGH (bovine growth hormone), *see* Bovine somatotropin
Bill of Rights, 41
Bonnen and Browne, 235, 248
Bovine somatotropin (BST), 238–241, 257
Boyle, Robert, 111, 217
Breimyer, Harold, 246, 247
Bromley, Daniel, 98
bt (Bacillus thurengensis), 111
Bumpers Amendment, 201, 202, 205–208

Positive rights, 44, 119
Potential Pareto improvement, 57, 95
Preference utilitarianism, 54, 55, 69, 70, 98
Preservations (-ist), 151, 153, 155–158, 160–163
Price supports, 81, 225, 227, 237, 238
Primary goods, 45, 46, 47, 71, 189, 257
Prisoners dilemma, 35, 59, 60–62, 67, 72, 161, 177, 234, 248
Problem identification, 15, 19, 30, 74, 79, 104, 224
Procedural law, 10–13, 18, 19
Procedural (ethical) theories, 36, 62–64, 66–68, 70, 72, 82, 104, 116, 119, 128, 229, 245
Production, 141, 143, 236
Productivity, 141–143, 236
Property rights, 11–13, 20, 21, 26, 45, 47, 58, 63, 69, 71, 76, 98, 150, 159, 162, 169, 190
Public law, 18
Pure Pareto improvement, 56, 94

Q

quantitative cost-benefit analysis, *see* cost-benefit analysis

R

Rawls/Rawlsian, 37, 45, 46–48, 71, 99, 177, 205, 206
Reagan, Ronald, 87, 194, 195, 202
Regan, Tom, 177, 179, 180, 185, 186
Reclamation Act, 138
Redistributive policies, 18
Regional Water Resources Plan, 146, 152
Registrations, of pesticides and food additives, 121
Regulated exchange (structure), 24
Regulatory policies, 19
Resource depletion, 131, 162, 234, 235
Rights, 11, 23, 24, 29, 30, 36, 38, 39, 41–45, 47–49, 51, 59, 76, 78, 82–86, 97, 98, 100, 101, 103–105, 141, 158, 160–162, 166, 169, 174, 175, 177–179, 184–186, 191, 194, 200–202, 206, 207, 226, 230, 250, 257

Rights-based theories, 36, 37, 39, 51, 57, 58, 77, 79, 82–86, 98, 100, 101, 104, 138–140, 162, 173, 193, 200, 226, 242, 245
Risk, 114, 121, 123, 138, 225–227
Rivalry, 20–23, 190
Roosevelt, Theodore, 1, 2, 5
Rule consequentialism, 52

S

Saccharin, 111
San Joaquin Valley, 131–134, 137, 141, 154
Save the Family Farm Act, 232
Scope, of utilitarian theories, 78, 79, 86, 87, 95, 143
Securities and Exchange Commission, 16
Selenium, 132, 135–138
Self-interest (theory), 26, 27, 38, 40, 41, 54, 216, 248, 258
Self-reliance, 254, 255
Sen, Amartya, 98, 189
Shadow pricing, 90, 95, 154
Shue, Henry, 50
Shurland, Elizabeth, 181
Sierra Club, 149, 150, 155
Sinclair, Upton, 108
Singer, Peter, 171, 175–177, 180, 185, 186, 193, 200
Situation, 8, 20, 28, 75, 76, 113, 190, 224
Social contract, 3, 6, 33, 35–40, 42–48, 51, 58, 59, 62–68, 70–72, 75, 79, 101–104, 140, 175, 177, 178, 190, 192, 202, 205, 208, 248, 250, 251, 254, 256–258
Social contract thesis, 205–207
Soil conservation, 57, 91, 232, 234
Soil Conservation Service, 216
Stagner, Steve, 147
State of nature, 35, 39–42, 44, 51, 58, 63, 67, 69, 71, 75, 160, 161, 177, 178, 202, 248
Status system, 23
Steinbeck, John, 131
Stewardship, 131, 141, 143, 160, 162
Strange, Marty, 235
Streep, Meryl, 124
Structure, 20, 23, 25, 28–30, 75, 78, 112, 114, 224, 226